ALEXANDER POPE

THE RAPE OF THE LOCK

OUR BOOKS ON LITERATURE

1. An Evaluation of His Poetry **JOHN KEATS**
2. The Rape of the Lock **ALEXANDER POPE**
3. An Evaluation of His Poetry **P.B. SHELLEY**
4. An Evaluation of His Poetry **W.B. YEATS**
5. The Prologue **GEOFFREY CHAUCER**
6. The Pardoner's Tale **GEOFFREY CHAUCER**
7. Songs of Innocence and of Experience **WILLIAM BLAKE**
8. Select Poems, Vol. I **ROBERT BROWNING**
9. Select Poems, Vol. II **ROBERT BROWNING**
10. Select Poems **ALFRED TENNYSON**
11. Select Poems **JOHN DONNE**
12. Select Poems **W.H. AUDEN**
13. An Evaluation of His Poetry **WILLIAM WORDSWORTH**
14. Preface to the Lyrical Ballads **WILLIAM WORDSWORTH**
15. Essays of Elia **CHARLES LAMB**
16. Bacon's Essays **FRANCIS BACON**
17. Doctor Faustus **CHRISTOPHER MARLOWE**
18. The Duchess of Malfi **JOHN WEBSTER**
19. Essays in Criticism **MATTHEW ARNOLD**
20. An Essay of Dramatic Poesy **JOHN DRYDEN**
21. An Apology for Poetry **PHILIP SIDNEY**
22. The Poetics **ARISTOTLE**
23. Biographia Literaria **S.T. COLERIDGE**
24. The Rime of Ancient Mariner **S.T. COLERIDGE**
25. An Evaluation of His Poetry **S.T. COLERIDGE**
26. Preface to Shakespeare **DR. JOHNSON**
27. Sons and Lovers **D.H. LAWRENCE**
28. The Rainbow **D.H. LAWRENCE**
29. Women in Love **D.H. LAWRENCE**
30. A Passage to India **E.M. FORSTER**
31. Oliver Twist **CHARLES DICKENS**
32. David Copperfield **CHARLES DICKENS**
33. Great Expectations **CHARLES DICKENS**
34. Hard Times **CHARLES DICKENS**
35. The Tale of Two Cities **CHARLES DICKENS**
36. Tess of the D'Urbervilles **THOMAS HARDY**
37. The Return of the Native **THOMAS HARDY**
38. Lord Jim **JOSEPH CONRAD**
39. Heart of Darkness **JOSEPH CONRAD**
40. The Secret Agent **JOSEPH CONRAD**
41. Vanity Fair **W.M. THACKERAY**
42. Arms and the Man **BERNARD SHAW**
43. To the Lighthouse **VIRGINIA WOOLF**
44. The Mill on the Floss **GEORGE ELIOT**
45. Middlemarch **GEORGE ELIOT**
46. Sceptical Essays **BERTRAND RUSSELL**
47. Unpopular Essays **BERTRAND RUSSELL**
48. Waiting for Godot **SAMUEL BECKETT**
49. The Waste Land & Other Poems **T.S. ELIOT**
50. The Critic **T.S. ELIOT**
51. Murder in the Cathedral **T.S. ELIOT**
52. The Cocktail Party **T.S. ELIOT**
53. History and Principles of Literary Criticism *Edited by* **LISA ROY**
54. The Old Man & the Sea **ERNEST HEMINGWAY**
55. A Farewell to Arms **ERNEST HEMINGWAY**
56. The Scarlet Letter **NATHANIELHAWTHORNE**
57. The Portrait of a Lady **HENRY JAMES**
58. The Adventures of Huckleberry Finn **MARK TWAIN**
59. Death of a Salesman **ARTHUR MILLER**
60. Select Poems **ROBERT FROST**
61. Select Poems **WALT WHITMAN**
62. Gitanjali **RAVINDRANATH TAGORE**
63. The Guide **R.K. NARAYAN**
64. The Serpent and the Rope **RAJA RAO**
65. Kanthapura **RAJA RAO**
66. Coolie **MULK RAJ ANAND**
67. Untouchable **MULK RAJ ANAND**
68. Nineteen Eighty Four **GEORGE ORWELL**
69. The Power & the Glory **GRAHAM GREENE**
70. Wuthering Heights **EMILY BRONTE**
71. Look Back in Anger **JOHN OSBORNE**
72. Gulliver's Travels **JONATHAN SWIFT**
73. Mansfield Park **JANE AUSTEN**
74. Pride and Prejudice **JANE AUSTEN**
75. Advanced Literary Essays *Edited by* **LISA ROY**
76. In Memoriam **ALFRED TENNYSON**
77. Paradise Lost, Book II **JOHN MILTON**
78. Paradise Lost, Book I **JOHN MILTON**
79. Paradise Lost, Book IV **JOHN MILTON**
80. Minor Poems **JOHN MILTON**
81. Paradise Lost, Book IX **JOHN MILTON**
82. Silver Poets of the Sixteenth Century *Edited by* **LISA ROY**
83. All for Love **JOHN DRYDEN**
84. Life of Pope **SAMUEL JOHNSON**
85. Life of Milton **SAMUEL JOHNSON**
86. The Pilgrim's Progress **JOHN BUNYAN**
87. The Man-Eater of Malgudi **R.K. NARAYAN**
88. Much Ado About Nothing **WILLIAM SHAKESPEARE**
89. The Winter's Tale **WILLIAM SHAKESPEARE**
90. King Lear (Text with Notes) **WILLIAM SHAKESPEARE**
91. Macbeth **WILLIAM SHAKESPEARE**
92. Othello **WILLIAM SHAKESPEARE**
93. Henry V **WILLIAM SHAKESPEARE**
94. Antony & Cleopatra **WILLIAM SHAKESPEARE**
95. A Midsummer Night's Dream **WILLIAM SHAKESPEARE**
96. As You Like It **WILLIAM SHAKESPEARE**
97. Richard II **WILLIAM SHAKESPEARE**
98. Hamlet (A Critical Study) **WILLIAM SHAKESPEARE**
99. Henry IV, Part I **WILLIAM SHAKESPEARE**
100. The Tempest **WILLIAM SHAKESPEARE**
101. Julius Caeser **WILLIAM SHAKESPEARE**
102. Twelfth Night **WILLIAM SHAKESPEARE**
103. The Merchant of Venice **WILLIAM SHAKESPEARE**
104. Jane Eyre **CHARLOTTE BRONTE**
105. The Way of the World **WILLIAM CONGREVE**
106. Lord of the Flies **WILLIAM GOLDING**
107. Crime and Punishment **FYODOR DOSTOYEVSKY**
108. Tom Jones **HENRY FIELDING**

Alexander Pope

THE RAPE OF THE LOCK

[A Complete Study Guide Including, Text, Analysis and Study Questions]

Mansi Sachdeva
B.A. English (Hons) , Delhi University;
M.A., M. Phil. (English), IGNOU

ANMOL PUBLICATIONS PVT. LTD.
NEW DELHI - 110 002 (INDIA)

ANMOL PUBLICATIONS PVT. LTD.

H.O.: 4374/4B, Ansari Road, Darya Ganj,
New Delhi-110 002 (India)
Ph.: 23278000, 23261597

B.O.: No. 1015, Ist Main Road, BSK IIIrd Stage
IIIrd Phase, IIIrd Block
Bangalore - 560 085 (India)
Visit us at: www.anmolpublications.com

The Rape of the Lock

First Published, 2009

PRINTED IN INDIA

Printed at Mehra Offset Press, Delhi.

Contents

Preface

The Rape of the Lock is the finest mock-heroic or mock-epic poem in English: written on the model of Boileau's Le Lutrin, it is an exquisitely witty and balanced burlesque displaying the literary virtuosity, the perfection of poetic "judgement," and the exquisite sense of artistic propriety, which was so sought after by Ne-classical artists. Repeatedly invoking classical epic devices to establish an ironic contrast between its structure and its content, it functions at once as a satire on the trivialities of fashionable life, as a commentary on the distorted moral values of polite society, and as an implicit indictment of human pride, and a revelation of the essentially trivial nature of many of the aspects of human existence which we tend to hold very dear.

The world of the beaux and belles of The Rape of the Lock is a an artificial one, a trivial realm of calm and decorum sustained by the strict observance of rigorous rules, a micrososm in which very real and very powerful human emotions and passions have been ignored or sublimated. The narcissistic inhabitants of this world assume that they are something more than human, but Pope shows us vulnerable, how fragile, their pretended perfection and their isolation from reality makes them. The Rape of the Lock, with all of its implicit and explicit sexual and emotional implications, shatters the calm, the order, the balance, and the decorum of their artificial world. They are undone by what Pope identifies—here, as in An Essay on Man and "An Essay on Criticism"—as their most important weakness: Pride.

Author

Chapter 1

Introduction

The Rape of the Lock had its origins in an actual, and trivial, incident in polite society: in 1711, the twenty-one year old Robert, Lord Peter, had, at Binfield, had surreptitiously cut a lock of hair from the head of the beautiful Arabella Fermor, whom he had been courting. Arabella took offense, and a schism developed between her family and Petre's. John Caryll, a friend of both familes and an old friend of Pope's, suggested that he work up a humourous poem about the episode which would demonstrate to both sides that the whole affair had been blown out of proportion and thus effect a reconciliation between them. Pope produced his poem, and it seemed to have achieved its purpose, though Petre never married Arabella. It became obvious over the course of time, however (especially after a revised and enlarged version of the poem, which existed at first only in manuscript copies, was published in 1714) that the poem, which Pope maintained "was intended only to divert a few young Ladies," was in fact something rather more substantial, and the Fermors again took offense—this time at Pope himself, who had to placate them with a letter, usually printed before the text, which explains that Arabella and Belinda, the heroine of the poem, are not identical.

The Rape of the Lock is the finest mock-heroic or mock-epic poem in English: written on the model of Boileau's Le Lutrin, it is an exquisitely witty and balanced burlesque displaying the literary virtuosity, the perfection of poetic "judgement," and the exquisite sense of artistic propriety, which was so sought after by Neo-classical artists.Repeatedly invoking classical epic devices to establish an ironic contrast between its structure and its content, it functions at once as a satire on the trivialities of fashionable life, as a commentary on the distorted moral values of polite society, and as an implicit indictment of human pride, and a revelation of the essentially trivial nature of many of the aspects of human existence which we tend to hold very dear.

The world of the beaux and belles of The Rape of the Lock is a an artificial one, a trivial realm of calm and decorum sustained by the strict observance of rigorous rules, a micrososm in which very real and very powerful human emotions and passions have been ignored or sublimated. The narcissistic inhabitants of this world assume that they are something more than human, but Pope shows us vulnerable, how fragile, their pretended perfection and their isolation from reality makes them. The Rape of the Lock, with all of its implicit and explicit sexual and emotional implications, shatters the calm, the order, the balance, and the decorum of their artificial world.

A final note: it is obvious that the poem was written for a limited and very specialized audience: in Pope's day, literary art was the province of the upper classes; the domain of a culture which was pervasively literary. Contemporary readers of The Rape of the Lock would, in consequence, recognize and delight in the enormous number of literary allusions which the poem contains. The readers of a poem so concerned with imitation ought, obviously, to be familiar with what is being imitated, and in Pope's day, if not in our own, this was largely the case. What else, though, does this pervasive emphasis on imitation, on distortion, on satire, on parody, and on irony tell us about the cultural milieu or context within which Pope created the poem, and about his relationship with the society he is reproducing in microcosm? In his postscript to his translation of the Odyssey, Pope noted that "Tis using a vast force to lift a feather": in The Rape of the Lock, however, the feather is heavier than one might suspect.

Chapter 2

Alexander Pope: Biography

Poet and satirist of the English Augustan period, best known for his poems *An Essay on Criticism* (1711), *The Rape of the Lock* (1712–14), *The Dunciad* (1728), and *An Essay on Man* (1733–34). He is one of the most epigrammatic of all English authors.

Pope's father, a wholesale linen merchant, retired from business in the year of his son's birth and in 1700 went to live at Binfield in Windsor Forest. The Popes were Roman Catholics, and at Binfield they came to know several neighbouring Catholic families who were to play an important part in the poet's life. Pope's religion procured him some lifelong friends, notably the wealthy squire John Caryll (who persuaded him to write *The Rape of the Lock*, on an incident involving Caryll's relatives) and Martha Blount, to whom Pope addressed some of the most memorable of his poems and to whom he bequeathed most of his property. But his religion also precluded him from a formal course of education, since Catholics were not admitted to the universities. He was trained at home by Catholic priests for a short time and attended Catholic schools at Twyford, near Winchester, and at Hyde Park Corner, London, but he was mainly self-educated.

He was a precocious boy, eagerly reading Latin, Greek, French, and Italian, which he managed to teach himself, and an incessant scribbler, turning out verse upon verse in imitation of the poets he read. The best of these early writings are the *Ode on Solitude* and a paraphrase of St. Thomas à Kempis, both of which he claimed to have written at age.

Early Works

Windsor Forest was near enough to London to permit Pope's frequent visits there. He early grew acquainted with former members of John Dryden's circle, notably William Wycherley, William Walsh, and Henry Cromwell. By 1705 his *Pastorals* were in draft and were circulating among the best literary judges of the day. In 1706 Jacob Tonson, the leading publisher of poetry, had solicited their publication, and they took the place of honour in his *Poetical Miscellanies* in 1709.

This early emergence of a man of letters may have been assisted by Pope's poor physique. As a result of too much study, so he thought, he acquired a curvature of the spine and some tubercular infection, probably Pott's disease, that limited his growth and seriously impaired his health. His full-grown height was 4 feet 6 inches (1.4 metres), but the grace of his profile and fullness of his eye gave him an attractive appearance. He was a lifelong sufferer from headaches, and his deformity made him abnormally sensitive to physical and mental pain. Though he was able to ride a horse and delighted in travel, he was inevitably precluded from much normal physical activity, and his energetic, fastidious mind was largely directed to reading and writing.

When the *Pastorals* were published, Pope was already at work on a poem on the art of writing. This was *An Essay on Criticism*, published in 1711. Its brilliantly polished epigrams (e.g., "A little learning is a dangerous thing," "To err is human, to forgive, divine," and "For fools rush in where angels fear to tread"), which have become part of the proverbial heritage of the language, are readily traced to their sources in Horace, Quintilian, Boileau, and other critics, ancient and modern, in verse and prose; but the charge that the poem is derivative, so often made in the past, takes insufficient account of Pope's success in harmonizing a century of conflict in critical thinking and in showing how nature may best be mirrored in art.

The well-deserved success of *An Essay on Criticism* brought Pope a wider circle of friends, notably Richard Steele and Joseph Addison, who were then collaborating on *The Spectator*. To this journal Pope contributed the most original of his pastorals, *The Messiah* (1712), and perhaps other papers in prose. He was clearly influenced by *The Spectator*'s policy of correcting public morals by witty admonishment, and in this vein he wrote the first version of his mock epic, *The Rape of the Lock* (two cantos, 1712; five cantos, 1714), to reconcile two Catholic families. A young man in one family had stolen a lock of hair from a young lady in the other. Pope treated the dispute that followed as though it were comparable to the mighty quarrel between Greeks and Trojans, which had been Homer's theme. Telling the story with all the pomp and circumstance of epic made not only the participants in the quarrel but also the society in which they lived seem ridiculous. Though it was a society where

...Britain's statesmen oft the fall foredoom
Of foreign tyrants, and of nymphs at home;

as if one occupation concerned them as much as the other, and though in such a society a young lady might do equally ill to ...Stain her honour, or her new brocade;

Forget her pray'rs, or miss a masquerade;

Pope managed also to suggest what genuine attractions existed amid the foppery. It is a glittering poem about a glittering world. He acknowledged how false the sense of values was that paid so much attention to external appearance, but ridicule and rebuke slide imperceptibly into admiration and tender affection as the heroine, Belinda, is conveyed along the Thames to Hampton Court, the scene of the "rape":

But now secure the painted vessel glides,
The sunbeams trembling on the floating tides:
While melting music steals upon the sky,
And soften'd sounds along the waters die;
Smooth flow the waves, the zephyrs gently play,
Belinda smil'd, and all the world was gay.

A comparable blend of seemingly incompatible responses—love and hate, bawdiness and decorum, admiration and ridicule—is to be found in all Pope's later satires. The poem is thick with witty allusions to classical verse and, notably, to Milton's *Paradise Lost*. The art of allusion is an element of much of Pope's poetry.

Pope had also been at work for several years on *Windsor-Forest*. In this poem, completed and published in 1713, he proceeded, as Virgil had done, from the pastoral vein to the georgic and celebrated the rule of Queen Anne as the Latin poet had celebrated the rule of Augustus. In another early poem, *Eloisa to Abelard,* Pope borrowed the form of Ovid's "heroic epistle" (in which an abandoned lady addresses her lover) and showed imaginative skill in conveying the struggle between sexual passion and dedication to a life of celibacy.

Homer and The Dunciad

These poems and other works were collected in the first volume of Pope's *Works* in 1717. When it was published, he was already far advanced with the greatest labour of his life, his verse translation of Homer. He had announced his intentions in October 1713 and had published the first volume, containing the *Iliad*, Books I–IV, in 1715. The *Iliad* was completed in six volumes in 1720. The work of translating the *Odyssey* (vol. i–iii, 1725; vol. iv and v, 1726) was shared with William Broome, who had contributed notes to the *Iliad*, and Elijah Fenton. The labour had been great, but so were the rewards. By the two translations Pope cleared about £10,000 and was able to claim that, thanks to Homer, he could "...live and thrive / Indebted to no Prince or Peer alive."

The merits of Pope's Homer lie less in the accuracy of translation and in correct representation of the spirit of the original than in the achievement of a heroic poem as his contemporaries understood it: a poem Virgilian in its dignity, moral purpose, and pictorial splendour, yet one that consistently kept Homer in view and alluded to him throughout. Pope offered his readers the *Iliad* and the *Odyssey* as he felt sure Homer would have written them had he lived in early 18th-century England.

Political considerations had affected the success of the translation. As a Roman Catholic, he had Tory affiliations rather than Whig; and though he retained the friendship of such Whigs as William Congreve, Nicholas Rowe, and the painter Charles Jervas, his ties with Steele and Addison grew strained as a result of the political animosity that occurred at the end of Queen Anne's reign. He found new and lasting friends in Tory circles—Jonathan Swift, John Gay, John Arbuthnot, Thomas Parnell, the earl of Oxford, and Viscount Bolingbroke. He was associated with the first five in the Scriblerus Club (1713–14), which met to write joint satires on pedantry, later to mature as *Peri Bathouse; or, The Art of Sinking in Poetry* (1728) and the *Memoirs of Martinus Scriblerus* (1741); and these were the men who encouraged his translation of Homer. The Whigs, who associated with Addison at Button's Coffee-House, put up a rival translator in Thomas Tickell, who published his version of the *Iliad*, Book I, two days after Pope's. Addison preferred Tickell's manifestly inferior version; his praise increased the resentment Pope already felt because of a series of slights and misunderstandings; and when Pope heard gossip of further malice on Addison's part, he sent him a satiric view of his character, published later as the character of Atticus, the insincere arbiter of literary taste in *An Epistle to Dr. Arbuthnot* (1735).

Even before the Homer quarrel; Pope had found that the life of a wit was one of perpetual warfare. There were few years when either his person or his poems were not objects of attacks from the critic John Dennis, the bookseller Edmund Curll, the historian John Oldmixon, and other writers of lesser fame. The climax was reached over his edition of Shakespeare. He had emended the plays, in the spirit of a literary editor, to accord with contemporary taste (1725), but his practice was exposed by the scholar Lewis Theobald in *Shakespeare Restored* (1726). Though Pope had ignored some of these attacks, he had replied to others with squibs in prose and verse. But he now attempted to make an end of the opposition and to defend his standards, which he aligned with the standards of civilized society, in the mock epic *The Dunciad* (1728). Theobald was represented in it as the Goddess of Dullness's favourite son, a suitable hero for those leaden times, and others who had given offense were preserved like flies in amber. Pope dispatches his victims with such sensuousness of verse and imagery that the reader is forced to admit that if there is petulance here, as has often been claimed, it is, to parody Wordsworth, petulance recollected in tranquillity. Pope reissued the poem in 1729 with an elaborate mock commentary of prefaces, notes, appendixes, indexes, and errata; this burlesque of pedantry whimsically suggested that *The Dunciad* had fallen a victim to the spirit of the times and been edited by a dunce.

Life at Twickenham

Pope and his parents had moved from Binfield to Chiswick in 1716. There his father died (1717), and two years later he and his mother rented a villa on the Thames at Twickenham, then a small country town where several Londoners had retired to live in rustic seclusion. This was to be Pope's home for the remainder of his life. There he entertained such friends as Swift, Bolingbroke, Oxford, and the painter Jonathan Richardson. These friends were all enthusiastic gardeners, and it was Pope's pleasure to advise and superintend their landscaping according to the best contemporary principles, formulated in his *Epistle to the Right Honourable Richard Earl of Burlington* (1731). This poem, one of the most characteristic works of his maturity, is a rambling discussion in the manner of Horace on false taste in architecture and design, with some suggestions for the worthier employment of a nobleman's wealth.

Pope now began to contemplate a new work on the relations of man, nature, and society that would be a grand organization of human experience and intuition, but he was destined never to complete it. *An Essay on Man* (1733–34) was intended as an introductory book discussing the overall design of this work. The poem has often been charged with shallowness and philosophical inconsistency, and there is indeed little that is original in its thought, almost all of which can be traced in the work of the great thinkers of Western civilization. Subordinate themes were treated in greater detail in *Of the Use of Riches, an Epistle to Bathurst* (1732), *An Epistle to Cobham, of the Knowledge and Characters of Men* (1733), and *Of the Characters of Women: An Epistle to a Lady* (1735).

Pope was deflected from this "system of ethics in the Horatian way" by the renewed need for self-defence. Critical attacks drove him to consider his position as satirist. He chose to adapt for his own defence the first satire of Horace's second book, where the ethics of satire are propounded, and, after discussing the question in correspondence with Dr. John Arbuthnot, he addressed to him an epistle in verse (1735), one of the finest of his later poems, in which were incorporated fragments written over several years. His case in *An Epistle to Dr. Arbuthnot* was a traditional one: that depravity in public morals had roused him to stigmatize outstanding offenders beyond the reach of the law, concealing the names of some and representing others as types, and that he was innocent of personal rancour and habitually forbearing under attack.

The success of his *First Satire of the Second Book of Horace, Imitated* (1733) led to the publication (1734–38) of 10 more of these paraphrases of Horatian themes adapted to the contemporary social and political scene. Pope's poems followed Horace's satires and epistles sufficiently closely for him to print the Latin on facing pages with the English, but whoever chose to make the comparison would notice a continuous enrichment of the original by parenthetic thrusts and compliments, as well as by the freshness of the imagery. The series was concluded with two dialogues in verse, republished as the *Epilogue to the Satires* (1738), where, as in *An Epistle to Dr. Arbuthnot,* Pope ingeniously combined a defence of his own career and character with a restatement of the satirist's traditional apology. In these imitations and dialogues, Pope directed his attack upon the materialistic standards of the commercially minded Whigs in power and upon the corrupting effect of money, while restating and illustrating the old Horatian standards of serene and temperate living. His anxiety about prevailing standards was shown once more in his last completed work, *The New Dunciad* (1742), reprinted as the fourth book of a revised *Dunciad* (1743), in which Theobald was replaced as hero by Colley Cibber, the poet laureate and actor-manager, who not only had given more recent cause of offense but seemed a more appropriate representative of the degenerate standards of the age. In *Dunciad*, Book IV, the Philistine culture of the city of London was seen to overtake the court and seat of government at Westminster, and the poem ends in a magnificent but baleful prophecy of anarchy. Pope had begun work on *Brutus*, an epic poem in blank verse, and on a revision of his poems for a new edition, but neither was complete at his death.

Assessment

Pope's favourite metre was the 10-syllable iambic pentameter rhyming (heroic) couplet. He handled it with increasing skill and adapted it to such varied purposes as the epigrammatic summary of *An Essay on Criticism*, the pathos of *Verses to the Memory of an Unfortunate Lady*, the mock heroic of *The Rape of the Lock*, the discursive tones of *An Essay on Man*, the rapid narrative of the Homer translation, and the Miltonic sublimity of the conclusion of *The Dunciad*. But his greatest triumphs of versification are found in the *Epilogue to the Satires*, where he moves easily from witty, spirited dialogue to noble and elevated declamation, and in *An Epistle to Dr. Arbuthnot*, which opens with a scene of domestic irritation suitably conveyed in broken rhythm:

Shut, shut the door, good John! fatigu'd, I said:
Tie up the knocker, say I'm sick, I'm dead.
The Dog-star rages! nay 'tis past a doubt,
All Bedlam, or Parnassus, is let out:
Fire in each eye, and papers in each hand,
They rave, recite, and madden round the land;

and closes with a deliberately chosen contrast of domestic calm, which the poet may be said to have deserved and won during the course of the poem:

Me, let the tender office long engage
To rock the cradle of reposing age,

With lenient arts extend a mother's breath,
Make languor smile, and smooth the bed of death,
Explore the thought, explain the asking eye,
And keep a while one parent from the sky!

Pope's command of diction is no less happily adapted to his theme and to the type of poem, and the range of his imagery is remarkably wide. He has been thought defective in imaginative power, but this opinion cannot be sustained in view of the invention and organizing ability shown notably in *The Rape of the Lock* and *The Dunciad*. He was the first English poet to enjoy contemporary fame in France and Italy and throughout the European continent and to see translations of his poems into modern as well as ancient languages.

Chapter 3

Alexander Pope: Major Works

CHRONOLOGICAL TABLE

- 1688 Pope born (21 May)
- 1709 *Pastorals*
- 1711 *An Essay on Criticism*
- 1712 *Messiah*
  The Rape of the Locke (2 canto verison)
- 1713 *Windsor Forest*
- 1714 *The Rape of the Lock* (revised; 5 canto version)
- 1715 *Temple of Fame Key to the Lock*
  Iliad (translation; Vols. I-VI published between 1715-1720)
- 1717 *Works* Includes *The Rape of the Lock* (with Clarissa's speech in Canto V) and *Eloisa to Abelard*
- 1725 Edition of Shakespeare
  Odyssey (Vols. I-III)
- 1726 *Odyssey* (Vols. IV-V)
- 1727-8 Pope-Swift *Miscellanies*
- 1728 *Peri Bathous*
  The first *Dunciad* (3 books, Theobald as hero)
- 1729 *Dunciad Variorum*
- 1731 *Epistle to Burlington (Moral Essay IV)*

- 1733 *Epistle to Bathurst (Moral Essay III)*
  First *Imitation of Horace* (Others 1734-8)
  An Essay of Man (Epistles I-III)
- 1734 *Epistle to Cobham (Moral Essay I)*
  Essay on Man (Epistle IV)
- 1735 *Epistle to Dr. Arbuthnot*
  Epistle to a Lady (Moral Essay II)
- 1742 *New Dunciad* (i.e., Book IV)
- 1743 *Dunciad* (4 books, Cibber as hero)
- 1744 Pope dies (30 May)

Chapter 4

Alexander Pope: Timeline

ALEXANDER POPE (1688 - 1744)

Timeline

- 1688: Born 21 May in London
- 1700: Family moves to Bonfield in Windsor Forest, Pope contracts tuberculosis
- 1704: Playwright William Wycherley introduces him into the circle of fashionable London wits and writers as a prodigy
- 1709: Publication of *Pastorals*
- 1711: *An Essay on Criticism* published
- 1712: Early version of *The Rape of the Lock* published
- 1713: *Windsor Forest* published
- 1717: Collected works published
- 1717: Moves to a villa in Twickenham
- 1728: *The Dunciad* published
- 1731: *Moral Essays* published
- 1733: *Imitations of Horace* published
- 1734: *Essay on Man* published
- 1744: Dies 30 May

Chapter 5

Alexander Pope: As an Artist

POPE'S WORKMANSHIP AND STYLE

Pope's literary activity in this first stretch of his career was singularly varied. Any dramatic work was confined to a share in Gay and Arbuthnot's *Three Hours after Marriage.* His *Ode for Music on Saint Cecilia's Day* marks the absence of the lyrical gift. His other attempts to sing were of the slightest; but there is enough variety in the rest to show the directions in which he could turn his extraordinary technical skill. We miss any indication of what was to be the main subject of his matured art. And, just when we might have expected him to plan a great original work, he binds himself to years of translation, and, this task over, we find him in a new field. Pope has been described, at this stage, as a potential romanticist, and we are conscious, in more than one of his poems, of feelings that faded away and a promise that was never fulfilled.

Something must be allowed to the spirit of the times, something to his long term of hard labour on his *Homer*, something to advancing years. For Pope aged early: to his gayer youth succeeded a more or less invalid middle age, which might itself account for a change of tone and a restriction in his choice of subject. The psychology of poetic creation is a perilous topic; but it would that his fervour was frequently kindled, not so much by the theme itself as by the consciousness of literary effort in treating it; that, in short, his inspiration grew in the course of composition. The main features of his style were now formed. Change of taste has done its worst with them; but it is unfair to construct an idea of the essential from the accidents of his art. At his best, he is signally direct, free from artificial balance, otiose epithets and pseudo-classical periphrasis. The nature of many of his winged words is responsible for the belief that Pope's qualities were hard and prosaic. But the exact matching of thought with speech, making any other mode of expression inconceivable, is not less remarkable in passages where the idea is more poetical. Pope did not restrict himself to conversational language: his style is exceptionally rich in apt reminiscences of other writers. But his acquaintance with men of the world, at a time when literature held little aloof from everyday life, made him sensitively aware what his audience demanded. In this respect, the age of Anne may be called Augustan.

Its chief men wrote primarily for the few. Pope has been compared to Horace, from whom he widely differs in much else. But the *curiosa felicitas* of both was connected with the same instinct. One of the conditions of Pope's correctness was that no extravagance or solecism should offend his reader's taste. His early devotion to books has been described. "I had rather," he confided to Spence, "be employed in reading than in the most agreeable conversation"; and, in all that he read, his tenacious memory and sense for apt expression never slumbered. Individual as his style remains, his fabric is many a time woven with threads drawn from another's web. But he was no plagiarist.

The form of words is borrowed or adapted to fit a thought of his own that already asked for utterance. We are reminded again and again of the advantage to which he had studied Milton and Waller and Dryden, and many another predecessor, besides taking hints from contemporaries. Many passages of this kind were noted by Warton and Wakefield and later editors, and a closer search will bring more to light. Pope is not one of those writers who are never at a loss for a word, still less for ten. His style rests on his oriental patience in elaborating his art. "I corrected," he observes in his preface of 1717, "because it was as pleasant to me to correct as to write," and a study of their gradual growth proves that, in many of his lines, the finest touches are due to second intentions. Thus owes its full effectiveness to an afterthought, and the inevitable couplet that tells of fit instruments of ill 5 is an improvement on an earlier attempt. Autographs, proof-sheets and revised editions all attest his passion for retouching. "I will make my enemy do me a kindness when he meant an injury," he writes to Caryll, "and so serve instead of a friend"; and he blotted lines that Dennis had condemned. In minute care of workmanship, he has not been outdone by Tennyson. The sense of the supreme importance of polish was a legacy from Augustan Rome. The endeavour for compactness makes Pope, at times, ungrammatical or obscure. Austin Dobson has characterised his age: But, in *An Essay on Criticism,* where there is need above all to be lucid, Pope, more than once, sins by ambiguity, as, again, in *An Essay on Man.* The metrical principles which he followed from an early period were expounded in a letter to Cromwell. He excepts against hiatus, the use of expletives, monosyllabic lines—unless very artfully managed—the repetition of the same rimes within four or six lines and the too frequent use of alexandrines; and recommends that the same pause in the verse should not to be continued for more than three lines in succession.

Pope has been charged with monotony in his management of the heroic couplet. The surprising thing is that he should have achieved so much variety. He was extraordinarily dexterous in varying the music of his verse within the limits he had set himself. The effect is due to change in pause and beat, a judicious attention to the number of syllables in his words, with an unobtrusive employment of every degree of alliteration and of what may be called the opposite of alliteration, as in The charge that, with Pope, the couplet is almost exclusively the unit of composition requires qualification. At his best, we find him working with the larger unit of the paragraph. As the ideas of a prose-writer using short independent sentences are not necessarily less consecutive than those developed in lengthy periods, so Pope, by avoiding *enjambement,* is not compelled to express a series of disconnected thoughts. A study of his more careful paragraphs shows, too, with what art he extended alliteration over the boundaries of the couplet and studied the music of the larger division. The most serious fault which can be detected is that his ear for rime was not so delicate as his sense of rhythm. When all allowance has been made for the pronunciation of his day, there still remain a large number of unsatisfactory rimes. Weakness, too, is shown in the repetition of the same set of rimes after too short an interval, and the employment of others too close in sound to those immediately preceding.

Chapter 6

Augustan Literature

Augustan literature is a style of English literature produced during the reigns of Queen Anne, King George I, and George II in the first half of the 18th century, ending in the 1740s with the deaths of Pope and Swift. It is a literary epoch that featured the rapid development of the novel, an explosion in satire, the mutation of drama from political satire into melodrama, and an evolution toward poetry of personal exploration. In philosophy, it was an age increasingly dominated by empiricism, while in the writings of political-economy it marked the evolution of mercantilism as a formal philosophy, the development of capitalism, and the triumph of trade.

The chronological anchors of the era are generally vague, largely since the label's origin in contemporary 18th century criticism has made it a shorthand designation for a somewhat nebulous age of satire. This new Augustan period exhibited exceptionally bold political writings in all genres, with the satires of the age marked by an arch, ironic pose, full of nuance, and a superficial air of dignified calm that hid sharp criticisms beneath.

As literacy (and London's population, especially) grew, literature began to appear from all over the kingdom. Authors gradually began to accept literature that went in unique directions rather than the formerly monolithic conventions and, through this, slowly began to honor and recreate various folk compositions. Beneath the appearance of a placid and highly regulated series of writing modes, many developments of the later Romantic era were beginning to take place — while politically, philosophically, and literarily, modern consciousness was being hewn out of hitherto feudal and courtly notions of ages past

Satire

A single name overshadows all others in 18th-century prose satire: Jonathan Swift. Swift wrote poetry as well as prose, and his satires range over all topics. Critically, Swift's satire marked the development of prose parody away from simple satire or burlesque. A burlesque or lampoon in prose would imitate a despised author and quickly move to *reductio ad absurdum* by having the victim say things coarse or idiotic. On the other hand, other satires would argue against a habit, practice, or policy by making fun of its reach or composition or methods. What Swift did was to combine parody, with its imitation of form and style of another, and satire in prose. Swift's works would pretend to speak in the voice of an opponent and imitate the style of the opponent and have the parodic work itself be the satire. Swift's first major satire was *A Tale of a Tub* (1703–1705), which introduced an ancients/ moderns division that would serve as a distinction between the old and new conception of value.

The "moderns" sought trade, empirical science, the individual's reason above the society's, while the "ancients" believed in inherent and immanent value of birth, and the society over the individual's determinations of the good. In Swift's satire, the moderns come out looking insane and proud of their insanity, and dismissive of the value of history. In Swift's most significant satire, *Gulliver's Travels* (1726), autobiography, allegory, and philosophy mix together in the travels. Thematically, *Gulliver's Travels* is a critique of human vanity, of pride. Book one, the journey to Liliput, begins with the world as it is. Book two shows that the idealized nation of Brobdingnag with a philosopher king is no home for a contemporary Englishman. Book four depicts the land of the

Houyhnhnms, a society of horses ruled by pure reason, where humanity itself is portrayed as a group of "yahoos" covered in filth and dominated by base desires. It shows that, indeed, the very desire for reason may be undesirable, and humans must struggle to be neither Yahoos nor Houyhnhnms, for book three shows what happens when reason is unleashed without any consideration of morality or utility (i.e. madness, ruin, and starvation).

There were other satirists who worked in a less virulent way, who took a bemused pose and only made lighthearted fun. Tom Brown, Ned Ward, and Tom D'Urfey were all satirists in prose and poetry whose works appeared in the early part of the Augustan age. Tom Brown's most famous work in this vein was *Amusements Serious and Comical, Calculated for the Meridian of London* (1700). Ned Ward's most memorable work was *The London Spy* (1704–1706). *The London Spy,* before *The Spectator,* took up the position of an observer and uncomprehendingly reporting back. Tom D'Urfey's *Wit and Mirth: or Pills to Purge Melancholy* (1719) was another satire that attempted to offer entertainment, rather than a specific bit of political action, in the form of coarse and catchy songs.

Particularly after Swift's success, parodic satire had an attraction for authors throughout the 18th century. A variety of factors created a rise in political writing and political satire, and Robert Walpole's success and domination of House of Commons was a very effective proximal cause for polarized literature and thereby the rise of parodic satire. The parodic satire takes apart the cases and plans of policy without necessarily contrasting a normative or positive set of values. Therefore, it was an ideal method of attack for ironists and conservatives—those who would not be able to enunciate a set of values to change toward but could condemn present changes as ill-considered. Satire was present in all genres during the Augustan period.

Perhaps primarily, satire was a part of political and religious debate. Every significant politician and political act had satires to attack it. Few of these were parodic satires, but parodic satires, too, emerged in political and religious debate. So omnipresent and powerful was satire in the Augustan age that more than one literary history has referred to it as the "Age of satire" in literature.

Poetry

In the Augustan era, poets wrote in direct counterpoint and direct expansion of one another, with each poet writing satire when in opposition. There was a great struggle over the nature and role of the pastoral in the early part of the century, reflecting two simultaneous movements: the invention of the subjective self as a worthy topic, with the emergence of a priority on *individual* psychology, against the insistence on all acts of art being *performance* and public gesture designed for the benefit of society at large. The development seemingly agreed upon by both sides was a gradual adaptation of all forms of poetry from their older uses. Odes would cease to be encomium, ballads cease to be narratives, elegies cease to be sincere memorials, satires no longer be specific entertainments, parodies no longer be performance pieces without sting, song no longer be pointed, and the lyric would become a celebration of the individual rather than a lover's complaint.

These developments can be seen as extensions of Protestantism, as Max Weber argued, for they represent a gradual increase in the implications of Martin Luther's doctrine of the priesthood of all believers, or they can be seen as a growth of the power and assertiveness of the bourgeoisie and an echo of the displacement of the worker from the home in growing industrialization, as Marxists such as E.P. Thompson have argued. It can be argued that the development of the subjective individual against the social individual was a natural reaction to trade over other methods of economic production. Whatever the prime cause, a largely conservative set of voices argued for a social person and largely emergent voices argued for the individual person.

The entire Augustan age's poetry was dominated by Alexander Pope. His lines were repeated often enough to lend quite a few clichés and proverbs to modern English usage.

Pope had few poetic rivals, but he had many personal enemies and political, philosophical, or religious opponents, and Pope himself was quarrelsome in print. Pope and his enemies (often called "the Dunces" because of Pope's successful satirizing of them in *The Dunciad*) fought over central matters of the proper subject matter for poetry and the proper pose of the poetic voice.

There was a great struggle over the nature and role of the pastoral in the early part of the century. After Pope published his *Pastorals* of the four seasons in 1709, an evaluation in the *Guardian* praised Ambrose Philips's pastorals above Pope's, and Pope replied with a mock praise of Philips's *Pastorals* that heaped scorn on them. Pope quoted Philips's worst lines, mocked his execution, and delighted in pointing out his empty lines. Pope later explained that any depictions of shepherds and their mistresses in the pastoral must not be updated shepherds, that they must be icons of the Golden Age: "we are not to describe our shepherds as shepherds at this day really are, but as they may be conceived then to have been, when the best of men followed the employment" (Gordon). Philips's *Pastorals* were not particularly awful poems, but they did reflect his desire to "update" the pastoral. In 1724, Philips would update poetry again by writing a series of odes dedicated to "all ages and characters, from Walpole, the steerer of the realm, to Miss Pulteney in the nursery." Henry Carey was one of the best at satirizing these poems, and his *Namby Pamby* became a hugely successful obliteration of Philips and Philips's endeavor. What is notable about Philips against Pope, however, is the fact that *both* poets were adapting the pastoral and the ode, both altering it. Pope's insistence upon a Golden Age pastoral no less than Philips's desire to update it meant making a political statement. While it is easy to see in Ambrose Philips an effort at modernist triumph, it is no less the case that Pope's artificially restricted pastoral was a statement of what the ideal should be.

Pope's friend John Gay also adapted the pastoral. Gay, working at Pope's suggestion, wrote a parody of the updated pastoral in *The Shepherd's Week*. He also imitated the Satires of

Juvenal with his *Trivia*. In 1728, his *The Beggar's Opera* was an enormous success, running for an unheard-of eighty performances. All of these works have in common a gesture of compassion. In *Trivia,* Gay writes as if commiserating with those who live in London and are menaced by falling masonry and bedpan slops, and *The Shepherd's Week* features great detail of the follies of everyday life and eccentric character. Even *The Beggar's Opera,* which is a satire of Robert Walpole, portrays its characters with compassion: the villains have pathetic songs in their own right and are acting out of exigency rather than boundless evil.

Throughout the Augustan era the "updating" of Classical poets was a commonplace. These were not translations, but rather they were imitations of Classical models, and the imitation allowed poets to veil their responsibility for the comments they made. Alexander Pope would manage to refer to the King himself in unflattering tones by "imitating" Horace in his *Epistle to Augustus.* Similarly, Samuel Johnson wrote a poem that falls into the Augustan period in his "imitation of Juvenal" entitled *London.* The imitation was inherently conservative, since it argued that all that was good was to be found in the old classical education, but these imitations were used for progressive purposes, as the poets who used them were often doing so to complain of the political situation.

In satire, Pope achieved two of the greatest poetic satires of all time in the Augustan period. *The Rape of the Lock* (1712 and 1714) was a gentle mock-heroic. Pope applies Virgil's heroic and epic structure to the story of a young woman (Arabella Fermor) having a lock of hair snipped by an amorous baron (Lord Petre). The *structure* of the comparison forces Pope to invent mythological forces to overlook the struggle, and so he creates an epic battle, complete with a mythology of sylphs and metempsychosis, over a game of Ombre, leading to a fiendish appropriation of the lock of hair. Finally, a deux ex machina appears and the lock of hair experiences an apotheosis. To some degree, Pope was adapting Jonathan Swift's habit, in *A Tale of a Tub,* of pretending that metaphors were literal truths, and he was inventing a mythos to go with the everyday. The poem was an enormous public success.

A decade after the gentle, laughing satire of *The Rape of the Lock,* Pope wrote his masterpiece of invective and specific opprobrium in *The Dunciad.* The story is that of the goddess Dulness choosing a new avatar. She settles upon one of Pope's personal enemies, Lewis Theobald, and the poem describes the coronation and heroic games undertaken by all of the dunces of Great Britain in celebration of Theobald's ascension. When Pope's enemies responded to *The Dunciad* with attacks, Pope produced the *Dunciad Variorum,* with a "learned" commentary upon the original *Dunciad.* In 1743, he added a fourth book and changed the hero from Lewis Theobald to Colley Cibber. In the fourth book of the new *Dunciad,* Pope expressed the view that, in the battle between light and dark (enlightenment and the Dark Ages), Night and Dulness were fated to win, that all things of value were soon going to be subsumed under the curtain of unknowing.

John Gay and Alexander Pope belong on one side of a line separating the celebrants of the individual and the celebrants of the social. Pope wrote *The Rape of the Lock,* he said, to settle a disagreement between two great families, to laugh them into peace. Even *The Dunciad,* which seems to be a serial killing of everyone on Pope's enemies list, sets up these figures as expressions of dangerous and *antisocial* forces in letters. Theobald and Cibber are marked by vanity and pride, by having no care for morality. The hireling pens Pope attacks mercilessly in the heroic games section of the *Dunciad* are all embodiments of avarice and lies. Similarly, Gay writes of political society, of social dangers, and of follies that must be addressed to protect the greater whole. Gay's individuals are microcosms of the society at large. On the other side of this line were people who agreed with the *politics* of Gay and Pope (and Swift), but not in approach.

They include, early in the Augustan Age, James Thomson and Edward Yonge. Thomson's *The Seasons* (1730) are nature poetry, but they are unlike Pope's notion of the Golden Age pastoral. Thomson's poet speaks in the first person from direct observation, and his own mood and sentiment colour the descriptions of landscape. Unlike Pope's *Windsor Forest*, Thomson's seasons have no mythology, no celebration of Britain or the crown. *Winter*, in particular, is melancholy and meditative. Edward Yonge's *Night Thoughts* (1742–1744) was immediately popular.

It was, even more than *Winter*, a poem of deep solitude, melancholy, and despair. In these two poets, there are the stirrings of the lyric as the Romantics would see it: the celebration of the private individual's idiosyncratic, yet paradigmatic, responses to the visions of the world.

These hints at the solitary poet were carried into a new realm with Thomas Gray, whose *Elegy Written in a Country Church-Yard* (1750) set off a new craze for poetry of melancholy reflection. It was written in the "country," and not in or as opposed to London, and the poem sets up the solitary observer in a privileged position. It is only by being solitary that the poet can speak of a truth that is wholly individually realised. After Gray, a group often referred to as the Churchyard Poets began imitating his pose, if not his style. Oliver Goldsmith (*The Deserted Village*), Thomas Warton, and even Thomas Percy (*The Hermit of Warkworth*), each conservative by and large and Classicist (Gray himself was a professor of Greek), took up the new poetry of solitude and loss.

When the Romantics emerged at the end of the 18th century, they were not assuming a radically new invention of the subjective self themselves, but merely formalizing what had gone before. Similarly, the later 18th century saw a ballad revival, with Thomas Percy's *Reliques of Ancient English Poetry*. The relics were not always very ancient, as many of the ballads dated from only the 17th century (e.g. the Bagford Ballads or The Dragon of Wantley in the Percy Folio), and so what began as an antiquarian movement soon became a folk movement. When this folk-inspired impulse combined with the solitary and individualistic impulse of the Churchyard Poets, Romanticism was nearly inevitable.

Drama

The "Augustan era" is difficult to define chronologically in prose and poetry, but it is very easy to date its end in drama. The Augustan era's drama ended definitively in 1737, with the Licensing Act. Prior to 1737, however, the English stage was changing rapidly from the Restoration comedy and Restoration drama and their noble subjects to the quickly developing melodrama.

George Lillo and Richard Steele wrote the trend-setting plays of the early Augustan period. Lillo's plays consciously turned from heroes and kings and toward shopkeepers and apprentices. They emphasized drama on a household scale, rather than a national scale, and the hamartia and agon in his tragedies are the common flaws of yielding to temptation and the commission of Christian sin. The plots are resolved with Christian forgiveness and repentance. Steele's *The Conscious Lovers* (1722) hinges upon his young hero avoiding fighting a duel. These plays set up a new set of values for the stage. Instead of amusing the audience or inspiring the audience, they sought to instruct the audience and ennoble it. Further, the plays were popular precisely because they seemed to reflect the audience's own lives and concerns.

Joseph Addison also wrote a play, entitled *Cato,* in 1713. *Cato* concerned the Roman statesman. The year of its première was important, for Queen Anne was in serious illness at the time, and both the Tory ministry of the day and the Whig opposition (already being led by Robert Walpole) were concerned about the succession. Both groups were contacting the Old Pretender about bringing the Young Pretender over. Londoners sensed this anxiety, for Anne had no heirs, and all of the natural successors in the Stuart family were Roman Catholic or unavailable. Therefore, the figure of Cato was a transparent symbol of Roman integrity, and the Whigs saw in him a champion of Whig values, while the Tories saw in him an embodiment of Tory sentiments. Both sides cheered the play, even though Addison was himself clearly Whig. John Home's play *Douglas* (1756) would have a similar fate to *Cato* in the next generation, after the Licensing Act.

As during the Restoration, economics drove the stage in the Augustan period. Under Charles II court patronage meant economic success, and therefore the Restoration stage featured plays that would suit the monarch and/or court. The drama that celebrated kings and told the history of Britain's monarchs was fit fare for the crown and courtiers. Charles II was a philanderer, and so Restoration comedy featured a highly sexualized set of plays. However, after the reign of William and Mary, the court and crown stopped taking a great interest in the playhouse. Theaters had to get their money from the audience of city dwellers, therefore, and consequently plays that reflected city anxieties and celebrated the lives of citizens drew and were staged.

Thus, there were quite a few plays that were, in fact, not literary that were staged more often than the literary plays. John Rich and Colley Cibber duelled over special theatrical effects. They put on plays that were actually just spectacles, where the text of the play was almost an afterthought. Dragons, whirlwinds, thunder, ocean waves, and even actual elephants were on stage. Battles, explosions, and horses were put on the boards. Rich specialized in pantomime and was famous as the character "Lun" in harlequin presentations. The plays put on in this manner are not generally preserved or studied, but their monopoly on the theaters infuriated established literary authors.

Additionally, opera made its way to England during this period. Inasmuch as opera combined singing with acting, it was a mixed genre, and this violated all the strictures of neo-classicism. Further, high melodies would cover the singers' expressions of grief or joy, thus breaking "decorum." To add insult to injury, the casts and celebrated stars were foreigners, and, as with Farinelli, castrati. The satirists saw in opera the *non plus ultra* of invidiousness. As Pope put it in *Dunciad B*:

"Joy to Chaos! let Division reign:

Chromatic tortures soon shall drive them [the muses] hence, Break all their nerves, and fritter all their sense:

One Trill shall harmonize joy, grief, and rage,
Wake the dull Church, and lull the ranting Stage;
To the same notes thy sons shall hum, or snore,
And all thy yawning daughters cry, encore." (IV 55–60)

John Gay parodied the opera with his satirical *Beggar's Opera* (1728) and offered up a parody of Robert Walpole's actions during the South Sea Bubble. Superficially, the play is about a man named Macheath who keeps being imprisoned by a thief named Peachum and who escapes prison over and over again because the daughter of the jailor, Lucy Lockitt, is in love with him. This is an obvious parallel with the case of Jonathan Wild (Peachum) and Jack Sheppard (Macheath). However, it was also the tale of Robert Walpole (Peachum) and the South Sea directors (Macheath). The play was a hit, and its songs were printed up and sold. However, when Gay wrote a follow up called *Polly*, Walpole had the play suppressed before performance

Playwrights were therefore in straits. On the one hand, the playhouses were doing without plays by turning out hack-written pantomimes. On the other hand, when a satirical play appeared, the Whig ministry would suppress it. This antagonism was picked up by Henry Fielding, who was not afraid to fight Walpole. His *Tom Thumb* (1730) was a satire on all of the tragedies written before him, with quotations from all the worst plays patched together for absurdity, and the plot concerned the eponymous tiny man attempting to run things. It was, in other words, an attack on Robert Walpole and the way that he was referred to as "the Great Man." Here, the Great Man is made obviously deficient by being a midget. Walpole responded, and Fielding's revision of the play was in print only. It was written by "Scribblerus Secundus," its title page announced, and it was the *Tragedy of Tragedies*, which functioned as a clearly Swiftian parodic satire. Anti-Walpolean sentiment also showed in increasingly political plays, and the theaters began to stage them. A particular play of unknown authorship entitled *A Vision of the Golden Rump* was cited when Parliament passed the Licensing Act of 1737. (The "rump" in question is Parliament, on the one hand, and buttocks on the other.)

The Licensing Act required all plays to go to a censor before staging, and only those plays passed by the censor were allowed to be performed. The first play to be banned by the new Act was *Gustavus Vasa,* by Henry Brooke. Samuel Johnson wrote a Swiftian parodic satire of the licensers, entitled *A Complete Vindication of the Licensers of the English Stage.* The satire was, of course, not a vindication at all, but rather a *reductio ad absurdum* of the position for censorship. Had the licensers not exercised their authority in a partisan manner, the Act might not have chilled the stage so dramatically, but the public was well aware of the bannings and censorship, and consequently any play that *did* pass the licensers was regarded with suspicion by the public. Therefore, the playhouses had little choice but to present old plays and pantomime and plays that had no conceivable political content. In other words, William Shakespeare's reputation grew enormously as his plays saw a quadrupling of performances, and sentimental comedy and melodrama were the only choices.

Very late in the Augustan period, Oliver Goldsmith attempted to resist the tide of sentimental comedy with *She Stoops to Conquer* (1773), and Richard Brinsley Sheridan would mount several satirical plays after Walpole's death, but to a large degree the damage had been done and would last for a century.

Chapter 7

Neoclassicism: An Introduction

The English Neoclassical movement, predicated upon and derived from both classical and contemporary French models, (see Boileau's L'Art Poetique (1674) and Pope's "Essay on Criticism" (1711) as critical statements of Neoclassical principles) embodied a group of attitudes toward art and human existence—ideals of order, logic, restraint, accuracy, "correctness," "restraint," decorum, and so on, which would enable the practitioners of various arts to imitate or reproduce the structures and themes of Greek or Roman originals. Though its origins were much earlier (the Elizabethan Ben Jonson, for example, was as indebted to the Roman poet Horace as Alexander Pope would later be), Neoclassicism dominated English literature from the Restoration in 1660 until the end of the eighteenth century, when the publication of Lyrical Ballads (1798) by Wordsworth and Coleridge marked the full emergence of Romanticism.

For the sake of convenience the Neoclassic period can be divided into three relatively coherent parts: the Restoration Age (1660-1700), in which Milton, Bunyan, and Dryden were the dominant influences; the Augustan Age (1700-1750), in which Pope was the central poetic figure, while Defoe, Richardson, Fielding, and Smollett were presiding over the sophistication of the novel; and the Age of Johnson(1750-1798), which, while it was dominated and characterized by the mind and personality of the inimitable Dr. Samuel Johnson, whose sympathies were with the fading Augustan past, saw the beginnings of a new understanding and appreciation of the work of Shakespeare, the development, by Sterne and others, of the novel of sensibility, and the emergence of the Gothic school—attitudes which, in the context of the development of a cult of Nature, the influence of German romantic thought, religious tendencies like the rise of Methodism, and political events like the American and French revolutions — established the intellectual and emotional foundations of English Romanticism.

To a certain extent Neoclassicism represented a reaction against the optimistic, exuberant, and enthusiastic Renaissance view of man as a being fundamentally good and possessed of an infinite potential for spiritual and intellectual growth. Neoclassical theorists, by contrast, saw man as an imperfect being, inherently sinful, whose potential was limited. They replaced the Renaissance emphasis on the imagination, on invention and experimentation, and on mysticism with an emphasis on order and reason, on restraint, on common sense, and on religious, political, economic and philosophical conservatism. They maintained that man himself was the most appropriate subject of art, and saw art itself as essentially pragmatic—as valuable because it was somehow useful—and as something which was properly intellectual rather than emotional.

Hence their emphasis on proper subject matter; and hence their attempts to subordinate details to an overall design, to employ in their work concepts like symmetry, proportion, unity, harmony, and grace, which would facilitate the process of delighting, instructing, educating, and correcting the social animal which they believed man to be. Their flavourite prose literary forms were the essay, the letter, the satire, the parody, the burlesque, and the moral fable; in poetry, the flavourite verse form was the rhymed couplet, which reached its greatest sophistication in heroic couplet of Pope; while the theatre saw the development of the heroic drama, the melodrama, the sentimental comedy, and the comedy of manners. The fading away of Neoclassicism may have appeared to represent the last flicker of the Enlightenment, but artistic movements never really die: many of the primary aesthetic tenets of Neoclassicism, in fact have reappeared in the twentieth century — in, for example, the poetry and criticism of T. S. Eliot — as manifestations of a reaction against Romanticism itself: Eliot saw Neo-classicism as emphasising poetic form and conscious craftsmanship, and Romanticism as a poetics of personal emotion and "inspiration," and pointedly preferred the former.

Neoclassical Style

Wit

The American Heritage Dictionary defines wit as "the ability to perceive and express in ingeniously humourous manner the relationship or similarity between seemingly incongruous or disparate things." A person who is noted for this ability is also known as a wit. These meanings, which gained currency in the age of Dryden and Pope, represent a marked change from the term's earlier definition.

According to authorities on the history of wit, the term had from earliest time the meaning of 'intellect' or 'mind'; not until the sixteenth century did it take on any slightest tinge of the meaning connected with surprise and amusement which we today normally associate with it. To the Elizabethan, 'wit' still meant primarily 'intellect' or 'mental capacity,' though it also had such meanings, apparently derivative of the central one, as 'understanding,' 'wisdom,' even 'power of imagination' [W. Lee Ustick and Hoyt H. Hudson, "Wit, 'Mixt Wit' and the Bee in Amber" Huntington Library Quarterly 8 (1935)].

These authors argue that Thomas Hobbes played a pivotal role in creating the modern sense of the term when he described.

that quick ranging of mind... joined with... comparing the things that come into the mind, one with another: in which comparison, a man delighteth himself either with finding unexpected similitude of things, otherwise unlike... from whence proceed those graceful similes, metaphors, and other tropes, by which both poets and orators have it in their power to make things please or displease... or else in discerning sudden dissimilitude in things that otherwise appear the same."

Heroic Couplet: A Brief Introduction

The hungry judges soon the Sentence sign, And Wretches hang that Jury-men may Dine.

The heroic couplet, lines in iambic pentameter rhymed in pairs, appeared early in English—it was Chaucer's flavourite meter—and came into vogue in poetic drama in the seventeenth century, but in the eighteenth century, in the hands of masters like Dryden, Pope, and Johnson, it became for many years the dominant English verse form. In the Neo-classical period the heroic couplet consisted of a couplet of end-stopped lines which formed a short stanza, and substituted for the Greek and Latin heroic hexameter.

Why should this meter, with its strongly symmetrical grammatical structure, be perceived by poets like Pope and Johnson as an ideal structure to embody and convey the emphasis on form and sense and wit which they sought so insistently in their work? And why would the rebellious Romantics, in their quest for personal and poetic freedom, (with a few important exceptions, such as Byron, and, to a lesser degree, Keats) react so strongly against these same qualities?

Chapter 8

The Rhetorical Organization of the Neoclassical Couplet

Parallel and Contrast

Know farther yet; Whoever FAIR and CHASTE Rejects [verb1: -] Mankind, is by some Sylph Embrac'd [verb1: +]:For Spirits, freed from mortal laws, with ease Assume WHAT Sexes and WHAT Shapes they please. What guards the purity of Melting Maids,In Courtly Balls [noun-adjective1a], and Midnight Masquerades [noun-adjective1b], The Glance by Day [obj1c], the Whisper in the Dark [obj1d]; WHEN kind Occasion prompts their warm Desires, WHEN Musick softens, and WHEN Dancing fires? – The Rape of the Lock, Canto I, lines 67-76

Note how Pope turns each set of two lines into a unit by closing it off with a strong rhyme. What kind of words and what parts of speech does he chose to create this closure? What kind does he avoid?

How many different kinds of parallels can you find in these lines?

How does Pope create variety so the form doesn't get monotonous? Hint: line 73 pairs "treach'rous Friend" and "daring Spark."

What does the second half of the couplet use for a similar parallel?

Rhetorical organization

An example of the way that the rhetorical organization of Pope's couplets generates his characteristic wit:

> Whether the Nymph shall break Diana's Law, Or some frail China Jar recieve a Flaw, Or stain her Honour, or her new Brocade, Forget her Prayer's, or miss a Masquerade, Or lose her Heart, or Necklace, at a Ball... — *The Rape of the Lock*, Canto II, lines 103-9

> What point does Pope make by placing side by side (and in similar grammatical forms) the important and the trivial?

> How does this establish tone, point of view, the subject of the poem?

Puns and Wordplay

> Here Britain's Statesmen oft the Fall foredoom Of Foreign Tyrants, and of Nymphs at Home; Here Thou, Great Anna! whom three Realms obey,Dost sometimes Counsel take and sometimes Tea. — *The Rape of the Lock*, Canto III, lines 5-9

Neoclassical Genres and Modes

The Mock Epic as Genre

As the name indicates, the Mock-Epic is a literary form that burlesques the Classical epic by bringing the formulas characteristic of the epic — the invocation of a deity, a formal statement of theme, the division of the work into books and cantos, grandiose speeches, battles, supernatural machinery, and so on — to bear upon a trivial subject. The main effect of thus employing techniques of the epic is, however, not so much to have fun with the epic as to deflate a subject or characters that by contrast appear particularly trivial. For example, Pope's Rape of the Lock uses its highly polished verses, mordantly satirical heroic couplets, wit depth, and intelligence to satirize the fuss that results when an idle young lord cuts a small lock of hair from the head of an idle young beauty.

By ludicrously overstating the importance of the whole affair (largely by parodying the epic, which readers in Pope's day knew well), he succeeds, paradoxically enough, in making the whole thing seem ridiculous and funny but also somehow tragic. As a result, Pope makes us aware of the fact that not only the participants in the drama but also the rest of humanity, including Pope himself and certainly his readers, are somehow ridiculous and funny — and tragic — too. Here are a few of the ways in which the plot and structure of The Rape of the Lock burlesques elements characteristic of the epic:

Epic	Mock Epic
Iliad, Aeneid	The Rape of the Lock
The Arming of the Hero	Toilet [dressing] scene.
Battle	Card Game.
The Statagem	The Pinch of Snuff.
Meddling Gods and Goddesses	Sylphs and Gnomes
The Journey to the Underworld	The Cave of Spleen
Dream	Dream

Satire

The word satire derives from the Latin satira, meaning "medley." A satire, either in prose or in poetic form, holds prevailing vices or follies up to ridicule: it employs humour and wit to criticize human institutions or humanity itself, in order that they might be remodeled or improved. Satire as an English literary form derives in large part from Greek and Roman literature. Aristophanes, Juvenal, Horace, Martial, and Petronius all wrote satires of one kind or another, and the tradition maintained a tenuous existence in England down through the Middle Ages in the form of the fabliau and the Beast-epic. The eighteenth century, however, in which poetry, drama, essays, and literary criticism were all imbued with the form, was the golden age of English satire. Dryden, Swift, Pope, Addison, Steele, and Johnson were all great satirists, and self-described heirs of the Roman poets Horace and Juvenal. Horatian satire tends to be gentler and more sympathetic than the more biting and bitter Juvenalian satire, in which the author‹Swift is the great example‹frequently rails savagely against the evil inherent in man and his institutions. Byron and Thackeray, in the nineteenth century, maintained and refined the satiric tradition, as did T. S. Eliot in the twentieth.

Alex Derwent Hope, the contemporary Australian poet, agrees with Pope that satire

> has a social function that places it on a level with Religion, Law, and Government. Though its tone may be light, its function is wholly serious; and as for passion, it is actuated by a fierce and strenuous moral and intellectual enthusiasm, the passion for order, justice, and beauty.... It keeps the public conscience alert, it exposes absurdity for what it is and makes those inclined to adopt foolish or tasteless fashions aware that they are ridiculous. It shows vice its own feature and makes it odious to others.... Satire is an aristocratic art. It is not afraid to tell unpopular truths, but its habit is to tell them with the assurance and detachment of ridicule, and ridicule is the weapon of contempt.

Narrators, Masks and Speakers in Satire

Satires employ a different kinds of narrators and speakers, and the reader cannot therefore assume that the speaker or storyteller is the author or speaks (directly) for the author. The Rape of the Lock (text of poem) has an omniscient third-person narrator, whereas the same author's "Epistle to Dr. Arbuthnot" presents an idealized version of Pope as the speaker. In contrast, Swift's "Gulliver's Travels uses a created character in a most complex and varying way. In the first book, which mocks England by having Gulliver describe six-inch beings whose customs resemble those of England, Swift's character usually presents the author's views, though indirectly; in the second, which mocks England by having Gulliver now the tiny figure, Gulliver becomes the target of satire as a means of mocking England; in the voyages of the third book, Gulliver again becomes more agent than target, but in the last, the darkest of the four, Gulliver, now a satiric everyman, becomes the target again. Similarly, in "A Modest Proposal" Swift creates a figure who becomes almost an allegorical representative of his audience

Hodgart on The Conditions of Political Satire

Richard Hodgart's Satire points out that "political satire requires special conditions for its appearance in strength:"

First, a degree of free speech either through design as in Greece or England, or through inefficiency as inlate eighteenth-century France and even in Czarist Russia.

Secondly, there must be a general readiness of the educated classes to take part in political affairs; this need not imply the existence of a democracy, but it does mean the spread of democratic ideas.

Thirdly, there must be some confidence on the part of writers that they can actually influence the conduct of affairs; and

Fourthly, there must be a wide audience that enjoys wit, imagination and the graces of literature, and that is sophisticated enough to enjoy their application to serious topics.

According to Hodgart, such conditions "existed to the full in England from about 1680 to 1820, and they have reappeared since in other parts of Europe, usually in pre-revolutionary rather than revolutionary situations; and as commonly associated with nationalistic as with social conflict".

Chapter 9

An Introduction to Eighteenth Century

Readers And Writers

I

Whatever may be true of other periods, the poets of the eighteenth century wrote their poetry fully intending that it should be read. It is therefore of some importance to know the sort of public they had in mind. If we know what people made a habit of reading the new poems as they came out we shall be in a better position to understand why the poets wrote as they did; for though they did not write *at* their public they did unquestionably write for a public whose tastes they knew, and probably shared, and whose views on poetry they would not normally wish to flout.

Who, then, read Pope and Gay and Johnson? Who read Tickell and Paul Whitehead and James Bramston, the Armstrongs and Somervilles, the Mallets and Mickles, and scores of other half-forgotten poets? We know that Lord Chesterfield and Lady Mary Wortley Montagu read and enjoyed the poetry of their contemporaries, but we also happen to know that Stephen Duck, the Wiltshire thresher, read *Paradise Lost* and Pope's *Messiah*, and that he had a friend who had been a footman for some years in London and who had there bought a number of books which they afterwards read together. Between those two extremes lies the greater part of the population of England, which in the first half of the eighteenth century amounted to about six millions. We may, however, reach some more definite conclusions if we can answer another question: Who *bought* eighteenth-century poetry? How many people in 1700 or i 750 could afford to buy modern poetry as it came from the press? For the contemporaries ofAddison and Pope there were almost no circulating libraries available, and though a number of the new poems might be found lying about on coffee-house tables along with the newspapers and other periodicals, it is safe to say that the reader of poetry had either to buy a copy for himself or else borrow one from a friend.

We can form a rough estimate of those who could afford to buy the new poems as they came out if we set the price of books opposite the average income of the period. There will always be Stephen Ducks who will go without food to purchase a book, but they may be safely left out of the calculation. On such evidence as is available it becomes clear that to most Englishmen in the eighteenth century poetry was economically a luxury, and that the public which habitually bought new books must have been confined to a relatively small class. For the lower ranges of income statistics are plentiful. We need go no lower in the scale than artisans and handicraftsmen, since with them we touch the fringe of illiteracy; their annual income averaged about œ40 throughout the century.

The average for the shopkeeper and tradesman class was only a little more, though obviously the upper limit might be a good deal higher. For this large lower-middle class an income of œ50 a year was above rather than below the average. The cost of living was a good deal lower than it is to-day, but clothing was not particularly cheap, and among the upper classes with their perukes, silk stockings, linen shirts, lace ruffles, and silver-buckled shoes (to confine the estimate to one sex) it was relatively dearer than it is to-day. Rents were lower, and servants' wages much lower; but then more servants were kept, and they had to be fed and to some extent clothed by their employers. The wonder is that lower-middle-class people lived as well as they did; but obviously they had little left over to spend on the last new poem or play, even if they had wanted to read it.

The book-buying public was therefore to be found mainly among the upper classes. Here, unfortunately, statistics of average income are far less plentiful, and much more subject to variation within the class. A contemporary estimate(2) still respected by economic historians (for want, perhaps, of anything better) puts the average income of temporal lords at œ2,800; of baronets at œ880; of esquires at œ450; and of other gentlemen at œ280. To this we might add that the Law was a profitable vocation, and that many of the gentlemen able to form extensive libraries were in fact lawyers. On the other hand, the great majority of the minor clergy were little better off than tradesmen, though their position was considerably better by 1800 than it had been in 1700. The esquire with œ450 might easily find that his various expenses left little over for the buying of books. When he came to Town with his family in the winter they expected him to find money for fashionable lodgings, for visits to the theatre, to the opera (where a seat, as the Branghtons in *Evelina* were to discover, might cost him a guinea), to concerts of vocal and instrumental music (tickets from five shillings to a guinea), to balls and ridottos, Ranelagh and other fashionable places of resort; and he himself would probably wish to dine with his friends at expensive eating-houses like Locket's or the Blue Posts. Even if he were unencumbered with a wife and family and preferred to spend his money in buying books rather than in running after the pleasures of the Town, poetry was only one of several sorts of literature he might wish to buy. Poetry competed in the literary market with political pamphlets, plays, travel books, history, sermons, technical and professional books (often expensive), the *Tatler*, the *Spectator*, and their successors, and, as the century advanced, with more and more prose fiction.

As for the cost of books in this age of low incomes, it was comparatively high. The average price of a new play, published in quarto and sold 'stitched', was eighteen pence; cheaper editions in duodecimo might follow. New poems of the length of Pope's *Epistle to Dr. Arbuthnot* (419 lines) were usually first published in folio or quarto and sold at eighteen pence. *The Dunciad Variorum* (1729) and *The Dunciad in Four Books* (1743), 7s. 6d.; but these were both large quarto volumes, swollen by Pope's prose commentary and intended, as part of the joke, to present a pompous appearance. Poetical miscellanies running to 250-300 pages in octavo usually cost five or six shillings. Such prices were prohibitive for a large section of the community, and must have acted as a serious deterrent to many gentlemen of middling means. In the circumstances the sale of poetry throughout the century is remarkable.

That there was a public willing to buy poetry and yet discouraged by the bookseller's prices may be seen from the many pirated editions of poems sold at cut prices. In the first decade of the century Henry Hills made a practice of pirating poems and printing them on cheap paper. Defoe's *Jure Divino*, published in folio and sold to subscribers at ten shillings, was promptly pirated in an octavo edition that sold at five shillings, and this edition was undercut not long afterwards by another in chapbook form selling at sixpence. In 1729 a number of booksellers pirated the *Dunciad*, and issued an advertisement claiming that the public had been 'insulted' by having to pay 6s. 6d. for 'the pompous Quarto Edition' when they could now have the same book for two shillings. Examples of such piracies could be multiplied.

In the later decades of the century cheap editions of the English classics became more numerous. The works of poets and prose writers were often issued serially, and the parts later bound together as a book. By 1782 the German traveller Moritz was able to remark on the familiarity of the English people with the great writers of their own country.

> The English national authors are in all hands, and read by all people, of which the innumerable editions they have gone through are a sufficient proof. My landlady, who is only a tailor's widow, reads her Milton; and tells me that her late husband first fell in love with her on this very account, because she read Milton with such proper emphasis.

He goes on to note how the quick sale of the classical authors is here promoted also by cheap and convenient editions. They have them all bound in pocket volumes, as well as in a more pompous style- and how, too, it is possible to pick up good books for a penny or a halfpenny on the stalls of second-hand dealers.

From this and other sources we know that the reading public was steadily increasing as the century advanced. But those new readers at the lower income-levels had little effect on the course of contemporary literature. What they had read had rarely been written for *them*; they were merely reading in a cheaper format what had already been published, and they had to take what the publisher in his wisdom thought fit to reprint for them. Occasionally an eighteenth-century poet deliberately sought the widest possible public. Sir Richard Blackmore claimed that he had adapted his *Creation* to 'the general apprehension and capacity of mankind', by trying to write as clearly as possible, by using 'easy and familiar expression', and by avoiding 'any term of art, or any phrase peculiar to the writing and conversation of learned men'. Defoe's *True-Born Englishman* and his *Jure Divino*, Isaac Watts's *Divine Songs attempted in Easy Language for the Use of Children*, the hymns of the Methodists, were all addressed to the unlearned, though their value is more often hortatory or educational than literary.

But then there is Swift. It was his practice, we are told, to have two of his men-servants brought in to listen to his poems being read, 'which, if they did not comprehend, he would alter and amend, until they understood it perfectly well, and then would say, *This will do; for I write to the vulgar, more than to the learned.*' How well he succeeded may be seen on almost any page of his poetical works, where the idiomatic and familiar style carries his meaning easily and forcibly to the least learned reader. But here, as in some other matters, Swift was not wholly at one with his age. This conscious ignoring of the polite was part of 'Dr. Swift's odd way', and aroused no protest because everyone knew that Swift was himself one of the polite, a learned man, and one used to courts and the conversation of gentlemen. Swift was a law to himself; he did not absolve other writers from their obligations to polite society. The eighteenth-century poet who wished his poems to make their way with the reading public, and the publisher who hoped to live by selling them, still counted-in the first instance, at least-on the patronage of the upper classes of society; and those polite readers had a clear, and in some respects limited, conception of what poetry was and how it should be written.

By the first decades of the nineteenth century a change was clearly on the way. The fact that John Murray could pay Crabbe £3,000 for his *Tales of the Hall* (1819), and that two years earlier Byron asked £ 2,500 for the fourth canto of *Childe Harold* and got £2,000, points unmistakably to a very considerable extension of the public for poetry, and also (it may be added) to a rise in the national income. In 1764 Goldsmith had received twenty guineas for *The Traveller*; Johnson had ten guineas for London (1738), and fifteen for *The Vanity of Human Wishes* (1749). Francis Jeffrey, who as editor of the Edinburgh Review was in a position to make a good guess, estimated in 1812 that there were probably 'not less than 200,000 persons who read for amusement or instruction, among the middling classes of society'. By the 'middling classes' he meant 'almost all those who are below the sphere of what is called fashionable or public life'. In) the higher ranks of society he reckoned 'not as many as 20,000'. He would certainly have arrived at a lower estimate in 1712-the year, incidentally, in which *The Rape of the Lock* first appeared in print. As late as 1753 the poet Armstrong was not prepared to put the fashionable class (in London alone) at much more than 12,000:

Range from Tower-hill all London to the Fleet,
Thence round the Temple t'utmost Grosvenor-street:
Take in your route both Gray's and Lincoln's Inn;
Miss not, be sure, my lords and gentlemen;
You'll hardly raise, as I with Petty guess,
Above twelve thousand men of taste; unless
In desperate times a connoisseur may pass.

It was those men and women of taste, whatever precisely their numbers may have been, who were the main supporters of Pope's poetry during his lifetime. It was for them that Nicholas Rowe wrote tragedies and Handel operas, and for them that Thomas Chippendale, a little later, designed furniture, Sir Joshua Reynolds painted portraits, and the Adam brothers built town and country houses. By the middle of the nineteenth century this aristocracy is no longer imposing its tastes so exclusively on the various arts; it is being displaced by a new moneyed class, and by a new middle class with less cultivated tastes and cruder responses.

It is not generally thought that this new middle class did much good to architecture (to take what is perhaps the most striking example) or indeed to any of the fine or the applied arts, but there is a widespread impression that the change which came over society in the nineteenth century brought with it nothing but good to poetry. It may be so; but if it is so, it requires more explanation than it appears ever to have been given. Why should the aristocratic taste that produced Bedford Square be so widely approved, and the aristocratic taste that produced Pope's *Eloisa to Abelard* be so often ridiculed and condemned? Have we one set of values for architecture and quite a different set for poetry? Or does the aristocratic taste express itself more satisfactorily in architecture than in poetry? For the present it is enough to note that the charge brought against eighteenth-century poetry by Wordsworth-that it is addressed to a particular class of society, and not to mankind in general- is on the whole justified. It distressed Wordsworth to find

How we mislead each other; above all
How books mislead us, seeking their reward
From judgments of the wealthy few, who see
By artificial lights; how they debase

The many for the pleasure of the few-how, too, they continually reflect the prejudices of this 'wealthy few' by emphasizing

Extrinsic differences, the outward marks
Whereby society has parted man
From man- and how, in so doing, they 'neglect the universal heart'. This heavy charge cannot be lightly dismissed. For good or for ill (and Wordsworth had no doubt which it was) eighteenthcentury poetry is fundamentally aristocratic. The poet of the period is not so much 'a man speaking to men' as a man speaking to men like himself, or to one rather higher in the social scale. His standards, his values, his emotions and intellectual interests, his mode of expressing himself are often characteristic of the upper class. To that class, or the upper-middle class, he almost certainly belonged himself by birth, or education, or both.

II

To get some idea of the education of the average poet of this period we may conveniently turn to those whose lives were written by Johnson. John Dryden (Westminster and Trinity College, Cambridge) died in 1700, and may therefore be omitted from our calculations. Of the forty-three poets in Johnson's collection whose lives fell either wholly or partially within the eighteenth century, sixteen were educated at Oxford, eleven at Cambridge, three at Trinity College, Dublin, and three at Edinburgh University. Of the remaining ten, three (Rowe, Dyer, Hammond) were Westminster boys. Two (John Hughes and Isaac Watts) were Dissenters, and one (Pope) a Roman Catholic: these were debarred by statute from matriculation at Oxford and Cambridge. Two (Dorset and Sheffield) were noblemen, and, as often happened with the sons of noblemen, were privately educated. This leaves us with only John Gay and Richard Savage, and Gay certainly got a good grounding in classics at his school in Barnstaple. If any of those forty-three poets can be spoken of as uneducated, it is Savage, and even he attended for some years a small grammar-school near St. Albans'. No fewer than ten of our poets were Westminster boys, five were at Winchester, four at Eton. Of their parents a considerable number were either noblemen or landed gentlemen, but rather more of them were professional men-lawyers, doctors, or clergymen. Eight of the poets (or about one in five) were the sons of parsons, and no less than thirteen of them (almost one in three) became parsons themselves.

In the eighteenth-century grammar-school the greater part of the young scholar's time was given to the study of Latin and Greek. Day after day, and week after week, he was Lashed into Latin by the tingling rod.

The contemporary curriculum was set forth, unsympathetically enough, by Thomas Sheridan in his *British Education: Or, The Source of the Disorders of Great Britain* (1756). Sheridan had his own axe to grind, but on the whole his picture is an accurate one.

When a boy can read English with tolerable fluency, which is generally about the age of seven or eight years, he is put to school to learn Latin and Greek; where seven years are employed in acquiring but a moderate skill in those languages. At the age of fifteen or thereabouts, he is removed to one of the universities, where he passes four years more in procuring a more competent knowledge of Greek and Latin, in learning the rudiments of logick, natural philosophy, astronomy, metaphysicks, and the heathen morality. At the age of nineteen or twenty a degree in the arts is taken, and here ends the education of a gentleman.

And what good comes of it? Sheridan asks:

Of the few who, from a love of the arts in which they have been trained, would still keep them alive in their memories, and display their talents to the world, much the greater part serve only to increase the number of bad versifiers, miserable essay writers, and minute philosophers.

It was all expressed more brilliantly in the *Dunciad*, where Pope brings on the ghost of Dr. Busby, the famous headmaster of Westminster School, to boast of his educational regime:

We ply the memory, we load the brain,
Bind rebel wit, and double chain on chain,

Confine the thought, to exercise the breath;
And keep them in the pale of words till death.

To the last line Pope appends a note: 'By obliging them to get the classic poets by heart, which furnishes them with endless matter for conversation, and verbal amusement for their whole lives.'

But Pope knew better than that. A classical education will produce pedants and bores if it works upon the insensitive and the superficial; but when a Gray or a Matthew Arnold comes in contact with classical literature it will permeate his intellectual and moral being. Something of this sort undoubtedly happened to Addison:

> He employed his first years in the study of the old Greek and Roman writers; whose language and manner he caught at that time of life, as strongly as other young people gain a French accent or a genteel air. An early acquaintance with the classics is what may be called the good-breeding of poetry, as it gives a certain gracefulness which never forsakes a mind that contracted it in youth, but is seldom or never hit by those who would learn it too late.

Addison was perhaps more thoroughly influenced by his classical studies than most men of his time; but if he was steeped in the literature of the ancient world, most of his literary contemporaries were at least strongly tinctured by it. Accustomed at school and college to get the Latin poets by heart, they could scarcely write English poetry without echoing, consciously or unconsciously, their Virgil and Horace, alluding to classical mythology, and employing classical idioms and turns of phrase. So completely was contemporary poetry in the hands of this educated class that when an outsider like Stephen Duck attempted to write poetry he set himself to learn the poetic idiom at second hand. He 'got English', we are told, 'just as *we* get Latin.... He study'd *Paradise Los*, as we study the classics.'So equipped, Duck was able to refer to the harvest as 'Ceres' gifts', and to say of the threshing with which his own arms had so often ached:

Nor with more heavy strokes could Aetna groan,
When Vulcan forg'd the arms for Thetis son.

Fifty years later, a greater than Duck resisted more stubbornly the contemporary idiom; but even Burns was sometimes prompted to show his paces as an orthodox English poet, almost always with unhappy consequences. Had he listened to the well-meant advice of Dr. John Moore, an Anglo-Scot who had made good in London both as a writer and a physician, his excursions into standard English poetry would have been more frequent and more thorough. After advising Burns to 'deal more sparingly, for the future, in the provincial dialect', since that was bound to limit the number of his admirers, Moore goes on to suggest a course of reading. Burns should study

> most of the best English poets, and read a little more of history. The Greek and Roman stories you can read in some abridgement, and soon become master of the most brilliant facts, which must highly delight a poetical mind. You *should* also, and very soon *may*, become master of the heathen mythology, to which there are everlasting allusions in all the poets, and which in itself is charmingly fanciful.

'You want to write poetry', Moore is saying to the young provincial. 'Well, this is what poetry is made of nowadays. This is what they want in London; and if you are going to become known outside Ayrshire you will have to remember that we are living in the eighteenth century now, and that polite readers have grown accustomed to a special kind of refined enjoyment when they read poetry. As a small farmer and a young man with only an elementary education, you start with grave disadvantages; but there are certain short cuts to knowledge, and with proper application to books you will soon equip yourself to write poetry that conforms to the recognized standards of the age.' Moore's letter to Burns might almost be called an early example of market research: this and this, he says, is what people are buying and reading to-day; these are the poetical wares that are most in demand in the literary market.

How accurate Dr. Moore was in his diagnosis of contemporary taste may be seen by anyone who takes the trouble to read through one of the most popular miscellanies of the century, Dodsley's *Collection of Poems by Several Hands*, first published in 1748 and reprinted frequently in the next thirty years. We are safe in taking the reader of this miscellany as the typical poetry-reader of the period. Not everything that he liked would be in Dodsley, but there was little in Dodsley that he would not enjoy. Dodsley's poets were men of culture writing for a reader who had enjoyed the same sort of education as their own, and who could therefore share their literary tastes and draw upon the same stock of knowledge. They assumed, for instance (as Dr. Moore assumed), that their readers would be tolerably familiar with at least the less recondite facts of ancient mythology. How far they were prepared to trust to his having this sort of knowledge may be judged from a passage in one of Burke's most popular pamphlets. Driving home one of his favourite points, that the State is an organism of slow growth, and that consequently we should be chary of any sudden innovation, he goes Oh to say:

> By this wise prejudice we are taught to look with horror on those children of their country, who arc prompt rashly to hack that aged parent in pieces, and put him into the kettle of magicians, in hopes that by their poisonous weeds, and wild incantations, they may regenerate the paternal constitution, and renovate their father's life.

No doubt there were some of Burke's readers for whom this reference to Medea and the daughters of Pelias meant nothing at all, but many-perhaps the majority-must have been better informed; Burke would hardly have risked clouding his argument with an allusion that was not likely to be fairly generally intelligible. The episode referred to is to be found in Ovid's *Metamorphoses*, Book VII, a work of which any boy who had been educated at an eighteenth-century grammar-school could hardly have been ignorant, and which indeed he probably knew well. This, then, was the sort of knowledge that an eighteenth-century poet or prose-writer counted upon your having. A twentieth-century writer, even if he had such knowledge at his finger-tips, would probably hesitate to make use of it, for he would be much less certain to make himself understood. A shift in the emphasis of education has left the modern reader only moderately equipped to respond to many of those literary associations-classical and Biblical, especially-to which neoclassical poetry confidently appeals, and on which in fact it relies for a good deal of its effect. The entire attitude to literary quotation has altered in the twentieth century; it is rare nowadays for an English author to be as allusive as Hazlitt, or (to take an example from more modern times) as the late Professor Saintsbury: Such a change is highly significant, and points to an unlettered reading public.

We can hardly suppose that the best contemporary writers are less well read than those of earlier periods; but to be allusive where only a few are likely to understand is bad manners, the mark of the literary snob. To quote Latin to-day in the House of Commons without self-consciousness is almost impossible; in Burke's day such quotation was a commonplace. When Wilkes argued that quotation was a sign of pedantry, Johnson resisted the suggestion: 'No, Sir, it is a good thing; there is a community of mind in it. Classical quotation is the *parole* of literary men all over the world.' Of literary men, it will be noticed; not specifically of the learned. It is just this 'community of mind' which is absent from the far larger and less select reading public of the twentieth century; and the knowledge that was once freely employed to diversify and deepen the significance of literature is rapidly being banished to the cross-word puzzle and the quiz. Such a change may leave the poetry of Wordsworth almost undamaged, but it is bound to impoverish the effect of the far more allusive literature of the eighteenth century.

Yet all the evidence from the eighteenth century does not point in the same direction. How, for instance, are we to interpret the fact that almost every classical poet of note was translated into English verse (some of them several times) during the century? We may readily suppose that a gentleman would often turn an ode of Horace into English verse, and that the more cultured among his friends would be able to appreciate the delicate modern application he had given to the original. But for what readers did Pope translate Homer? The frequent reprinting of this great work in the eighteenth century points rather to a public that could not read Homer in the original than to one which read the translation for the pleasure of comparing the English version with the Greek.

The study of Greek, it is true, was less general than the study of Latin. But the frequent translation of the *Aeneid*-by Dryden, Nicholas Brady, Trapp, Pitt, and some half-dozen others-suggests again a public that could enjoy the poem only in English. At the same time, the remarkable popularity of Dryden's *Virgil* and Pope's *Homer*, and the fact that publishers found it worth their while to put out other translations both in verse and in prose, would suggest that Homer and Virgil in English were among the favourite authors of the eighteenth century.

There is no comparable demand for them to-day. We must not, of course, make a hard-and-fast division between those who could enjoy Virgil in the original and those who had no Latin at all; many of the readers of Dryden's *Virgil* were probably somewhere between those two extremes. Again, the publication in 1712 of *Mottoes in Five Volumes of the Tatler and to the Two Volumes of the Spectators, Latin and English* indicates, perhaps, an attempt on the part of a publisher to profit from the exasperation of the uninitiated. It was followed by a similar publication in 1737, which included the mottoes to the *Guardian* and the *Freeholder*.

Not to know Latin at all was undoubtedly a handicap to the reader of eighteenth-century poetry. That this was recognized at the time is borne out by an advertisement inserted in the *Craftsman* of 19 April 1729, announcing a new (and comparatively painless) method of learning Latin. The course was intended as a means of gentlemen's being qualified to receive the truest and utmost diversion and entertainment that can arise from those books that are in polite learning, as essays, plays, poetry etc. by judiciously discerning the fine thoughts, arguments, images, figurative expressions, and elegancies, many of which are taken from the classical writers.

In short, a course in Latin to enable a reader to understand and enjoy English poetry, since so much of the enjoyment must lie in a reader's ability to recognize immediately the conscious echo of Virgil or Horace or Ovid. No one in the eighteenth century doubted that this was one of the *legitimate* pleasures of poetry. Indeed, it extended, as the *Craftsman* advertisement indicates, to all polite literature. In the Preface to *Joseph Andrews* Fielding remarks of the burlesque passages that many instances will occur in this work, as in the description of battles, and some other places, not necessary to be pointed out to the classical reader; for whose entertainment those parodies or burlesque imitations are chiefly calculated.

It may be that eighteenth-century writers relied overmuch on literary allusion. Johnson has an interesting passage on Gilbert West's imitations of Spenser. They are highly successful performances of their kind; but- such compositios are not to be reckoned among the great achievements of intellect, because their effect is local and temporary; they appeal not to reason or passion, but to memory, and presuppose an accidental or artificial state of mind. An Imitation of Spenser is nothing to a reader, however acute, by whom Spenser has never been perused.... The noblest beauties of art are those of which the effect is co-extended with rational nature, or at least with the whole circle of polished life; what is less than this can be only pretty, the plaything of fashion and the amusement of a day.

Johnson was more conscious than most contemporary critics of the 'common reader', and he realised better than most that much eighteenth-century poetry passed slightly above the common reader's head. But if imitations of Spenser fail to meet the supreme test of great literature, are imitations of Horace- or Juvenal-any better? Johnson might have replied that Horace and Juvenal are comprehended in 'the whole circle of polished life', but in fact he did not choose to make that claim. In discussing Pope's imitations of Horace (the 'relaxations of his genius') he still insisted on the limitations of this kind of literature:

The man of learning may be sometimes surprised and delighted by an unexpected parallel; but the comparison requires knowledge of the original....

And that knowledge, Johnson implies, cannot be fairly *asked* of the reader. (If he already has it, of course, so much the better for him; but the enjoyment of English literature should not depend on one's ability to read a Latin author in the original.) The imitation of classical authors, however, though common enough in eighteenth-century poetry, is an extreme case of that literary inspiration which was so widespread in the period. That modern English poetry could fairly draw some of its nourishment from classical literature Johnson would never have doubted.

III

If a knowledge of classical literature and mythology was the most important element in the eighteenth-century reader's intellectual equipment, it was far from being the only knowledge required of him or of the poet. Dryden makes several significant pronouncements about the sort of education which he considered essential for the good poet.

A man should be learned in several sciences, and should have a reasonable, philosophical, and in some measure a mathematical head, to be a complete and excellent poet; and besides this, should have experience in all sorts of humours and manners of men; should be thoroughly skilled in conversation, and should have a great knowledge of mankind in general.

In the *Essay of Dramatic Poesy* Neander [Dryden] argues that one 'would be loth to say that he who is endued with a sound judgment has no need of history, geography, or moral philosophy to write correctly'. Elsewhere he insists that many who understand Greek and Latin are ignorant of their mother-tongue, and that there is little chance for an English poet to acquire and appreciate the delicacies of the English language without the help of a liberal education, long reading, and digesting of those few good authors we have amongst us, the knowledge of men and manners, the freedom of habitudes and conversation with the best company of both sexes; and, in short, without wearing off the rust which he contracted while he was laying in a stock of learning.

A poet, Addison told the readers of the *Spectator*, 'should take as much pains in forming his imagination, as a philosopher in cultivating his understanding'. For pastoral poetry he will require some knowledge of country life and the works of nature.

> If he would go beyond pastoral, and the lower kinds of poetry, he ought to acquaint himself with the pomp and magnificence of courts. He should be very well versed in everything that is noble and stately in the productions of art, whether it appear in painting or statuary, in the great works of architecture which are in their present glory, or in the ruins of those which flourished in former ages.

Johnson's Imlac has similar large demands to make. 'To a poet nothing can be useless'; the poet must 'store his mind with inexhaustible variety'. In the same spirit Reynolds repeatedly advised the young artist to 'amass a stock of ideas', to prepare his mind by 'laying in proper materials' and to see that it was 'continually fertilized and enriched by foreign matter'. 'Nothing can come of nothing', he warned his students.

> The greatest natural genius cannot subsist on its own stock: he who resolves never to ransack any mind but his own, will soon be reduced, from mere barrenness, to the poorest of all imitations; he will be obliged to imitate himself.

All through our period, then, the consensus of opinion is that the poet must be an educated man, well read, far travelled, accustomed to the best society. The list of requirements might be considerably extended, but it will be enough here to mention one more: the poet should know the Rules. In the *Dunciad* there is a contemptuous note on James Ralph:

> This low writer... was wholly illiterate, and knew no language, not even French. Being advised to read the rules of

dramatick poetry before he began a play, he smiled and reply'd, *Shakespeare writ without rules.*

In poetry and drama Pope found a growing number of those upstarts who 'writ without rules', and he resented their intrusion into polite letters. He saw in them a threat to the whole tradition of literary culture that he and his friends represented. His opposition to the Ralphs, therefore, resembled that of the registered practitioner to the chiropractors: such men had not taken the recognized training, they had not graduated.

To Hobbes, writing in 1675, it seemed self-evident that the 'readers of poesie are commonly persons of the best quality' The spread of education to all classes of society, more especially in the present century, may tend to conceal from us the chasm that yawned two hundred years ago between the educated and the uneducated. They spoke a different language. They still do, but the number of the educated is much larger. In commending the ballad of 'Chevy Chase' to the sympathetic attention of his readers, Addison had argued that human nature was the same in all reasonable creatures, 'and whatever falls in with it, will meet with admirers among readers of all qualities and conditions'.

He then proceeds to cite the 'little old woman' to whom Moliere used to read his comedies, and whose reactions were always confirmed by the polite when the play was performed. To this specious argument John Dennis replied that the taste of Moliere's old woman was really beside the point. She might, indeed, have a true taste for comedy, since comedy is 'an imitation of human nature depraved'; but we should hardly care to accept her as ajudge of poetry. 'What can be more absurd than to conclude, that because the rabble, that is, such as never had any education, are tolerable judges of human nature depraved, that therefore they are judges of human nature exalted, of which none can be judges but they who have had the best education?' Addison had thought to propitiate his polite readers by suggesting a resemblance between

The hounds ran swiftly thro' the wood
The nimble deer to take,
And with their cries the hills and dales
An eccho shrill did make.
and Virgil's _vocat ingenti clamore Cithacron
Taygetique canes, domitrixque Epidaurus equorum
Et vox assensu nemorum ingeminata remugit.

But Dennis appealed equally confidently to *his* polite readers: 'What is there in the first but what is vile and trivial? What ploughman, what tinker, what trull is not capable of saying the like?'

Some fifty years later the same point of view was expressed, but rather more soberly, by Shenstone. In his essay 'On the Test of Popular Opinion' he introduces to us a citizen, a courtier, and an academic. The citizen says that he hears a lot of talk about taste, refinement, and politeness,

but methinks the vulgar and illiterate generally approve the same productions with the connoisseurs. One rarely finds a landskip, a building, or a play that has charms for the critick exclusive of the mechanick.

To this the courtier replies that he cannot answer for every individual instance, 'but I think, moderately speaking, the vulgar are generally in the wrong'. He meets the argument that the vulgar find the same beauties in poetry as the man of reading with a flat denial.

Now half or more of the beauties of poetry depend on metaphor or allusion, neither of which by a mind uncultivated can be applied to their proper counterparts. Their beauty of consequence is like a picture to a blind man. How many of these peculiarities in poetry turn upon a knowledge of philosophy and history; and let me add these latent beauties give the most delight to such as can unfold them.

The academic, with characteristic timidity, takes up a middle position, but in the main he sides with the courtier. An author, he thinks, should not flatter himself with a confused expectation of pleasing both the vulgar and the polite: few things, in comparison, being capable of doing both in any great degree.

His finest things will probably 'escape the organs' of the mob, but he will find his reward in the praise of the discriminating (the 'judicious few'), and in due course the few will impose their values on the many.

Most eighteenth-century critics would have agreed with the courtier and the academic. In that aristocratic age it seemed almost self-evident that 'opinions, like fashions, always descend from those of quality to the middle sort, and thence to the vulgar'. But whether innate or acquired, taste had to be cultivated. A true taste in poetry involved wide general reading, for (as Shenstone's courtier said) it was upon allusion and reference that the contemporary poets depended for most of their overtones. It is frequently suggested by critics that the poetry of Dryden and Pope is too much a poetry of plain statement, and that the denotation of words is for them more important than the connotation. This may be true (but only to a limited extent) of the way in which individual words were used, but behind the surface statement there are often layers of literary or historical reference. When, for instance, Dryden brought his alteration of *The Tempest* upon the stage in 1667, his Prologue contained a reference which could hardly be intelligible to anyone who had not read Shakespeare's play:

But Shakespear's magick could not cmopy'd be;
Within that circle none durst walk but he.

The imaginative identification of Shakespeare with his own Prospero, suggested by the circle drawn by magicians when they cast a spell, gives a delicate 'turn' to the thought. The poetry of Dryden and Pope is full of such confident yet subtle suggestion. How far the allusive habit had entered into the mind of the age may be seen from a characteristic reflection of Shenstone's on gardens. After remarking on the advantage enjoyed by some Italian noblemen and gentlemen whose estates are situated 'on ground mentioned in the classicks', he continues:

And, even in England, wherever a park or garden happens to have been the scene of any event in history, one would surely avail one's self of that circumstance, to make it more interesting to the imagination. Mottoes should allude to it, columns, etc. record it; verses moralize upon it; and curiosity receive it's share of pleasure.

IV

What, then, are we to conclude about the relationship of the poet to his readers in the eighteenth century? Are we to assume that he was quite out of touch with his unlearned readers? In a more democratic or less scholarly age would they have found poets to express their deepest thoughts and feelings in language that all might understand? In view of the esoteric poetry now being written by many poets in the less scholarly and more democratic twentieth century, it would be rash to make any such assumption. Yet it has often been suggested that in the time of Pope the hungry sheep looked up and were not fed. Pope and his contemporaries have been accused of cultivating poetry for a small and exclusive clique. 'Poetry was in the hands of a few', we are told, 'who kept it within the limits of their narrow interests; it was poetry in a park surrounded by high walls.

The people were ignored, not admitted.'If this is so, the people must have made a habit of climbing the walls: few poets have been read and admired by so large a proportion of their fellow countrymen as was Pope in his own day. It is true that his poetry was fully intelligible only to men and women who had reached a certain level of education; but that was well understood at the time, and the contemporary reader, looking on poetry as a special sort of pleasure which demanded from him a special sort of awareness, was at some pains to equip himself for the enjoyment of it.

The demands made upon his literary knowledge differed from poem to poem: at one extreme was Gray's *Elegy*, in which the field of reference was tolerably familiar to the common reader, and at the other, 'The Bard' and 'The Progress of Poesy', which most of Gray's contemporaries, with some justification, found dreadfully obscure. But there is little evidence to show that the eighteenth-century reader was disappointed with the poetry which his poets were providing. As the century advanced, taste was modified in a variety of ways, the range of sensibility shifted slightly, new types of experience were desired; but the poets on the whole seem to have kept in touch with their readers. The notion of a parched and thirsty nation waiting eagerly for the prophet Wordsworth to smite the rock and let forth the living water is at variance with the facts. Wordsworth had first to persuade the public that it was thirsty before he could get it to drink his pure mountain streams at allL

Poetry In 18 th Century

T0 say that eighteenth-century poetry was patronized for the I most part by the upper classes of society is to say less than enough to account for its predominantly aristocratic tone. A really extensive middle-class public for poetry can hardly be said to have existed in England until the days of Tennyson and Browning. If we go back to the seventeenth century, and still more to the sixteenth, the reading public grows steadily smaller, while the proportion of readers belonging to the upper class correspondingly increases. Yet the poetry of Donne and Herbert, of Jonson and Drayton, while not noticeably the expression of a middle-class mind, does not give the impression of being addressed to the upper-class reader, or for that matter to any specific reader at all. Why, then, does the upper class exert so marked a pressure on the writers and artists of the eighteenth century?

The explanation is to be found in a new and closer relationship between the writer and his patrons. In the years that followed the Restoration the English upper class was much better organized for the task of keeping itself amused and supporting 'le pénible fardeau de n' avoir rien a faire' than it had ever been before. The great landowners still had their noble mansions in the country, and still passed a few months of the summer there; but the lords and the country gentlemen were beginning to spend more of their time in London, for long the great centre of culture and fashionable amusement, but never more so than since the Restoration. This movement into Town had not perhaps reached its full significance until the 1670s and 1680s, when London was being rebuilt after the Great Fire. Writing in 1667 Thomas Sprat could still say of the French that 'their nobility live commonly close together in their cities, and ours for the most part scattered in their country houses'. But even in 1667 there was a 'season', when Parliament and the law courts were sitting, when the two theatres were open and the places of resort were crowded by men and women of fashion. Out of the season society still kept together at Bath, Tonbridge, and the other spas and seaside resorts which were one by one coming into prominence. Society, in fact, was more compact, more conscious of itself than it had been in Elizabethan or Jacobean days.

This new gregariousness is reflected in the vastly increased number of eating-houses, and of the comparatively new coffee-houses and chocolate-houses, some of which (like Will's, and, a little later, Button's) were the recognized haunts of literary men. Conversation, that most social of all the arts, was cultivated there, and the discussion of new books and new authors proceeded at different levels of urbanity and wit. After the Restoration, too, the men of letters appear to have enjoyed increased opportunities of mixing on easy terms with the aristocracy. Dryden and Shadwell, Wycherley and Congreve, Swift and Pope and Gay, were all familiar with some of the great noblemen of their day, who were often amateurs of letters themselves.

For a proper understanding of the eighteenth century we should never forget the value then placed upon good conversation. This was the most universal of all the arts, cultivated by all but the most boorish. The writers are never tired of discussing it. Steele gives much of his space in *Tatlers, Spectators*, and *Guardians* to explaining the nature and significance of polite conversation; Swift satirizes conversational cliches; Fielding writes a long essay and Cowper a long poem on conversation; Johnson deals with it in the *Rambler* and practises it continually, while Boswell and others record it ; Jane Austen counts it among the essential qualifications of a hero or heroine. Whatever the Englishman may have been in the seventeenth century or was to become in the nineteenth and twentieth, there can be no question that in the eighteenth century he was a person of genuinely sociable habits; and the high value placed upon the art of polite conversation is the clearest indication of it. As he became more and more urban, the Englishman grew a little more urbane. 'We polish one another', Shaftesbury had noticed in 1709, 'and rub off our corners and rough sides by a sort of *amicable collision*.'

The art of polite conversation, then, was the special grace of the lady and gentleman; it depended upon the finest qualities of intelligence and character. Restraint, propriety, an absence of emphasis, consideration for others and the desire to give them pleasure, a willingness to subordinate what is merely personal or private or a matter of 'self-expression' in favour of what is generally interesting and universally intelligible in polite society, a sense of proportion, the avoidance of mere display, the conscious imitation of the best models (in this case the conversation of the fine lady and the fine gentleman)-these are some of the qualities of good conversation as the eighteenth century understood and practised it.

They are also the qualities of the best eighteenth-century architecture, and they are everywhere present in its most characteristic prose. They are also, to a remarkable extent, the qualities of its most characteristic poetry. The poetry of that century, however remote its diction may sometimes be from the idiom of contemporary speech, has at least this in common with conversation that it is consciously addressed to someone else. The eighteenth-century poet is addressing the reader in a variety of ways, and with different ends in view, but he is not murmuring to himself alone. Poetry was to him, like good conversation, a social activity; it exacted from him a consideration for the reader and a corresponding restraint upon himself.

II

Social intercourse would be almost impossible if the individuals forming a society were not willing to accept certain restrictions on their freedom of expression. In dress, behaviour, conversation, and 'all the little intercourses of life', as Steele insists, 'there is a certain deference due to custom; and... a man ought to sacrifice his private inclinations and opinions to the practice of the public'. No doubt our manners to-day are a good deal freer than those of the upper classes in the eighteenth century; yet even to-day most people adjust themselves, whether consciously or not, to the company in which they find themselves. But society would become excessively tedious if there were no nonconformists, no eccentrics. Dr. Johnson's reputation in the eighteenth century as a formidable talker was partly due to his habit in a conventional and artificial age of being remarkably unconventional.

He resented any doubts being cast on his good manners, but it is clear that he sometimes offended against the contemporary standards of politeness. You never could tell what he would say next, and polite society can only survive on the understanding that truth will not be pursued too eagerly into awkward places. Johnson's conversation was not, in fact, wholly characteristic of his century; the measure of his originality as a talker is that he continually overstepped the limitations that Lord Chesterfield accepted with habitual self-control. How severe those restraints could be may be seen from the kind of advice that Lord Chesterfield used to give his son. He went so far as to warn the boy against laughing:

Having mentioned laughing, I must particularly warn you against it: and I could heartily wish that you may often be seen to smile, but never heard to laugh while you live. Frequent and loud laughter is the characteristic of folly and ill manners: it is the manner in which the mob express their silly joy at silly things; and they call it being merry. In my mind there is nothing so illiberal and so ill bred, as audible laughter.... I am neither of a melancholy, nor a cynical disposition, and am as willing, and as apt, to be pleased as anybody; but I am sure that, since I had the full use of reason, nobody has ever heard me laugh.

Behind Chesterfield's advice to his son, here and elsewhere, lies his consciousness of that society in which all our actions are mirrored. We are in the presence of others, and we must act accordingly.

If Johnson was occasionally hurried into an extravagance of thought or a violence of expression it was when he was carried away by the excitement of conversation; it did not happen in his poetry. His poetry was more deliberately submitted to the public. The eighteenth-century poet's consciousness of this public inhibited the expression of emotion, unless it was of a recognized and acceptable kind. It is absurd to contend that eighteenth-century poetry is lacking in feeling; it is still more naive to suppose that the poets of that century did not feel as men. Nothing had happened to England or to Englishmen that prevented them feeling the loss of a wife or a child with as much intensity as Englishmen in the reign of Queen Elizabeth or Queen Victoria; nothing had intervened to prevent them from delighting in a warm spring day or from falling in love or from looking back with regret on their lost youth. They felt such things as those, and much more, but they rarely gave *direct* expression to such feelings in their poetry. Certain more public emotions, such as the love of country or the sense of national grief at the death of some illustrious soldier or statesman, they found little difficulty in expressing adequately. But it is clear that the more private and personal emotions aroused a certain self-consciousness; a man kept those to himself, or unburdened his soul only to a friend. It is not therefore an eighteenth-century poet who writes:

But she is in her grave, and, oh,
The difference to me!
or
'0 mercy!' to myself I cried,
'If Lucy should be dead!'

Such revelations of feeling would have seemed to the eighteenth century altogether too naive. Wordsworth's poems, in fact, made their way very slowly into public favour in the face of a criticism that complained of their silliness and childishness. Francis Jeffrey in particular, doggedly upholding the standards of the eighteenth century at a time when they were gradually beginning to disintegrate, puts perhaps more clearly than it had ever been put before a view of poetry that his own father and grandfather would certainly have endorsed. In all large and polished societies, he tells his readers, there is such a thing as a general taste. There is, too, 'a certain tact, which informs us at once that many things, which we still love and are moved by in secret, must necessarily be despised as childish, or derided as absurd'. In this tact he finds Wordsworth woefully deficient.

> If Mr. Wordsworth, instead of confining himself almost entirely to the society of the dalesmen and cottagers, and little children, who form the subjects of his book, had condescended to mingle a little more with the people that were to read and judge of it, we cannot help thinking that its texture might have been considerably improved.

There, unflinchingly expressed, is the attitude of the eighteenth century to the poet and his poetry. The poet's readers are men and women who have arrived at a certain standard of culture, and it is a culture of an urban and aristocratic kind; they have certain well-defined interests, a characteristic (and, though they do not know this, peculiar) mode of thinking and feeling, and when they read poetry they expect a specific kind of pleasure and no other. Their way of thinking is not that of a Covent Garden porter or a Cumberland shepherd; but they, after all-and not the porter or the shepherd-are the readers of poetry, and until they change their nature 'it will remain the poet's office to proceed upon that state of association which actually exists as *general*'.The readers of poetry (in Jeffrey's words, the people who are 'to read and judge of it') are accustomed to a certain reticence in the expression of all feeling, and to a complete silence about some feelings which it is not considered proper to disclose to the world at large. How heavily eighteenth-century manners weighed upon some of the more impulsive souls of the period may be seen from a characteristic outburst of Rousseau's:

In our day, now that more subtle study and a more refined taste have reduced the art of pleasing to a system, there prevails in modern manners a servile and deceptive conformity; so that one would think every mind had been cast in the same mould. Politeness requires this thing; decorum that; ceremony has its forms, and fashion its laws, and these we must always follow, never the promptings of our own nature.

And he continues:

We no longer dare seem what we really are, but lie under a perpetual restraint; in the meantime the herd of men, which we call society, all act under the same circumstances exactly alike, unless very particular and powerful motives prevent them.

If Rousseau were to return to-day he would find less ground for complaint; he might conceivably feel embarrassed at the length to which the twentieth-century writer is prepared to go in exposing to the public his most private thoughts and feelings. That there are still some limits recognized may be deduced from the embarrassment that most people feel when confronted in a railway carriage or a restaurant by some stranger who insists on confessing his sins. But in literature we have grown accustomed to almost every kind of self-display. This breaking down of the once solid barriers between public and private life (the process has not yet been carried so far in Europe as in America) is one of the reasons why eighteenth-century poetry is apt to seem deficient in feeling and intimacy to the modern reader. He misses the personal note with which he has nowadays grown so familiar. When Gray writes an ode 'On a Distant Prospect of Eton College' there is no direct expression of his feelings, except in the second stanza:

Ah happy hills, ah pleasing shade,
Ah fields belov'd in vain,
Where once my careless childhood stray'd,
A stranger yet to pain!

Yet the whole poem is about Gray's feelings, a Gray who has already experienced the vicissitudes of life, and who now feels as a man what, as a schoolboy at Eton, he had only construed- 'Sunt lacrimae rerum et mentem mortalia tangunt'. But Gray is an artist of exquisite restraint; his feelings steal upon us imperceptibly as he recalls, but hardly seeks to individualize, particular experiences:

> *Who foremost now delight to cleave*
> *With pliant arm thy glassy wave?*
> *The captive linnet which enthrall?*

Gray never walks boldly up to the front door and rattles on the knocker. His personal feeling is almost never stated, it emerges; and the eighteenth century hiked him the better for it.

Naturally enough men and women could not always live up to those severe standards even in the eighteenth century; and among the novelists Fielding delighted, with a humanity which seemed to Richardson perverse and 'low', to depict those moments of crisis when all restraint is thrown aside. But a poet could not decently plead overpowering feelings as an excuse for some emotional indiscretion *in print*. Whatever he might be driven to write in the warmth or hurry of feeling, there was no compulsion on him to publish it in cold blood. It is significant that some of Johnson's most personal poems were written, not in English but in Latin: the dead language was almost a cipher by means of which he could express himself more freely and frankly than he would have cared to do in English. Nor did he think of publishing those poems; he was writing for himself alone.

So little was the eighteenth-century poet habituated to the free expression of spontaneous emotions that when a writer like Edward Young attempts to 'give a loose' to feeling in his *Night Thoughts*, we are apt to-day to doubt his sincerity and deplore his exhibitionism. We feel almost as if we had come unawares upon the poet in his underclothes; there is nothing to be done but close the door and tiptoe away as softly as possible. What came naturally enough to Wordsworth was difficult and even embarrassing to the eighteenth-century poet: if one has grown accustomed, like public-school boys, to conceal rather than express the feelings it becomes more and more troublesome to express them naturally and without self-consciousness. It was therefore *natural* for Gray to write impersonally about 'the wretch' who long had tossed on the thorny bed of pain, and to express his sense of returning vitality through the discoveries of this anonymous convalescent:

The meanest flowret of the vale,
The simplest note that swells the gale,
The common Sun, the air, the skies,
To him are opening Paradise.

It would have been unnatural for Wordsworth to write on such impersonal terms. He would have written in the first person, speaking either for himself, or more probably, perhaps, for some aged cottager-simple, garrulous, and direct, using the language really spoken by men:

Oh Sir! I get about a bit,
I see the blessed sun on high;
And I must think, do all I can,
'Tis Paradise in yon blue sky.

Wordsworth's poetry continually takes the form of a personal statement of what he had thought or felt ('And much it grieved my heart to think...'; 'And, oh, the difference to me!'; 'My heart leaps up when I behold...'; 'I thought of Chatterton, the marvellous boy'; 'Ne'er saw I, never felt, a calm so deep!'): Gray's poetry is almost uniformly impersonal. But the difference is not one of feeling and not-feeling; it is a difference mainly in the conventions of expression, which turns ultimately on a different relationship with the reader.

A curious and interesting example of the eighteenth-century expression of feeling is the poem which Lord Lyttelton wrote to the memory of his first wife, who died in childbed. There can be no doubt about the sincerity of his grief, as those who read the poem in the *Oxford Book of Eighteenth Century*

Verse will readily agree. The poem opens in a vein of unforced simplicity, which would be the natural expression of sorrow in any age.

In vain I look around
O'er the well-known ground,
My Lucy's wonted footsteps to descry;
Where oft we us'd to walk,
Where oft in tender talk
We saw the summer sun go down the sky;
Nor by yon fountain's side,
Nor where its waters glide
Along the valley, can she now be found:

In all the wide-stretch'd prospect's ample bound No more my mournful eye

Can aught of her espy,
But the sad sacred earth where her dear relics lie.

But the Oxford editor has given us the poem that Lyttelton should have written, not the one that he actually wrote. After two more stanzas in the same strain (his Lucy preferred the quiet retirement of Hagley to the glitter of courts; she devoted herself to her children, guiding their infant steps; how will the unhappy father, alone and oppressed with his griefs, bring up those infants without her?) Lyttelton suddenly breaks out into:

Where were ye, Muses, when relentless Fate
From these fond arms your fair disciple tore?

and in succeeding stanzas we meet with 'Castalia's plain', 'the Thespian vallies', 'Mincio's bank', Petrarch and his Laura, and much else. All this the Oxford editor judiciously omits, together with the most purple of all Lyttelton's patches, the stanza of the orange-tree:

So where the silent streams of Liris glide,
In the soft bosom of Campania's vale,
When now the wintry tempests all are fled,
And genial Summer breathes her gentle gale,
The verdant orange lifts its beauteous head:
From every branch the balmy flowerets rise,

On every bough the golden fruits are seen;
With odours sweet it fills the smiling skies,
The wood-nymphs tend it, and th' Idalian queen.
But in the midst of all its blooming pride,
A sudden blast from Apenninus blows,
Cold with perpetual snows:
The tender blighted plant shrinks up its leaves, and dies.

Towards the close Lyttelton returns to his earlier and happier manner:

O best of wives! O dearer far to me
Than when thy virgin charms
Were yielded to my arms,
How can my soul endure the loss of thee?
How in the world, to me a desart grown,
Abandon'd and alone,
Without my sweet companion can I live?...

Two voices are there in this monody: one giving us the natural unaffected melody that corresponds to Lyttelton's real feelings, the other supplying the sort of orchestration that an eighteenth-century poet considered proper. Among contemporary comments on the poem, two may be cited for the light they throw on eighteenth-century taste. 'If it were all like the fourth stanza,' Gray wrote to Horace Walpole, 'I should be excessively pleased. Nature and sorrow, and tenderness, are the true genius of such things; and something of these I find in several parts of it (not in the orange-tree): poetical ornaments are foreign to the purpose, for they only shew a man is not sorry.' Gray's attitude here is the same as Johnson's on similar occasions, and it would probably be endorsed by most readers of poetry to-day. But to Lyttelton's friend, Dr. Philip Doddridge, it was the simplicity that let the poem down, and the orange-tree stanza that was most admirable. In replying to Doddridge's criticism, Lyttelton not unnaturally defended both simplicity and orange-tree.

Simplicity [he argues] if it does not descend into *vulgarism*, is the chief excellence of all kinds of writing, but above all of those in which the heart is to speak. Without the utmost simplicity, both of thought and diction, the *pathos* cannot be preserved; and I would admit no ornaments into such a work, but merely as pauses at proper intervals, to relieve the reader from the emotions of grief, which are excited by the more passionate parts. In those parts, figures, or metaphors, or any high colouring, or hardness of style, are quite improper; and points, or *concetti*, are insupportable faults, however witty and brilliant they may be....

As for the orange-tree, the 'high colouring' of that simile would have been 'very improper in those [parts] where grief alone could find room to speak'.

How little eighteenth-century poetry was 'the spontaneous overflow of powerful feelings' may be guessed from an unlucky episode in the poetical career of Pope. In the summer of 1718 he was staying at Stanton Harcourt as the guest of Lord Harcourt. One day a thunderstorm broke over the district, and Lord Harcourt's servants, who were haymaking at the time, scattered in all directions to seek shelter. Among them were two young lovers, John Hewet and Sarah Drew-two names very common in the Berkshire villages to this day. Sarah was terrified and sank down on a haycock, and her lover hurriedly raked together some heaps of hay to cover her, and then lay down beside her. The thunder rolled, the lightning flashed; and when the storm had blown over the other labourers came out to look for John and Sarah.

They found John Hewet with one arm about his Sarah's neck, as if to screen her from the lightning. But both of them were dead. There was no mark or discolouring on either of them, except that Sarah's eyebrows were a little singed, and there was a small spot between her breasts. This sad event so preyed on the poet's mind (as well it might) that he told the story, quite unaffectedly and with genuine concern, to several different correspondents, and- what was quite unusual for him-set himself almost immediately to mourn the event in verse. The situation with which he had to deal was one that Wordsworth would have had no difficulty in handling; it was the perfect theme for a lyrical ballad. But for Pope it was not nearly so easy; indeed, it was the wrong material altogether. He did not attempt to present the death of the lovers as a moving accident, and still less as an experience that had come to *him*. Instead, he suggested to Lord Harcourt that he should erect a monument to the memory of the unhappy lovers, and himself set about writing their epitaph. The result, to say the least of it, was not a triumph for decorum:

When Eastern lovers feed the fun'ral fire,
On the same pile their faithful fair expire:
Here pitying Heav'n that virtue mutual found,
And blasted both, that it might neither wound.
Hearts so sincere th' Almighty saw well pleas'd,
Sent his own lightning, and the victims seiz'd.

To this Pope added gallantly in a letter to Lady Mary Wortley Montagu:

The greatest honour people of this low degree could have was to be remembered on a little monument; unless you will give them another, -that of being honoured with a tear from the finest eyes in the world.

An epitaph is not (or certainly was not with Pope) a cry of the heart, and it would be unfair to blame Pope for not giving what he never intended to give. But we could hardly find a better example of the way in which the raw materials of human experience were habitually transmuted in eighteenth-century poetry. A Burns, a Blake, a Wordsworth constantly succeed to a remarkable degree in finding the words that will enable them to hand on their experience to the reader, who re-experiences it in all its original freshness. Pope's epitaph, though it had its origin in a genuine and moving experience, is not intended to be a mere statement of it, but a decorative rendering of0 it, or, more accurately, of ideas arising from it. The sharp impact of the experience has been lost; indeed, it has never been desired. Pope's own feelings have been decently veiled; he has concentrated on the memorial. The event and its accompanying emotions have been formalized and made impersonal to the poet. But that, of course, is what the polite reader of the period wanted. He had no desire for naked experience; about *that* he felt much as the lady in the stage-coach did about Joseph Andrews: '0 J-sus! A naked man! Dear coachman, drive on and leave him.'

This sort of preference is one of the most difficult things for the modern reader to understand, let alone to accept or enjoy. What is characteristically absent from eighteenth-century poetry (and, indeed, from all the arts of the period) is the sense of immediate, direct contact with experience. Eighteenth-century poetry had almost always been submitted to a process in the poet's mind analogous to what went on in the kitchen before dinner was served in the dining-room. Mr. Knightley's dislike of picnics is characteristic of the whole century. His idea of the simple and natural, it will be recalled, was 'to have the table spread in the dining-room. The nature and the simplicity of gentlemen and ladies, with their servants and furniture,... is best observed by meals within doors.' The reader of poetry in Mr. Knightley's day liked his poetry that way too.

To Wordsworth, on the other hand, the important thing is always the experience in all its original purity. If his poem is successful he has made us feel exactly what he himself felt at the time: the very wind of it passes across our brow, the taste of it is on our lips. Like the strawberries that poor Mrs. Elton wanted to pick. ('we are to walk about your gardens, and gather the strawberries ourselves, and sit under trees;... it is to be all out of doors') the experience in each poem of Wordsworth's is fresh and unspoilt; it has not been fingered, nothing has been 'done' to it.

To see Wordsworth at work we could not do better than turn to 'The Idiot Boy', where he is transmitting an imaginative experience in all its uniqueness and unexpectedness: what it feels like to be an idiot boy riding on a pony in bright moonlight; what it feels like to be a mother who has lost her idiot son-the whole palpitating, bewildering, agonizing experience of a rather weak-witted woman driven nearly crazy by the loss of her child. Almost everything is seen from the point of view of the idiot ('But when the pony *moved his legs*...'), or from the standpoint of the distracted mother:

She looks again-her arms are up-
She screams-she cannot move for joy....

These astonishing lines have all the force of a primitive painting: human action and human passion have been reduced to their simplest terms. Sometimes the experience comes to us from neither mother nor son. The stillness of the night, the silent town with the moon riding high above it in the blue sky, the queer hush before dawn-

The streams with softest sound are flowing,
The grass you almost hear it growing-the hooting of the owlets, the little birds beginning to stir sleepily in the hedgerows, the gradual fading of the moon ('so pale you scarcely looked at her'), the return of the travellers to their cottage: everything is given with a remarkable directness that even Wordsworth never surpassed.

In Donne's poem 'The Calme' or in Coleridge's 'Frost at Midnight' we again meet with an experience just as sharply individualized, and one from which (as with 'The Idiot Boy') the original glow and colour have not departed. Why do we so rarely find anything comparable in the poetry of the eighteenth century? The answer, it has already been suggested, can scarcely be that the poets of that century never had such matters to express. To suppose so is to postulate a quite unprecedented break in the continuity of human experience. Even if we committed ourselves to so rash a theory the poets themselves would disprove it, since they occasionally give us poems, hike Ambrose Philips's 'Winter Piece', of the kind in question.

Normally, however, they drew a clear distinction between what they considered to be private and what could be made public, what was merely a matter of personal memoranda and what might be worked into a regular poem. That some such distinction was widely accepted, and that it was not peculiar to the poets, may be seen from the remarkable sketches of nature made by Gains-borough, but made by him as private records for his own use. In those sketches, so obviously dashed off at speed, Gains-borough seized with remarkable intimacy the momentary appearance, the atmosphere of a sunny morning, the look of the wind passing through a clump of trees. But a picture was another thing altogether: that was a work of art, based on the recollection of many sunny mornings and many wind-swept clumps of trees. In the finished picture the sense of immediacy has largely disappeared; instead, many separate observations and much artistic experience are blended into one harmonious composition. It is much the same with the poet Gray. What he wrote in his *Journal* was for his own eye, and what he wrote in letters to his friends was for their eyes alone; in both journal and letters he is far freer and far closer to the momentary appearance of things and to the thoughts and feelings that take shape in his consciousness as he writes than he ever cared to be in his poetry.

It is significant that when his friend Mason came to publish Gray's letters he felt compelled to prepare them for the public. It was never his intention to present the public with Gray's letters (private letters, not written for publication) exactly as they stood. 'I will promise my reader', he said, 'that he shall, in the following pages, seldom behold Mr. Gray in any light than that of a scholar and poet'-the very light, in fact, in which Gray had always presented himself to the public, in so far as he had ever allowed himself to publish what he had written. He therefore prepared the letters for publication by eliminating Gray's slang, his contractions, and many of his little intimacies and indiscretions. About such editing the twentieth century is apt to express indignation, and many people to-day probably feel that Mason cut out all the most interesting bits; but Mason was publishing a *book*, and he drew the distinction, usual in that century, between what was and what was not fit for the public.

Boswell's *Life of Johnson* had not yet appeared to accustom readers to a new range of intimacy; still less Rousseau's *Confession*. When Boswell's *Life* did appear, its intimacies startled many readers; they startled even XVordsworth. 'The Life of Johnson by Boswell', he wrote, 'had broken through many pre-existing delicacies, and afforded the British public an opportunity of acquiring experience, which before it had happily wanted.'The twentieth-century writer and his readers are scarcely aware of any such inhibitions, and when they meet with restraint and formality in eighteenth-century poetry are too apt to assume a want of feeling or an obtuseness of perception. In an age of publicity we have almost no private life left; the newspaper reporter enters the cottage and the palace, views the body and gets the widow's story, photographs the fatal mansion and marks the window with a cross. Whether we wish to or not, whether we are tender or unfeeling, we are 'condemn'd alike to groan' for the pains of others. But in the eighteenth century this curiosity about what was happening to other people had not yet become intense; men were left to live their own private lives, they were not expected to unbosom their feelings to strangers, they did not obtrude their personal concerns upon society.

In his essay on Gray, Matthew Arnold makes a good deal, after his fashion, of the observation made about Gray by his Swiss friend, Bonstetten: 'He would never talk of himself never would allow me to speak to him of his poetry. If I quoted lines to him, he kept silence like an obstinate child.' On which Arnold reiterates, 'He never spoke out', and goes on to explain that 'Gray, a born poet, fell upon an age of prose'. The truth is surely less depressing than that: Gray's misfortune-if it was a misfortune-was only that he did not fall upon an age of romantic poetry. A. E. Housman behaved in much the same way to young men who quoted *A Shropshire Lad* at him-not because he fell in an age of prose, but because he was an Englishman and a don, and found it difficult to bring himself to such intimacies with men much younger than himself.

In his Epitaph on John Hewet and Sarah Drew Pope had felt very sincerely and expressed his feelings very badly. A far happier instance of his ability to transmit his feeling is the 'Epistle to Miss Blount on her leaving the Town after the Coronation'. The poet daydreams about his mistress in the country, confined to the society of 'dull aunts and croaking rooks', and with nothing whatever to do except

muse and spill her solitary tea;
Or o'er cold coffee trifle with the spoon,
Count the slow clock, and dine exact at noon....

When *she* muses it is of the Town she is thinking, the Coronation celebrations, the lords and earls, the balls and assemblies- and then, one flirt of her fan and all the vision disappears! But the poet, too, has his vision as he languishes in the Town:

So when your slave, at some dear, idle time,
(Not plagu'd with headachs, or the want of rhime)
Stands in the streets, abstracted from the crew,
And while he seems to study, thinks of you:
Just when his fancy points your sprightly eyes,
Or sees the blush of Parthenissa rise,
Gay pats my shoulder, and you vanish quite;
Streets, chairs, and coxcombs, rush upon my sight;
Vext to be still in town, I knit my brow,
Look sow'r, and hum a song-as you may now.

Pope can manage his feeling perfectly here, because it never goes beyond the studied carelessness of fashionable society. It is what an intelligent young diarist noticed and duly entered in his diary in the year 1715, after watching some people of fashion playing at ombre at Lady Pilkington's: 'I don't find among these fine folks that their conversation is better or more improving or diverting than others', only they have a certain genteel way of carrying it and saying very ordinary things without concern.' But if Pope has caught to perfection this unconcern of manner, the feeling is there beyond doubt-as anyone with an ear for rhythm could tell at once. As a love poem this Epistle of Pope's is a less passionate and a far less direct expression of feeling than

I sigh'd, and said amang them a',
'Ye are na Mary Morison'-but it is none the less a love-poem, and there can be little doubt that the lady, who was well versed in the artificialities of polite society, had no difficulty whatever in recognizing the accents of genuine feeling. We must not

allow the mothers of idiot boys to make us suspect the emotions of others more happily placed.

On the other hand, it would be useless to deny that the eighteenth-century poet generally makes poor work of the expression of his 'natural' feelings. He can give us 'Sally in our Alley' and Cowper's 'Lines on the Receipt of his Mother's Picture', but such poems, if not uncommon, are not very numerous during the period. Occasionally we get conscious exercises in feeling. The eighteenth-century poet, *in his character as a poet,* felt justified in departing very far from the ordinary prose levels of thought and feeling. Some interesting evidence on this aspect of the poet's profession comes from Coleridge, who had a good deal more of the eighteenth century in him than Wordsworth. In a letter to Southey Coleridge replies to a request for permission to reprint the 'Monody on the Death of Chatterton' in a forthcoming edition of Chatterton's poems. He has been re-reading his own poem, and he has now a poor opinion of it: the emotion he had felt when he wrote the poem was genuine enough, but it had hurried him into extravagance and hyperbole.

A young man by strong feelings is impelled to write on a particular subject, and this is all his feelings do for him. They set him upon the business, and then they leave him. He has such a high idea of what poetry ought to be, that he cannot conceive that such things as his natural emotions may be allowed to find a place in it; his learning, therefore, his fancy, or rather conceit, and all his powers of buckram are put on the stretch.

In this devastatingly honest analysis of the 'Monody' Coleridge is, in fact, describing an attitude to poetry which (if kindlier expressed) most eighteenth-century poets would have found little difficulty in accepting. The poets (and their readers) had 'a high idea of what poetry ought to be', and consciously braced themselves at times to what they considered an adequate emotional state. Poetry, said Steele, with the air of a man stating a truism, 'is in itself an elevation above ordinary and common sentiments'. It was not at times the poet's natural feelings as a man that were called into play so much as his elevated emotions as a poet. It was surely something of this sort that happened when Pope wrote *Eloisa to Abelard*: that poem is a conscious exercise in emotional utterance, similar in kind to the passionate monologues in the tragedies of his friend, Nicholas Rowe. In Rowe's tragedy, *The Royal Convert*, Rodogune is in love with Aribert, but Aribert loves Ethelinda. Rodogune is torturing herself with thoughts of her rival.

Rodogune: How is she form'd? With what superior grace,This rival of my love? What envious God,In scorn of Nature's wretched works below,Improv'd and made her more than half divine?How has he taught her lips to breathe ambrosia?How dy'd her blushes with the morning's red,And cloath'd her with the fairest beams of light,To make her shine beyond me?

Aribert: Spare the theme.

But Rowe cannot afford to spare the theme; he is writing poetic drama, and this is what it required of him in the reign of Queen Anne. The trouble here is not that he is using a poetic diction (there is little of that), but that this highfalutin emotional utterance is what he believes to be proper to tragic drama. Rodogune's speech is over-wrought, over-coloured, remote from natural human expression. Rowe is constantly decorating ideas in this sumptuous fashion; his language has all the pomp of velvet trappings and elaborate folds of drapery. It belongs to the period just as much as the elaborate funeral processions with the mourners following the escutcheoned hearse in their ponderous and ill-sprung coaches.

Feeling such as that expressed by Rowe's Rodogune, rhetorical feeling, is common enough in eighteenth-century tragedy. It is perhaps to be found at its best just before the century opened, in some of Dryden's Heroic plays. The celebrated passage in *The Indian Emperor* (iii. ii) will show how good rhetoric can be at its best:

All things are hush'd, as Nature's self lay dead;
The mountains seem to nod their drowsy head;
The little birds, in dreams, their songs repeat,

And sleeping flow'rs beneath the night-dew sweat.
Ev'n Lust and Envy sleep; yet Love denies
Rest to my soul, and slumber to my eyes.

Such passages as this serve the same purpose, in a more refined form, as the drums and trumpets and the stage battles to which critics of the Heroic Drama took exception; they 'raise the imagination of the audience' and help the dramatist to obtain 'an absolute dominion over the minds of the spectators'. It is not in the nature of rhetoric to be precise; its purpose is to induce an emotional state in the mind of the reader or listener so that certain other more specific purposes may be served. There is little *crude* rhetoric in eighteenth-century poetry. When we do come upon it, as in Young's *Night Thoughts,* we are reading what is essentially a dramatic monologue. Eighteenth-century poetry, though it has normally a rhetorical basis, is usually a good deal quieter and more restrained than Young's; for that consciousness of an audience which encouraged extravagance *in the theatre* had usually the very opposite effect in the poetry of that milder Muse to which most of the poets owed their inspiration.

Poetry In A Polite Society:Refinement

Polite society not only exercises certain restraints on its members; it expects certain refinements. These can only be obtained at a cost. Refinement frequently comes into conflict with expressiveness; you must avoid some statements and some expressions because they are too crude, too forthright, because they arouse sensations of disgust. The point at which anything becomes disgusting will vary enormously with different individuals and different nations; it will vary, too, from one century to another, and from one class of society to another.

There can be no question that the formal manners of upper-class society in the eighteenth century were often abnormally fastidious. No doubt the coarseness, both of thought and expression, which becomes immediately apparent in this century as soon as we step among the middle or lower classes had a good deal to do with the exaggerated refinement of polite society. The artificial dikes which had been built to hold back the encroaching flood of vulgarity had to be maintained in strict repair; the muddy boots of the squire, the aroma of stable-dung and tobacco which he brought with him, his horse-laugh and coarse jests, had to be kept out of the drawing-room. Millamant coping distastefully with her country cousin, drunk and boisterous—'Sir Wilfull grows very powerful. Eh! how he smells! I shall be overcome if I stay' —is an epitome of the whole period. Where manners are artificial rather than natural one cannot be too careful, and the more careful one is the greater is the effect of a *faux pas*. In any case the culture of the Millamants and the Mirabells was rarely much more than skin-deep.

The century never achieved more than a precarious balance: the second book of the *Dunciad* and some of the verses which Swift allowed himself to write would alone show how precarious it was. The combination of an exquisitely delicate artistry with a coarseness of spiritual fibre is one of the paradoxes of the period. Little wonder, then, that the polite, beset on all sides, were driven in self-protection to an excessive refinement and artificiality which end only too often in a refusal to accept the ordinary facts of existence.

The effect of this upon poetry—and particularly in the first half of the century—is curious. Partly owing to this excessive refinement, and partly to the widespread notion that poetry, like the church service, necessitated a conscious withdrawal from everyday concerns and a certain remoteness from ordinary life, the eighteenth-century poet was often driven to exclude from his poetry much of his normal environment. That could be done, and was done, quite easily; but it necessarily narrowed the range of the instrument on which the poet played and the tunes he might play on it. He was beset by inhibitions, and from a good deal of what was going on in the street or in the human heart he had to avert his eyes.

It was not merely the thought that had to be refined to satisfy the contemporary reader; language, too—the 'dress of thought' —had also to be decontaminated from all mean or vulgar associations. The eighteenth-century point of view on this important matter was put by Addison with his customary lucidity:

> If clearness and perspicuity were only to be consulted the poet would have nothing else to do but to clothe his thoughts in the most plain and natural expressions. But, since it often happens that the most obvious phrases, and those which are used in ordinary conversation, become too familiar to the ear, and contract a kind of meanness by passing through the mouths of the vulgar, a poet should take particular care to guard himself against idiomatic ways of speaking.

So far from thinking that it is an advantage to the poet to write in 'a selection of the language really used by men', Addison is of opinion that Homer and Virgil may be counted fortunate to have written their poetry in what are now dead languages:

> Were there any mean phrases or idioms in Virgil and Homer, they would not shock the ear of the most delicate modern reader so much as they would have done that of an old Greek or Roman, because we never hear them pronounced in our streets, or in ordinary conversation.

Elsewhere Addison notes that the names of English rivers— because of their familiarity—are less poetical than those of the ancient world; and in his remarks on the ballad of 'Chevy Chase', after quoting two stanzas recounting the deaths of Earl Douglas, Sir Hugh Montgomery, Sir Charles Carrel, Sir Charles Murrel of Ratcliff, and Sir David Lamb, he observes with entire consistency that 'the familiar sound in these names destroys the majesty of the description'. Three of his own poems, 'The Battle of the Pygmies and Cranes', 'The Barometer', and 'A Bowling-green', are concerned with 'mean' or trivial subjects, and Addison has written them in Latin. Commenting on this, Johnson remarks that 'when the matter is low or scanty a dead language, in which nothing is mean because nothing is familiar, affords great conveniences'. But English poets must, of course, write most of their poetry in English; and since English is not a dead language, Addison and his contemporaries felt that—for epic and certain other kinds of poetry— they had to deaden it or anaesthetize it by suitable injections of words not used in the street or market-place.

In the Postscript to his translation of the *Odyssey* Pope echoes Addison; he, too, seems half to regret that English is not a dead language, but only too disconcertingly alive:

It must also be allowed that there is a majesty and harmony in the Greek language, which greatly contribute to elevate and support the narration. But I must also observe, that this is an advantage grown upon the language since Homer's time: for things are removed from vulgarity by being out of use; and if the words we could find in any present language were equally sonorous or musical in themselves, they would still appear less poetical and uncommon than those of a dead one, from this only circumstance, of being in every man's mouth.

Some thirty years earlier Dryden had also had occasion to remark on the difficulties that beset the poet writing in what was still a living language. Virgil's *mollis amaracus*, for instance; how should a modern English poet translate that sonorous phrase?

If I should translate it *sweet marjoram*, as the word signifies, the reader would think I had mistaken Virgil: for those village words, as I may call them, give us a mean idea of the thing; but the sound of the Latin is so much more pleasing, by the just mixture of the vowels with the consonants, that it raises our fancies to conceive somewhat more noble than a common herb, and to spread roses under him, and strew lilies over him; a bed not unworthy the grandson of the goddess.

Dryden's Venus, therefore, crowns the head of the young Ascanius with a wreath of myrtle, and softly lays him, not on marjoram, but on 'a flowery bed'. In Dryden's dilemma we can catch a glimpse of the influence—here, at any rate, a baleful influence—of constantly reading poetry in a dead language. The reason that Dryden gives for preferring *mollis amaracus* to sweet marjoram' ('the sound of the Latin is so much more pleasing, by the just mixture of the vowels with the consonants') will scarcely bear examination; the English words sound as pleasingly in the ear as the Latin. His real reason for shrinking from 'sweet marjoram' is that it is a 'village word', and that means, for Dryden, that it is too humble for epic poetry. Worse still, it brings with it too sharp an air of actuality; it disturbs that calm and remote atmosphere which he associates with classical poetry. But the calm and the remoteness are at least partly due to the passage of the centuries, and if Virgil was not afraid of *mollis amaracus* his translator should not refuse 'sweet marjoram'. The twentieth-century translator would not hesitate for a moment; it would need something much more prosaic-like, say, 'bachelor's buttons'—to drive him to such a periphrasis as 'flowery bed'.

It cannot be denied that eighteenth-century refinement is often a false and exaggerated refinement, or that the poet and his readers had an almost morbid dread of mean or ludicrous associations radiating from the words used in everyday life. The more poetry refused those everyday words, the greater was the danger that the unguarded introduction of some quite natural expression might break the poetical circuit between poet and reader. To-day—such is the gap between us and the eighteenth century—the situation is almost completely reversed: the modern poet must guard himself against 'poetical' words. But we must accept here a genuine difference of poetical conventions, a difference in the sort of expectations present in the mind of a reader when he opens a volume of poetry. There is no lack of evidence as to how the eighteenth century felt in those matters. In a well-known passage Johnson singles out a speech of Lady Macbeth's to illustrate the unfortunate effect of low expressions. After telling us that 'words become low by the occasions to which they are applied, or the general character of them who use them; and the disgust which they produce arises from the revival of those images with which they are commonly united', he proceeds to quote Lady Macbeth's words—

Come, thick night!
And pall thee in the dunnest smoke of hell,
That my keen knife see not the wound it makes;
Nor heav'n peep through the blanket of the dark,
To cry, Hold, hold!

To the language of this passage Johnson has three objections to offer: 'dun' is an epithet 'now seldom heard but in the stable', 'knife' makes him think of butchers, and the expression 'peep through the blanket' has such a ludicrous sound in his ears that he can 'scarce check [his] risibility'. We cannot suppose that Johnson is thinking up those objections to support a thesis: Shakespeare's language was continually giving such shocks to a century accustomed to a poetic diction which, like Dante's, had been passed through a kind of linguistic sieve. A contemporary of Johnson's, the Scottish poet William Hamilton of Bangour, undertook on one occasion to show what might be done by way of refining Shakespeare. He chose for his experiment some words uttered by Lear in his agony: 'Thou owest the worm no silk, the beast no hide, the sheep no wool, the cat no perfume....' Meditating on this, Hamilton produced his own version for an age of greater refinement:

For thee, the skilful worm, of specious hue,
No shining threads of ductile radiance drew;
For thee no sun the ripening gem refin'd;
No bleating innocence the fleece resign'd:
The hand of luxury ne'er taught to pour
O'er thy faint limbs the oil's refreshing show 'r....

Perhaps the fairest comment on those remarkable lines is a passage from one of Lord Chesterfield's letters to his son. In those modern days, he tells the boy, elegance is all:

People know very little of the world, and talk nonsense, when they talk of plainness and solidity unadorned; they will do nothing: mankind has been long out of a state of nature, and the golden age of native simplicity will never return. Whether for the better or the worse, no matter; but we are refined; and plain manners, plain dress, and plain.diction, would as little do in life, as acorns, herbage, and the water of the neighbouring spring, would do at table.

Low thoughts and low expressions, then, were to be avoided. The eighteenth-century poet, writing his own original poetry, had little difficulty in complying with the taste of the age. But when he was translating the poetry of an earlier and less refined age, he might, as we have seen, encounter serious difficulties. When Pope undertook to translate the *Odyssey* he secured the assistance of two friends, Elijah Fenton and the Rev. William Broome. On his way through Book XX Fenton ran into trouble, and wrote to Broome about it:

How I shall get over the bitch and her puppies, the roasting of the black puddings, as Brault translated it, and the cow-heel that was thrown at Ulysses' head, I know not. (11)

The bitch that Fenton found to be a poetical liability appears in a simile near the beginning of the book:

And as a bitch stands over her tender whelps growling, when she sees a man she does not know, and is eager to fight, so his [sc. Ulysses'] heart growled within him.... (12)

In his rendering of the passage Fenton avoids the word 'bitch', but succeeds, by a departure from English idiom, in indicating the sex; the puppies are generalized, and both the growling and the person growled at are dignified:

As o'er her young the mother-mastiff growls,
And bays the stranger groom: so wrath compress'd,
Recoiling, mutter'd thunder in his breast...

The cow-heel which Ctesippus flung at the head of Ulysses presented Fenton with a stiffer problem of devitalization. This unheroic action, which took place when the suitors were at dinner, is described by Homer quite simply and directly:

So saying, he hurled with strong hand the hoof of an ox, taking it up from the basket where it lay.

Fenton does not dare to omit the incident altogether, but he tries his best to veil its indecency with an elaborate periphrasis:

He said: and of the steer before him plac'd,
That sinewy fragment at Ulysses cast,
Where to the pastern-bone, by nerves combin'd,
The well-horn'd foot indissolubly join'd.

If the missile has not become even yet entirely heroic it is not the fault of the translator. He, at least, has wrapped it up in a napkin of poetic diction. To introduce humble and undignified facts into epic poetry was to Fenton like bringing pots and pans into the dining-room and setting them on the glossy sideboard with worthier and more polite vessels. The eighteenth-century poet believed in rendering unto Apollo the things he reckoned to be Apollo's; and whatever might be proper to the familiar epistle or the mock-heroic, the epic was held to demand from the poet a heightening of thought and expression well above the ordinary. In the same spirit eighteenth-century sculptors were accustomed to portraying contemporary English statesmen in the Roman toga. 'We go so far', Reynolds admits, 'as hardly to bear a statue in any other drapery.'It is not, therefore, surprising to find him assuring his students that the manner in which poetry is offered to the ear, the tone in which it is recited, should be as far removed from the tone of conversation, as the words of which that poetry is composed.... Whatever is familiar, or in any way reminds us of what we see and hear every day, perhaps does not belong to the higher provinces of art, either in poetry or painting.

Pope was well aware that a translator must accept the simplicities of Homer, and not try to write him up where the original does not justify such treatment.

There is a real beauty [he saw] in an easy, pure, perspicuous description, even of a low action.... Whenever the poet is obliged by the nature of his subject to descend to the lower manner of writing, an elevated style would be affected, and therefore ridiculous.

But when it came to the pinch Pope seems to have become conscious of the ladies and gentlemen who had subscribed (at a guinea a volume) for his translation, and he usually spares them too sharp a contact with the actual. Broome, too, was equally circumspect. Where Homer had written:

Now so long as my men had grain and red wine they kept their hands from the cattle, for they were eager to save their lives. But when all the stores had been consumed from out the ship, they must needs roam about in-search of game, fishes, and fowl, and whatever might come to their hands, fishing with bent hooks, for hunger pinched their bellies(19)-

Broome feels impelled to translate:
Unhurt the beeves, untouch'd the woolly train
Low through the grove, or range the flowery plain:
Then fail'd our food; then fish we make our prey,
Or fowl that screaming haunt the watery way.
Till now, from sea or flood no succour found,
Famine and meagre want besieg'd us round.
Or again:

The mother sat at her hearth with her handmaidens, spinning the yarn of purple dye...

becomes in Fenton:
the Queen her hours bestow'd
In curious works; the whirling spindle glow'd
With crimson threads, while busy damsels cull
The snowy fleece, or twist the purpled wool.

The process here is not simply one of refining: Fenton has amplified, and he has also managed to impart a rhetorical excitement ('whirling', 'glowed', 'busy') which is perhaps endemic in the heroic couplet. In Homer's less emphatic hexameters it is no doubt easier to say simple things simply. Yet refinement is certainly responsible for many of the modifications made by Pope and his assistants.

It is the same when he tries his hand at modernizing Chaucer. When Chaucer has a thing to say he goes the shortest way about it; the thing felt or thought is expressed with the minimum of fuss. But Pope, for a variety of reasons—because 'old Chaucer' is too naive, or too frank, or too unadorned—feels bound to give him a different turn. So we have Chaucer's

And folwed ay his bodily delyt
On wommen, there—as was his appetyt—
softened by Pope to
Yet led astray by Venus' soft delights,
He scarce cou'd rule some idle appetites;
and Chaucer's
Now wolde God that it were waxen night:
And that the night wolde lasten evermo!
conventionalized to
Restless he sate, invoking ev'ry pow'r
To speed his bliss, and haste the happy hour.

Pope is here turning Chaucer's natural (and therefore *perpetually* fresh) English into the fashionable idiom of a later century, the sort of idiom that softens the blow of actuality by referring to a birth in the family as 'a happy event'. We are not therefore surprised to find Pope in his ironical *Art of Sinking in Poetry* counselling the poet who wishes to excel in bathos to be sure to paint nature 'in her lowest simplicity' (ch. v), and to 'familiarize his mind to the lowest objects' (ch. vii). To this end, he adds, 'vulgar conversation will greatly contribute'.

As might be expected, the eighteenth-century reader had some difficulty in taking the old English and Scottish ballads seriously. He was the victim of his own 'good taste'. If one has gone to the best masters in pianoforte it seems ridiculous to sit and listen to a penny whistle, and still more so to take it senously. In his two interesting attempts to gain a hearing for the ballads of 'Chevy Chase' and 'The Two Children in the Wood', it is significant that Addison did not offer to defend the way in which they were expressed. In his discussion of the first he cautioned the reader not to let the simplicity of the style blind him to the greatness of the thought. In the second, he admitted that there is 'a despicable simplicity in the verse', and that the author has told his story 'in such an abject phrase and poorness of expression' that to quote him would only invite a laugh. But the thoughts are natural, 'and therefore cannot fail to please those who are not judges of language'. Not knowing any better, he implies, they will not be disgusted by the familiarity and naked simplicity of the expression.

Those who are judges of languages will inevitably (Addison supposes) be put off by the humble expressions, but they should still be able to appreciate the natural thoughts, if they have 'a true and unprejudiced taste of nature.

If Chaucer could be modernized, why not the ballads? If language is only 'the dress of thought' we can have a new dress whenever we want one, and the ballad—a sort of Cinderella among the literary Kinds—can come sparkling forth in a new gown and in the latest fashion. So, more than once, it did, and in so doing it completely lost its original character.

One of the most interesting examples of an eighteenth-century poet transmuting the work of an earlier day is Prior's treatment of 'The Nut-Brown Maid'. Prior had a genuine admiration for this old poem, or he would not have set to work upon it; he must have admired the natural feeling so simply and directly expressed. But in his 'Henry and Emma' this feeling has all but evaporated. What Prior has done is not so much to translate the poem into modern English as to inject it with some sort of poetical serum which completely alters the blood-content. He has treated it as a modern choreographer might treat some fairy-tale so as to evolve from it a delicate and sophisticated ballet. Emma, who undergoes a transformation similar to that of Liza in Shaw's *Pygmalion*, has become 'the dame' at whose feet Henry has often breathed his 'amorous vows. Upon a spreading beech-tree

Henry, in knots involving Emma's name,
Had half express'd, and half conceal'd his flame.

When, in the old poem, the Man asks the Maid if she could bear to marry an outlaw, a banished man—

Yet take good hede; for ever I drede that ye coude nat susteyne
The thornie wayes, the depe valeies, the snowe, the frost, the rayne,
The colde, the hete: for, drye or wete, we must lodge on the playne;
And us above, none other rofe, but a brake, bush, or twayne:
Which sone sholde greve you, I beleve, and ye wolde gladly than
That I had to the grene wode go, alone, a banyshed man—

Prior's Henry inquires:

But canst thou, tender maid, canst thou sustain
Afflictive want, or hunger's pressing pain?
Those limbs, in lawn and softest silk array'd,
From sunbeams guarded, and of winds afraid;
Can they bear angry Jove ? can tney resist
The parching dog-star, and the bleak north-east?
When, chill'd by adverse snows and beating rain,
We tread with weary steps the longsome plain;
When with hard toil we seek our evening food,
Berries and acorns, from the neighbouring wood;
And find among the cliffs no other house,
But the thin covert of some gather'd boughs;
Wilt thou not then reluctant send thine eye
Around the dreary waste; and weeping try
(Though then, alas! that trial be too late)
To find thy father's hospitable gate,
And seats, where ease and plenty brooding sate?

If it is asked whether the eighteenth-century lover talked to his mistress like this, the answer is, No; nor did the Elizabethan lover talk like Romeo. But in so far as Henry's language is the language of gallantry it would be perfectly well understood by the eighteenth-century fine lady, to whom it would also be, in its own affected fashion, the language of the heart. To Johnson, it is true, Prior's love poetry was in general 'unaffecting or remote', and 'Henry and Emma' in particular 'a dull and tedious dialogue'. But Johnson's reactions were not always typical of his century, and his poor opinion of Prior's love poetry is partly accounted for by his inveterate distaste for the mythological trimmings of Venus, Cupid, and the rest which Prior introduced so profusely into his work.

To set against Johnson's adverse criticism there is the testimony not only of Horace Walpole (who was, of course, the sort of reader that Prior had in mind) but also the poet Cowper, who can hardly be accused of any want of natural feeling. 'There are few readers of poetry of either sex in this country', Cowper wrote, 'who cannot remember how that entertaining piece has bewitched them.' There are not many of whom those words could be spoken today. Indeed, 'Henry and Emma' is to eighteenth-century poetry what 'The Idiot Boy' or 'Simon Lee' are to the poetry of Wordsworth: a test which only the initiated are likely to pass. To the open-minded reader, however, Prior's poem has still some of the charm of a period piece, if nothing more.

Why so many people come with an open and receptive mind to eighteenth-century furniture, architecture, or music, and yet approach the poetry of that period with a closed and even hostile mind is something of a mystery. A Chippendale chair is a period piece and is willingly accepted as such; but when the reader of poetry comes upon some equally perfect period piece in the work of John Gay he is, as often as not, far less ready to' respond to the fashion of an earlier age.

The average reader of poetry, it may be, is not content with a purely aesthetic pleasure; he looks for some reflection, or at least adumbration, of his own habitual thoughts and feelings in the poem he happens to be reading. It is in the poetry of his own generation that he has most chance of finding it—or, if he is not quite abreast of his own day, in that of a generation back. If he does read the poetry of past ages he is apt to prefer what comes nearest in spirit to the poetry of his own day. If this is his habitual approach to poetry, then a good deal of the most characteristic work of the eighteenth-century poets will seem remote enough from his field of interest.

But much of it—at its most remote, and even because of that remoteness—is capable of yielding a genuine aesthetic pleasure, the sort of pleasure that he may be accustomed to receiving from a Chelsea shepherdess or a conversation-piece by Zoffany. Gay at his best is among the most finished artists in that sophisticated and artificial style. He transmutes the raw materials of life into something at once delicate and artificial and remote. As with the chef in the *Dunciad*, working his culinary miracles, Beeves, at his touch, at once to jelly turn.

When Gay thinks of summer days in London he sees the lovers lying in the long grass beyond 'the dusty town', but before he has finished with them they have merged in his gentle mockery into the setting for a modern pastoral:

When the sweet-breathing spring unfolds the buds,
Love flys the dusty town for shady woods...
Then Chelsea's meads o'erhear perfidious vows,
And the prest grass defrauds the grazing cows.

Perhaps no eighteenth-century poet got so much fun and so much beauty out of the poetic diction of the period as Gay. In *Rural Sports* and *Trivia* he revels in its absurdity, its dangerous dignity, its exquisite artificiality, and its serenity. He takes it seriously—more so, for example, than Cowper—but not too seriously; he delights in it, he has a delicate understanding of its possibilities, and so he can produce *objets d'art* in verse, completely satisfying to the aesthetic sense, and with no more (but no less) importance than a vase from the workshops of Josiah Wedgewood.

III

If the twentieth-century reader is prepared to smile at Fenton's nervous approach to the cow-heel and the black puddings, he is not so ready to forgive another aspect of eighteenth-century refinement—the tacit assumption that the poor and the humble were not worth taking very seriously. It was an assumption that the novelists—from Defoe, Richardson, and Fielding onwards—were steadily undermining, but that the poets, for various reasons, were slower to discard.

The normal attitude of the eighteenth-century poet to the peasant ought not to shock or surprise us; it does not differ noticeably from the attitude of the Oxford or Cambridge undergraduate of to-day to his scout or gyp, or of the average Londoner to a 'cabby', or of the normal housewife to her 'char'. In all but exceptional circumstances the usual relationship is still one of good-natured condescension to an inferior: a gentleman will take care that his condescension does not become too apparent, but when he is alone with his friends he will be quite undemocratically facetious about the cabby or the scout or the gyp.

The twentieth-century novelist still considers himself entitled to make fun of butlers and taxi-drivers and charwomen; it has always been the most important literary function of the poor to provide comic relief. If you make fun of a cabinet minister that is satire; if you make fun of a taxi-driver or a country bumpkin it is comedy. But we no longer permit our poets to make that sort of fun. Since the days of Wordsworth it has become customary to assume that to any real poet not only the meanest flower that blows, but the humblest man that walks the earth, ought invariably to give 'thoughts that do often lie too deep for tears'. It is a remarkable tribute to Wordsworth that we should think so. To that great poet it seemed self-evident that pride,

Howe'er disguised in its own majesty,
Is littleness; that he who feels contempt
For any living thing, hath faculties
Which he has never used; that thought with him
Is in its infancy.

There was little of this feeling in the eighteenth century, and the poets did not do much to encourage its growth. What, for instance, are we to make of Lady Mary Wortley Montagu ? When Pope, still troubled by the sudden death of John Hewet and Sarah Drew, told her all about it in his letter and enclosed the epitaph he had written, Lady Mary (who was on her way home from Paris) replied in a letter so devastatingly facetious that we can scarcely read it to-day without a feeling of discomfort.

I must applaud your good-nature [she tells Pope] in supposing that your pastoral lovers (vulgarly called haymakers) would have lived in everlasting joy and harmony if the lightning had not interrupted their scheme of happiness.... Since you desire me to try my skill in an epitaph, I think the following lines perhaps more just, though not so poetical as yours:

Here lie John Hughes and Sarah Drew;
Perhaps you'll say, what's that to you?
Believe me, friend, much may be said
On this poor couple that are dead.
On Sunday next they should have married;
But see how oddly things are carried!
On Thursday last it rained and lighten'd;
These tender lovers, sadly frighten'd,
Shelter'd beneath the cocking hay,
In hopes to pass the storm away;
But the bold thunder found them out
(Commission'd for that end, no doubt),
And, seizing on their trembling breath,
Consign'd them to the shades of death.
Who knows if 'twas not kindly done?
For had they seen the next year's sun,
A beaten wife and cuckold swain
Had jointly curs'd the marriage chain;
Now they are happy in their doom,
For P. has wrote upon their tomb.

I confess these sentiments are not altogether so heroic as yours; but I hope you will forgive them in favour of the two last lines....

Perhaps if Lady Mary, and not Pope, had been staying at Stanton Harcourt when the storm broke she might have felt differently about John Hewet (not Hughes, as she has it) and Sarah Drew. Something, too, should be allowed for the fact that most of us tend to resist a direct call upon our sympathy, though we may respond readily enough if we are not so prompted. But Lady Mary's reaction to Pope's rural tragedy is quite clear: she thinks that he is making altogether too much fuss over a couple of mere villagers. These are people that one would scarcely notice at all if they were alive: why grow heroic about them merely because they have come to a sudden end ? If the bolt had struck Lord Harcourt, that *would* have been something! Her response does at least indicate how such an incident was apt to strike an aristocratic lady in the eighteenth century. Pope had asked her to take his rustic lovers seriously;

but his epitaph was not nearly good enough to persuade her to alter her habitual attitude to such folk.

What prevented the average eighteenth-century poet from being fully conscious of his common humanity with the poor was not so much an economic inequality as an inequality in education. He talked a different language from the poor man, he had a wider range of ideas and interests. For a century in which polite expression meant so much, the barrier erected between the classes by a different mode of' speech was almost insuperable. The full significance of Wordsworth's heresy about adopting or adapting the language of humble and rustic life for poetry will not be apparent unless we can realise what such a suggestion would have meant to Lady Mary Wortley Montagu or Lord Chesterfield, or even to a man of such comprehensive sympathies as Edmund Burke. The normal attitude to the poor in the eighteenth century was, as has been suggested, one of good-natured condescension to Goody Smith or Gaffer Brown or Granny White. So Goldsmith, the kindly but amused spectator from a different *monde,* recalls the village inn, where the country innocents were to be seen relaxing in characteristic attitudes—

Where grey-beard mirth, and smiling toil retired,
Where village statesmen talked with looks profound,
And news much older than their ale went round.

No one would question the kindliness of that, but the rustics are not Simon Lees or Betty Foys; they are much nearer to being the fauna of the place—only a little more important to Goldsmith than the flora, or the noisy geese that gabbled o'er the pool, or the varnished clock that clicked behind the door. Goldsmith makes more of his rustics than most eighteenth-century poets, but he remains aware of their limitations as poetic material. Those limitations were set forth by Johnson with all his customary candour:

The state of a man confined to the employments and pleasures of the country, is so little diversified, and exposed to so few of those accidents which produce perplexities, terrors, and surprises, in more complicated transactions, that he can be shown but seldom in such circumstances as attract curiosity. His ambition is without policy, and his love without intrigue. He has no complaints to make of his rival, but that he is richer than himself; nor any disasters to lament, but a cruel mistress or a bad harvest.

All of which, Johnson suggests, makes for dull poetry, since a man only becomes interesting when he has arrived at a stage of some emotional and intellectual complexity. In direct opposition to this statement of Johnson's may be placed the equally downright assertion of Wordsworth about humble and rustic people. 'From their rank of society and the sameness and narrow circle of their intercourse'—they are not just dull or boring with the tedious repetition of their unsophisticated notions, but—'being less under the influence of social vanity, they convey their feelings and notions in simple and unelaborated expressions.' And what they have to convey—'the essential passions of the heart'—is what interests Wordsworth, as man and poet. Johnson and Wordsworth, it will be noticed, start from precisely the same premiss (that rustic life is simple, unvaried, and narrow in scope), and arrive at exactly the opposite conclusions. It is not that Johnson did not know a good deal about the essential passions of the heart; it is certainly not that he lacked any feeling of common humanity with the poor. He had known poverty, and he never ceased to know the poor. It is therefore all the more significant that it is Johnson—and not Lord Chesterfield or Horace Walpole—who undertakes to demonstrate that the rustic poor have only a limited value for poetry. They failed to interest the eighteenth century deeply in the same way, and for much the same reason, as children failed to interest Pope or Gray: they were not fully adult, they were intellectually immature, and their sentiments and expressions were crude. The century's normal attitude here was that expressed by Hume in his essay on 'Refinement in Writing':

Sentiments which are merely natural affect not the mind with any pleasure, and seem not worthy of our attention. The pleasantries of a waterman, the observations of a peasant, the ribaldry of a porter or hackney coachman, all of these are natural, and disagreeable.... Nothing can please persons of taste, but nature drawn with all her graces and ornaments, *La belle nature*; or if we copy low life, the strokes must be strong and remarkable, and must convey a lively image to the mind.

It follows therefore that if pastoral poetry is to be made tolerable to a polite age the poet must shun any strict adherence to the sort of life actually led by shepherds, since (as Johnson observed) 'according to the customs of modern life, it is improbable that shepherds should be capable of harmonious numbers, or delicate sentiments'(38)—and both were required by the eighteenth-century reader. Shepherds are accordingly to be described 'as they may be conceived then to have been, when the best of men followed the employment'. What to an eighteenth-century poet was the logical outcome of describing country folk 'as at this day they really are' Gay showed in *The Shepherd's Week*, and Pope demonstrated even more hilariously in the mock ballad of Roger and Cicely which he inserted in his *Guardian* essay on Philips's *Pastorals*:

But the most beautiful example of this kind that I ever met with, is in a very valuable piece, which I chanced to find among some old manuscripts, entitled, *A Pastoral Ballad*: which I think, for its nature and simplicity, may (notwithstanding the modesty of the title) be allowed a perfect pastoral: It is composed in the *Somersetshire* dialect, and the names such as are proper to the country people. It may be observed, as a further beauty of this pastoral, the words *Nymph, Dryad, Naiad, Fawn, Cupid*, or *Satyr*, are not once mentioned through the whole. I shall make no apology for inserting some few lines of this excellent piece. *Cicely* breaks thus into the subject, as she is going a-milking:

Cicely	Rager go vetch tha kee, or else tha zunWill quite be go,. be yore c' have half a don.
Roger	Thou shouldst not ax ma tweece, but I've a be To dreave our bull to bull tha parson's kee.

And so forth, ending with the lines:
So Rager parted vor to vetch tha kee,
And vor her bucket in went Cicely.

That, then, is Pope's *reductio ad absurdum* of Ambrose Philips's *simplesse.* John Hewet and Sarah Drew might qualify for an epitaph, but Pope would see to it that they never strayed into pastoral poetry.

As the century wore on, this attitude to the poor began very gradually to change. In his *Elegy* Gray is reminding his readers that the great and the important must die like everyone else; death is not a fate reserved only for the poor and humble. *Some* of the humble folk, it is true, might in more affluent circumstances have become famous, but 'their lot forbad'. Never mind: it also forbade them to grow great in wickedness. The poor, then, are taken seriously in the *Elegy*; but it is rather the deadness of the dead, and the universality of death (made all the more apparent by the anonymity of the mouldering heaps distinguished by no 'storied urn or animated bust'), that the poet's imagination has seized most firmly. As a man of culture Gray still has a decent respect for the storied urn, and is even prepared to be slightly apologetic about the frail memorials of the villagers, with 'their uncouth rhymes and shapeless sculpture deck'd' — the lapidary equivalent of ballads and broadsides in literature. He is still, in fact, thinking of 'the rude forefathers of the hamlet'. Goldsmith is perhaps more democratic, a humourous soul who was probably quite as much at ease with his landlady as with Burke or Johnson; but Goldsmith, too, with his smith who 'relaxes his pond'rous strength and leans to hear', or his swain 'mistrustless of his smutted face', or his awed rustics listening to the polysyllabic disputation of parson and schoolmaster, is hardly taking his rustics quite seriously. You do not feel that anyone in the village is quite adult. Cowper, too, is still (for all his sympathy and interest) one of the gentlefolk writing naturally of 'swains' and 'boors' and of the woodman with 'the short tube that fumes beneath his nose.

The change comes, when it does come, not so much in the habitual way of seeing the poor as a different race (for that continues) as in a greater readiness to feel for them *when they are in distress*. This may be seen, as early as 1730, in some lines of James Thomson:

Ah! little think the gay licentious proud,
Whom pleasure, power, and affluence surround-
They, who their thoughtless hours in giddy mirth,
And wanton, often cruel, riot waste-
Ah! little think they, while they dance along,
How many feel, this very moment, death
And all the sad variety of pain;...
How many pine in want, and dungeon-glooms;...
... sore pierced by wintry winds,
How many sink into the sordid hut
Of cheerless poverty....

If men would only think of these things, and of the 'incessant struggle' that life means for so many unfortunate wretches,

The social tear would rise, the social sigh;
And into clear perfection, gradual bliss,
Refining still, the social passions work.

In the same way Goldsmith's voice changes when he pictures to himself 'yon widow'd, solitary thing', the last survivor of the now depopulated village,

Forced in age, for bread,
To strip the brook with mantling cresses spread,
To pick her wintry faggot from the thorn,
To seek her nightly shed, and weep till morn....

Cowper, too, has his Crazy Kate in The Task.

Such miseries and such destitution made Goldsmith and Cowper sad; it is not until we come to Crabbe that we find a poet whom they make positively angry. The anger may not lead to better poetry, but it does suggest that the point of view has altered. Yet even Crabbe is still for the most part the *spectator ab extra,* moved by the hard lot of the poorer classes, and distressed by their shiftlessness and improvidence, but not particularly interested in their minds.

For that sort of interest (if we except Burns, who was one of them) we have to wait till Wordsworth. We never really get it in Coleridge, Byron, Shelley, or Keats. It was Wordsworth, almost alone among the Romantic poets, who saw into the depth of human souls, Souls that appear to have no depth at allTo careless eyes.

But it is a common mistake to assume that we are all Wordsworths now, and that the common human attitude to the poor (as distinct from the provision made for them) has radically, altered since the days of Pope and Swift. We are all Wordsworths now only when Wordsworth has shown us the way. Left to ourselves, most of us still approach a tramp or a charwoman with meagre expectations, and with a conscious or unconscious adjustment of our mental attitude.

Chapter 10

The Rape of the Lock: Introduction

Introduction: The Mock-Epic

At the beginning of "The Rape of the Lock," Pope identifies the work as a "heroi-comical poem." Today, the poem–and others like it–is referred to as a *mock-epic* and sometimes as a *mock-heroic*. Such a work parodies the serious, elevated style of the classical epic poem–such as *The Iliad* or *The Odyssey*, by Homer–to poke fun at human follies. Thus, a mock-epic is a type of satire; it treats petty humans or insignificant occurrences as if they were extraordinary or heroic, like the great heroes and events of Homer's two great epics. In writing "The Rape of the Lock," Pope imitated the characteristics of Homer's epics, as well as later epics such as *The Aeneid* (Vergil), *The Divine Comedy* (Dante), and *Paradise Lost* (Milton). Many of these characteristics are listed below, under "Epic Conventions."

Setting

The action takes place in London and its environs in the early 1700's on a single day. The story begins at noon (Canto I) at the London residence of Belinda as she carefully prepares herself for a gala social gathering. The scene then shifts (Canto II) to a boat carrying Belinda up the Thames. To onlookers she is as magnificent as Queen Cleopatra was when she traveled in her barge. The rest of the story (Cantos III-V) takes place where Belinda debarks–Hampton Court Palace, a former residence of King Henry VIII on the outskirts of London–except for a brief scene in Canto IV that takes place in the cave of the Queen of Spleen.

Source: A Real-Life Incident

Pope based *The Rape of the Lock* on an actual incident in which a British nobleman, Lord Petre, cut off a lock of hair dangling tantalizingly from the head of the beautiful Arabella Fermor. Petre's daring theft of the lock set off a battle royal between the Petre and Fermor families. John Caryll–a friend of Pope and of the warring families–persuaded the great writer to pen a literary work satirizing the absurdity and silliness of the dispute. The result was one of the greatest satirical poems in all of literature. In writing the poem, Pope also drew upon ancient classical sources–notably Homer's great epics, *The Iliad* and *The Odyssey*–as models to imitate in style and tone. He also consulted the texts of medieval and Renaissance epics.

Chapter 11

Characters in the Poem

Belinda: Belinda is based on the historical Arabella Fermor, a member of Pope's circle of prominent Roman Catholics. Robert, Lord Peter (the Baron in the poem) had precipitated a rift between their two families by snipping off a lock of her hair.

The Baron: This is the pseudonym for the historical Robert, Lord Petre, the young gentleman in Pope's social circle who offended Arabella Fermor and her family by cutting off a lock of her hair. In the poem's version of events, Arabella is known as Belinda.

Caryl: The historical basis for the Caryl character is John Caryll, a friend of Pope and of the two families that had become estranged over the incident the poem relates. It was Caryll who suggested that Pope encourage a reconciliation by writing a humourous poem.

Goddess: The muse who, according to classical convention, inspires poets to write their verses

Shock: Belinda's lapdog

Ariel: Belinda's guardian sylph, who oversees an army of invisible protective deities

Umbriel: The chief gnome, who travels to the Cave of Spleen and returns with bundles of sighs and tears to aggravate Belinda's vexation

Brillante: The sylph who is assigned to guard Belinda's earrings

Momentilla: The sylph who is assigned to guard Belinda's watch.

Crispissa: The sylph who is assigned to guard Belinda's "favourite Lock"

Clarissa: A woman in attendance at the Hampton Court party. She lends the Baron the pair of scissors with which he cuts Belinda's hair, and later delivers a moralizing lecture.

Thalestris: Belinda's friend, named for the Queen of the Amazons and representing the historical Gertrude Morley, a friend of Pope's and the wife of Sir George Browne (rendered as her "beau," Sir Plume, in the poem). She eggs Belinda on in her anger and demands that the lock be returned.

Sir Plume: Thalestris's "beau," who makes an ineffectual challenge to the Baron.

Chapter 12

The Rape of the Lock: Text

TO MRS. ARABELLA FERMOR

Madam,

It will be vain to deny that I have some Value for this Piece, since I dedicate it to You. Yet you may bear me Witness, it was intended only to divert a few young Ladies, who have good Sense and good humour enough, to laugh not only at their Sex's little unguarded Follies, but at their own. But as it was communicated with the Air of a Secret, it soon found its Way into the World. An imperfect Copy having been offered to a Bookseller, You had the good-Nature for my Sake to consent to the Publication of one more correct: This I was forced to before I had executed half my Design, for the *Machinery* was entirely used to complete it.

The *Machinery*, Madam, is a term invented by the Critics, to signify that Part which the Deities, Angels, or Daemons, are made to act in a Poem: For the ancient Poets are in one Respect like many modern Ladies: Let an Action be never so trivial in itself, they always make it appear of the utmost Importance. These Machines I determined to raise on a very new and odd Foundation, the *Rosicrucian* Doctrine of Spirits.

I know how disagreeable it is to make use of hard Words before a Lady: but 'tis so much the Concern of a Poet to have his works understood, and particularly by your Sex, that you must give me leave to explain two or three difficult Terms.

The *Rosicrucians* are a People I must bring you acquainted with. The best Account I know of them is in a French book called *Le Comte de Gabalis,* which both in its Title and Size is so like a Novel, that many of the Fair Sex have read it for one by Mistake. According to these Gentlemen the four Elements are inhabited by Spirits, which they call *Sylphs, Gnomes, Nymphs,* and *Salamanders.* The *Gnomes,* or Daemons of Earth, delight in Mischief: but the *Sylphs,* whose Habitation is Air, are the best-conditioned Creatures imaginable. For they say, any Mortals may enjoy the most intimate Familiarities with these gentle Spirits, upon a Condition very easy to all true *Adepts,* an inviolate Preservation of Chastity.

As to the following Canto's, all the Passages of them are as Fabulous, as the vision at the Beginning, or the Transformation at the End; (except for the Loss of your Hair, which I always name with Reverence.) The Human Persons are as Fictitious as the Airy ones; and the Character of *Belinda,* as it is now managed, resembles you in nothing in beauty.

If this Poem had as many Graces as there are in Your Person, or in Your Mind, yet I could never hope it should pass thro' the World half so uncensored as you have done. But let its Fortune be what it will, mine is happy enough, to have given me this Occasion of assuring You that I am, with the truest Esteem,

Madam,

Your most Obedient

Humble Servant,
A. POPE

Canto 1

What dire Offence from am'rous Causes springs,
What mighty Contests rise from trivial Things,
I sing — This Verse to C—, Muse! is due;
This, ev'n Belinda may vouchsafe to view:
Slight is the Subject, but not so the Praise,
If She inspire, and He approve my Lays.

Say what strange Motive, Goddess! cou'd compel
A well-bred Lord t'assault a gentle Belle?
Oh say what stranger Cause, yet unexplor'd,
Cou'd make a gentle Belle reject a Lord?
And dwells such Rage in softest Bosoms then?
And lodge such daring Souls in Little Men?

Sol thro' white Curtains shot a tim'rous Ray,
And op'd those Eyes that must eclipse the Day;
Now Lapdogs give themselves the rowzing Shake,
And sleepless Lovers, just at Twelve, awake:
Thrice rung the Bell, the Slipper knock'd the Ground,
And the press'd Watch return'd a silver Sound.
Belinda still her downy Pillow prest,
Her Guardian Sylph prolong'd the balmy Rest.
'Twas he had summon'd to her silent Bed
The Morning-Dream that hover'd o'er her Head.
A Youth more glitt'ring than a Birth-night Beau,
(That ev'n in Slumber caus'd her Cheek to glow)
Seem'd to her Ear his winning Lips to lay,
And thus in Whispers said, or seem'd to say.
Fairest of Mortals, thou distinguish'd Care
Of thousand bright Inhabitants of Air!
If e'er one Vision touch'd thy infant Thought,
Of all the Nurse and all the Priest have taught,
Of airy Elves by Moonlight Shadows seen,
The silver Token, and the circled Green,
Or Virgins visited by Angel-Pow'rs,
With Golden Crowns and Wreaths of heav'nly Flowers,
Hear and believe! thy own Importance know,
Nor bound thy narrow Views to Things below.
Some secret Truths from Learned Pride conceal'd,
To Maids alone and Children are reveal'd:
What tho' no Credit doubting Wits may give?
The Fair and Innocent shall still believe.
Know then, unnumbered Spirits round thee fly,
The light Militia of the lower Sky;
These, tho' unseen, are ever on the Wing,

Hang o'er the Box, and hover round the Ring.
Think what an Equipage thou hast in Air,
And view with scorn Two Pages and a Chair.
As now your own, our Beings were of old,
And once inclos'd in Woman's beauteous Mold;
Thence, by a soft Transition, we repair
From earthly Vehicles to these of Air.
Think not, when Woman's transient Breath is fled,
That all her Vanities at once are dead:
Succeeding Vanities she still regards,
And tho' she plays no more, o'erlooks the Cards.
Her Joy in gilded Chariots, when alive,
And Love of Ombre, after Death survive.
For when the Fair in all their Pride expire,
To their first Elements the Souls retire:
The Sprights of fiery Termagants in Flame
Mount up, and take a Salamander's Name.
Soft yielding Minds to Water glide away,
And sip with Nymphs, their Elemental Tea.
The graver Prude sinks downward to a Gnome,
In search of Mischief still on Earth to roam.
The light Coquettes in Sylphs aloft repair,
And sport and flutter in the Fields of Air.

Know farther yet; Whoever fair and chaste
Rejects Mankind, is by some Sylph embrac'd:
For Spirits, freed from mortal Laws, with ease
Assume what Sexes and what Shapes they please.
What guards the Purity of melting Maids,
In Courtly Balls, and Midnight Masquerades,
Safe from the treach'rous Friend, and daring Spark,
The Glance by Day, the Whisper in the Dark;
When kind Occasion prompts their warm Desires,
When Musick softens, and when Dancing fires?
'Tis but their Sylph, the wise Celestials know,
Tho' Honour is the Word with Men below.

Some Nymphs there are, too conscious of their Face,
For Life predestin'd to the Gnomes Embrace.

These swell their Prospects and exalt their Pride,
When Offers are disdain'd, and Love deny'd.
Then gay Ideas crowd the vacant Brain;
While Peers and Dukes, and all their sweeping Train,
And Garters, Stars, and Coronets appear,
And in soft Sounds, Your Grace salutes their Ear.
'Tis these that early taint the Female Soul,
Instruct the Eyes of young Coquettes to roll,
Teach Infants Cheeks a bidden Blush to know,
And little Hearts to flutter at a Beau.

Oft when the World imagine Women stray,
The Sylphs thro' mystick Mazes guide their Way,
Thro' all the giddy Circle they pursue,
And old Impertinence expel by new.
What tender Maid but must a Victim fall
To one Man's Treat, but for another's Ball?
When Florio speaks, what Virgin could withstand,
If gentle Damon did not squeeze her Hand?
With varying Vanities, from ev'ry Part,
They shift the moving Toyshop of their Heart;
Where Wigs with Wigs, with Sword-knots
Sword-knots strive,

Beaus banish Beaus, and Coaches Coaches drive.
This erring Mortals Levity may call,
Oh blind to Truth! the Sylphs contrive it all.

Of these am I, who thy Protection claim,
A watchful Sprite, and Ariel is my Name.
Late, as I rang'd the Crystal Wilds of Air,
In the clear Mirror of thy ruling Star
I saw, alas! some dread Event impend,
E're to the Main this Morning Sun descend.
But Heav'n reveals not what, or how, or where:
Warn'd by thy Sylph, oh Pious Maid beware!
This to disclose is all thy Guardian can.
Beware of all, but most beware of Man!

He said; when Shock, who thought she slept too long,
Leapt up, and wak'd his Mistress with his Tongue.

'Twas then Belinda, if Report say true,
Thy Eyes first open'd on a Billet-doux.
Wounds, Charms, and Ardors, were no sooner read,
But all the Vision vanish'd from thy Head.

And now, unveil'd, the Toilet stands display'd,
Each Silver Vase in mystic Order laid.
First, rob'd in White, the Nymph intent adores
With Head uncover'd, the cosmetic Pow'rs.
A heav'nly Image in the Glass appears,
To that she bends, to that her Eyes she rears;
Th' inferior Priestess, at her Altar's side,
Trembling, begins the sacred Rites of Pride.
Unnumber'd Treasures ope at once, and here
The various Off'rings of the World appear;
From each she nicely culls with curious Toil,
And decks the Goddess with the glitt'ring Spoil.
This Casket India's glowing Gems unlocks,
And all Arabia breathes from yonder Box.

The Tortoise here and Elephant unite,
Transform'd to Combs, the speckled and the white.
Here Files of Pins extend their shining Rows,
Puffs, Powders, Patches, Bibles, Billet-doux.
Now awful Beauty puts on all its Arms;
The Fair each moment rises in her Charms,
Repairs her Smiles, awakens ev'ry Grace,
And calls forth all the Wonders of her Face;
Sees by Degrees a purer Blush arise,
And keener Lightnings quicken in her Eyes.
The busy Sylphs surround their darling Care;
These set the Head, and those divide the Hair,
Some fold the Sleeve, while others plait the Gown;
And Betty's prais'd for Labours not her own.

Canto 2

NOT with more Glories, in th' Etherial Plain,
The Sun first rises o'er the purpled Main,
Than issuing forth, the Rival of his Beams
Lanch'd on the Bosom of the Silver Thames.

Fair Nymphs, and well-drest Youths around her shone,
But ev'ry Eye was fix'd on her alone.
On her white Breast a sparkling Cross she wore,
Which Jews might kiss, and Infidels adore.
Her lively Looks a sprightly Mind disclose,
Quick as her Eyes, and as unfix'd as those:
Favours to none, to all she Smiles extends,
Oft she rejects, but never once offends.
Bright as the Sun, her Eyes the Gazers strike,
And, like the sun, they shine on all alike.
Yet graceful Ease, and Sweetness void of Pride,
Might hide her Faults, if Belles had faults to hide:
If to her share some Female Errors fall,
Look on her Face, and you'll forget 'em all.

This Nymph, to the Destruction of Mankind,
Nourish'd two Locks, which graceful hung behind
In equal Curls, and well conspir'd to deck
With shining Ringlets her smooth Iv'ry Neck.
Love in these Labyrinths his Slaves detains,
And mighty Hearts are held in slender Chains.
With hairy Sprindges we the Birds betray,
Slight Lines of Hair surprize the Finny Prey,
Fair Tresses Man's Imperial Race insnare,
And Beauty draws us with a single Hair.

Th' Adventrous Baron the bright Locks admir'd,
He saw, he wish'd, and to the Prize aspir'd:
Resolv'd to win, he meditates the way,
By Force to ravish, or by Fraud betray;
For when Success a Lover's Toil attends,
Few ask, if Fraud or Force attain'd his Ends.

For this, e're Phoebus rose, he had implor'd
Propitious Heav'n, and ev'ry Pow'r ador'd,
But chiefly Love—to Love an Altar built,
Of twelve vast French Romances, neatly gilt.
There lay three Garters, half a Pair of Gloves;
And all the Trophies of his former Loves.
With tender Billet-doux he lights the Pyre,

And breathes three am'rous Sighs to raise the Fire.
Then prostrate falls, and begs with ardent Eyes
Soon to obtain, and long possess the Prize:
The Pow'rs gave Ear, and granted half his Pray'r,
The rest, the Winds dispers'd in empty Air.

But now secure the painted Vessel glides,
The Sun-beams trembling on the floating Tydes,
While melting Musick steals upon the Sky,
And soften'd Sounds along the Waters die.
Smooth flow the Waves, the Zephyrs gently play
Belinda smil'd, and all the World was gay.
All but the Sylph—With careful Thoughts opprest,
Th' impending Woe sate heavy on his Breast.
He summons strait his Denizens of Air;
The lucid Squadrons round the Sails repair:

Soft o'er the Shrouds Aerial Whispers breathe,
That seem'd but Zephyrs to the Train beneath.
Some to the Sun their Insect-Wings unfold,
Waft on the Breeze, or sink in Clouds of Gold.
Transparent Forms, too fine for mortal Sight,
Their fluid Bodies half dissolv'd in Light.
Loose to the Wind their airy Garments flew,
Thin glitt'ring Textures of the filmy Dew;
Dipt in the richest Tincture of the Skies,
Where Light disports in ever-mingling Dies,
While ev'ry Beam new transient Colours flings,
Colours that change whene'er they wave their Wings.
Amid the Circle, on the gilded Mast,
Superior by the Head, was Ariel plac'd;
His Purple Pinions opening to the Sun,
He rais'd his Azure Wand, and thus begun.

Ye Sylphs and Sylphids, to your Chief give Ear,
Fays, Fairies, Genii, Elves, and Daemons hear!
Ye know the Spheres and various Tasks assign'd,
By Laws Eternal, to th' Aerial Kind.
Some in the Fields of purest AEther play,
And bask and whiten in the Blaze of Day.

Some guide the Course of wandring Orbs on high,
Or roll the Planets thro' the boundless Sky.
Some less refin'd, beneath the Moon's pale Light
Hover, and catch the shooting stars by Night;
Or suck the Mists in grosser Air below,
Or dip their Pinions in the painted Bow,
Or brew fierce Tempests on the wintry Main,
Or o'er the Glebe distill the kindly Rain.
Others on Earth o'er human Race preside,
Watch all their Ways, and all their Actions guide:
Of these the Chief the Care of Nations own,
And guard with Arms Divine the British Throne.

Our humbler Province is to tend the Fair,
Not a less pleasing, tho' less glorious Care.
To save the Powder from too rude a Gale,
Nor let th' imprison'd Essences exhale,
To draw fresh Colours from the vernal Flow'rs,
To steal from Rainbows ere they drop in Show'rs
A brighter Wash; to curl their waving Hairs,
Assist their Blushes, and inspire their Airs;
Nay oft, in Dreams, Invention we bestow,
To change a Flounce, or add a Furbelo.

This Day, black Omens threat the brightest Fair
That e'er deserv'd a watchful Spirit's Care;
Some dire Disaster, or by Force, or Slight,
But what, or where, the Fates have wrapt in Night.
Whether the Nymph shall break Diana's Law,
Or some frail China Jar receive a Flaw,
Or stain her Honour, or her new Brocade,
Forget her Pray'rs, or miss a Masquerade,
Or lose her Heart, or Necklace, at a Ball;
Or whether Heav'n has doom'd that Shock
must fall.
Haste then ye Spirits! to your Charge repair;
The flutt'ring Fan be Zephyretta's Care;
The Drops to thee, Brillante, we consign;
And Momentilla, let the Watch be thine;
Do thou, Crispissa, tend her fav'rite Lock;
Ariel himself shall be the Guard of Shock.

To Fifty chosen Sylphs, of special Note,
We trust th' important Charge, the Petticoat.
Oft have we known that sev'nfold Fence to fail;
Tho' stiff with Hoops, and arm'd with Ribs of Whale.
Form a strong Line about the Silver Bound,
And guard the wide Circumference around.

Whatever spirit, careless of his Charge,
His Post neglects, or leaves the Fair at large,
Shall feel sharp Vengeance soon o'ertake his Sins,
Be stopt in Vials, or transfixt with Pins.
Or plung'd in Lakes of bitter Washes lie,

Or wedg'd whole Ages in a Bodkin's Eye:
Gums and Pomatums shall his Flight restrain,
While clog'd he beats his silken Wings in vain;
Or Alom-Stypticks with contracting Power
Shrink his thin Essence like a rivell'd Flower.
Or as Ixion fix'd, the Wretch shall feel
The giddy Motion of the whirling Mill,
In Fumes of burning Chocolate shall glow,
And tremble at the Sea that froaths below!

He spoke; the Spirits from the Sails descend;
Some, Orb in Orb, around the Nymph extend,
Some thrid the mazy Ringlets of her Hair,
Some hang upon the Pendants of her Ear;
With beating Hearts the dire Event they wait,
Anxious, and trembling for the Birth of Fate.

Canto 3

CLOSE by those Meads for ever crown'd with Flow'rs,
Where Thames with Pride surveys his rising Tow'rs,
There stands a Structure of Majestick Frame,
Which from the neighb'ring Hampton takes its Name.
Here Britain's Statesmen oft the Fall foredoom
Of Foreign Tyrants, and of Nymphs at home;
Here Thou, great Anna! whom three Realms obey,
Dost sometimes Counsel take—and sometimes Tea.

Hither the Heroes and the Nymphs resort,
To taste awhile the Pleasures of a Court;
In various Talk th' instructive hours they past,
Who gave the Ball, or paid the Visit last:
One speaks the Glory of the British Queen,
And one describes a charming Indian Screen.
A third interprets Motions, Looks, and Eyes;
At ev'ry Word a Reputation dies.
Snuff, or the Fan, supply each Pause of Chat,
With singing, laughing, ogling, and all that.

Mean while declining from the Noon of Day,
The Sun obliquely shoots his burning Ray;
The hungry Judges soon the Sentence sign,
And Wretches hang that Jury-men may Dine;
The Merchant from th'exchange returns in Peace,
And the long Labours of the Toilette cease ——
Belinda now, whom Thirst of Fame invites,
Burns to encounter two adventrous Knights,
At Ombre singly to decide their Doom;
And swells her Breast with Conquests yet to come.
Strait the three Bands prepare in Arms to join,
Each Band the number of the Sacred Nine.
Soon as she spreads her Hand, th' Aerial Guard
Descend, and sit on each important Card,
First Ariel perch'd upon a Matadore,
Then each, according to the Rank they bore;
For Sylphs, yet mindful of their ancient Race,
Are, as when Women, wondrous fond of place.

Behold, four Kings in Majesty rever'd,
With hoary Whiskers and a forky Beard;
And four fair Queens whose hands sustain a Flow'r,
Th' expressive Emblem of their softer Pow'r;
Four Knaves in Garbs succinct, a trusty Band,
Caps on their heads, and Halberds in their hand;
And Particolour'd Troops, a shining Train,
Draw forth to Combat on the Velvet Plain.

The skilful Nymph reviews her Force with Care;
Let Spades be Trumps, she said, and Trumps they were.

Now move to War her Sable Matadores,
In Show like Leaders of the swarthy Moors.
Spadillio first, unconquerable Lord!
Led off two captive Trumps, and swept the Board.
As many more Manillio forc'd to yield,
And march'd a Victor from the verdant Field.
Him Basto follow'd, but his Fate more hard
Gain'd but one Trump and one Plebeian Card.
With his broad Sabre next, a Chief in Years,
The hoary Majesty of Spades appears;
Puts forth one manly Leg, to sight reveal'd;
The rest his many-colour'd Robe conceal'd.
The Rebel-Knave, who dares his Prince engage,
Proves the just Victim of his Royal Rage.
Ev'n mighty Pam that Kings and Queens o'erthrow,
And mow'd down Armies in the Fights of Lu,
Sad Chance of War! now, destitute of Aid,
Falls undistinguish'd by the Victor Spade.

Thus far both Armies to Belinda yield;
Now to the Baron Fate inclines the Field.
His warlike Amazon her Host invades,
Th' Imperial Consort of the Crown of Spades.
The Club's black Tyrant first her Victim dy'd,

Spite of his haughty Mien, and barb'rous Pride:
What boots the Regal Circle on his Head,
His Giant Limbs in State unwieldy spread?
That long behind he trails his pompous Robe,
And of all Monarchs only grasps the Globe?

The Baron now his Diamonds pours apace;
Th' embroider'd King who shows but half his Face,
And his refulgent Queen, with Pow'rs combin'd,
Of broken Troops an easie Conquest find.
Clubs, Diamonds, Hearts, in wild Disorder seen,
With Throngs promiscuous strow the level Green.
Thus when dispers'd a routed Army runs,
Of Asia's Troops, and Africk's Sable Sons,
With like Confusion different Nations fly,

In various habits and of various Dye,
The pierc'd Battalions dis-united fall,
In Heaps on Heaps; one Fate o'erwhelms them all.

The Knave of Diamonds now tries his wily Arts,
And wins (oh shameful Chance!) the Queen of Hearts.
At this, the Blood the Virgin's Cheek forsook,
A livid Paleness spreads o'er all her Look;
She sees, and trembles at th' approaching Ill,
Just in the Jaws of Ruin, and Codille.
And now, (as oft in some distemper'd State)
On one nice Trick depends the gen'ral Fate.
An Ace of Hearts steps forth: The King unseen
Lurk'd in her Hand, and mourn'd his captive Queen.
He springs to Vengeance with an eager pace,
And falls like Thunder on the prostrate Ace.
The Nymph exulting fills with Shouts the Sky,
The Walls, the Woods, and long Canals reply.

Oh thoughtless Mortals! ever blind to Fate,
Too soon dejected, and too soon elate!
Sudden these Honours shall be snatch'd away,
And curs'd for ever this Victorious Day.

For lo! the Board with Cups and Spoons is crown'd,
The Berries crackle, and the Mill turns round.
On shining Altars of Japan they raise
The silver Lamp; the fiery Spirits blaze.
From silver Spouts the grateful Liquors glide,
And China's Earth receives the smoking Tyde.
At once they gratify their Scent and Taste,
While frequent Cups prolong the rich Repast.
Strait hover round the Fair her Airy Band;
Some, as she sip'd, the fuming Liquor fann'd,
Some o'er her Lap their careful Plumes display'd,
Trembling, and conscious of the rich Brocade.
Coffee, (which makes the Politician wise,
And see thro' all things with his half shut Eyes)
Sent up in Vapours to the Baron's Brain
New Stratagems, the radiant Lock to gain.

Ah cease rash Youth! desist e'er 'tis too late,
Fear the just Gods, and think of Scylla's Fate!
Chang'd to a Bird, and sent to flit in Air,
She dearly pays for Nisus' injur'd Hair!

But when to Mischief Mortals bend their Will,
How soon they find fit Instruments of Ill!
Just then, Clarissa drew with tempting Grace
A two-edg'd Weapon from her shining Case;
So Ladies in Romance assist their Knight,
Present the Spear, and arm him for the Fight.
He takes the Gift with rev'rence, and extends
The little Engine on his Finger's Ends:
This just behind Belinda's Neck he spread,
As o'er the fragrant Steams she bends her Head:
Swift to the Lock a thousand Sprights repair,
A thousand Wings, by turns, blow back the Hair,
And thrice they twitch'd the Diamond in her Ear,
Thrice she look'd back, and thrice the Foe drew near.
Just in that instant, anxious Ariel sought
The close Recesses of the Virgin's Thought;
As on the Nosegay in her Breast reclin'd,

He watch'd th' Ideas rising in her Mind,
Sudden he view'd, in spite of all her Art,
An Earthly Lover lurking at her Heart.
Amaz'd, confus'd, he found his Pow'r expir'd,
Resign'd to Fate, and with a Sigh retir'd.

The Peer now spreads the glitt'ring Forfex wide,
T'inclose the Lock; now joins it, to divide.
Ev'n then, before the fatal Engine clos'd,
A wretched Sylph too fondly interpos'd;
Fate urg'd the Sheers, and cut the Sylph in twain,
(But Airy Substance soon unites again)
The meeting Points that sacred Hair dissever
From the fair Head, for ever and for ever!

Then flash'd the living Lightnings from her Eyes,
And Screams of Horror rend th' affrighted Skies.
Not louder Shrieks to pitying Heav'n are cast,

When Husbands or when Lap-dogs breath their last,
Or when rich China Vessels, fal'n from high,
In glittring Dust and painted Fragments lie!

Let Wreaths of Triumph now my Temples twine,
(The Victor cry'd) the glorious Prize is mine!
While Fish in Streams, or Birds delight in Air,
Or in a Coach and Six the British Fair,
As long as Atalantis shall be read,
Or the small Pillow grace a Lady's Bed,
While Visits shall be paid on solemn Days,
When numerous Wax-lights in bright Order blaze,
While Nymphs take Treats, or Assignations give,
So long my Honour, Name, and Praise shall live!

What Time wou'd spare, from Steel receives its date,
And Monuments, like Men, submit to Fate!
Steel cou'd the Labour of the Gods destroy,
And strike to Dust th' Imperial Tow'rs of Troy.
Steel cou'd the Works of mortal Pride confound,
And hew Triumphal Arches to the Ground.
What Wonder then, fair Nymph! thy Hairs shou'd feel
The conqu'ring Force of unresisted Steel?

Canto 4

BUT anxious Cares the pensive Nymph opprest,
And secret Passions labour'd in her Breast.
Not youthful Kings in Battel seiz'd alive,
Not scornful Virgins who their Charms survive,
Not ardent Lovers robb'd of all their Bliss,
Not ancient Ladies when refus'd a Kiss,
Not Tyrants fierce that unrepenting die,
Not Cynthia when her Manteau's pinn'd awry,
E'er felt such Rage, Resentment and Despair,
As Thou, sad Virgin! for thy ravish'd Hair.

For, that sad moment, when the Sylphs withdrew,
And Ariel weeping from Belinda flew,
Umbriel, a dusky melancholy Spright,
As ever sully'd the fair face of Light,

Down to the Central Earth, his proper Scene,
Repairs to search the gloomy Cave of Spleen.

Swift on his sooty Pinions flitts the Gnome,
And in a Vapour reach'd the dismal Dome.
No cheerful Breeze this sullen Region knows,
The dreaded East is all the Wind that blows.
Here, in a Grotto, sheltred close from Air,
And screen'd in Shades from Day's detested Glare,
She sighs for ever on her pensive Bed,
Pain at her side, and Megrim at her Head.

Two Handmaids wait the Throne: Alike in Place,
But diff'ring far in Figure and in Face.
Here stood Ill-nature like an ancient Maid,

Her wrinkled Form in Black and White array'd;
With store of Pray'rs, for Mornings, Nights, and Noons,
Her Hand is fill'd; her Bosom with Lampoons.

There Affectation with a sickly Mien
Shows in her Cheek the Roses of Eighteen,
Practis'd to Lisp, and hang the Head aside,
Faints into Airs, and languishes with Pride;
On the rich Quilt sinks with becoming Woe,
Wrapt in a Gown, for Sickness, and for Show.
The Fair ones feel such Maladies as these,
When each new Night-Dress gives a new Disease.

A constant Vapour o'er the Palace flies;
Strange Phantoms rising as the Mists arise;
Dreadful, as Hermit's Dreams in haunted Shades,
Or bright as Visions of expiring Maids.
Now glaring Fiends, and Snakes on rolling Spires,
Pale Spectres, gaping Tombs, and Purple Fires:
Now Lakes of liquid Gold, Elysian Scenes,
And Crystal Domes, and Angels in Machines.

Unnumber'd Throngs on ev'ry side are seen
Of Bodies chang'd to various Forms by Spleen.
Here living Teapots stand, one Arm held out,
One bent; the Handle this, and that the Spout:

A Pipkin there like Homer's Tripod walks;
Here sighs a Jar, and there a Goose Pie talks;
Men prove with Child, as pow'rful Fancy works,
And Maids turn'd Bottels, call aloud for Corks.

Safe past the Gnome thro' this fantastick Band,
A Branch of healing Spleenwort in his hand.
Then thus addrest the Pow'r—Hail wayward Queen!
Who rule the Sex to Fifty from Fifteen,
Parent of Vapours and of Female Wit,
Who give th' Hysteric or Poetic Fit,
On various Tempers act by various ways,
Make some take Physick, others scribble Plays;
Who cause the Proud their Visits to delay,
And send the Godly in a Pett, to pray.
A Nymph there is, that all thy Pow'r disdains,
And thousands more in equal Mirth maintains.
But oh! if e'er thy Gnome could spoil a Grace,
Or raise a Pimple on a beauteous Face,
Like Citron-Waters Matron's Cheeks inflame,
Or change Complexions at a losing Game;
If e'er with airy Horns I planted Heads,
Or rumpled Petticoats, or tumbled Beds,
Or caus'd Suspicion when no Soul was rude,
Or discompos'd the Head-dress of a Prude,
Or e'er to costive Lap-Dog gave Disease,
Which not the Tears of brightest Eyes could ease:
Hear me, and touch Belinda with Chagrin;
That single Act gives half the World the Spleen.

The Goddess with a discontented Air
Seems to reject him, tho' she grants his Pray'r.
A wondrous Bag with both her Hands she binds,
Like that where once Ulysses held the Winds;
There she collects the Force of Female Lungs,
Sighs, Sobs, and Passions, and the War of Tongues.
A Vial next she fills with fainting Fears,
Soft Sorrows, melting Griefs, and flowing Tears.
The Gnome rejoicing bears her Gift away,
Spreads his black Wings, and slowly mounts to Day.

Sunk in Thalestris' Arms the Nymph he found,
Her Eyes dejected and her Hair unbound.
Full o'er their Heads the swelling Bag he rent,
And all the Furies issued at the Vent.
Belinda burns with more than mortal Ire,
And fierce Thalestris fans the rising Fire.
O wretched Maid! she spread her hands, and cry'd,
(While Hampton's Ecchos, wretched Maid reply'd)
Was it for this you took such constant Care
The Bodkin, Comb, and Essence to prepare;

For this your Locks in Paper-Durance bound,
For this with tort'ring Irons wreath'd around?
For this with Fillets strain'd your tender Head,
And bravely bore the double Loads of Lead?
Gods! shall the Ravisher display your Hair,
While the Fops envy, and the Ladies stare!
Honour forbid! at whose unrival'd Shrine
Ease, Pleasure, Virtue, All, our Sex resign.
Methinks already I your Tears survey,
Already hear the horrid things they say,
Already see you a degraded Toast,
And all your Honour in a Whisper lost!
How shall I, then, your helpless Fame defend?
'Twill then be Infamy to seem your Friend!
And shall this Prize, th' inestimable Prize,
Expos'd thro' Crystal to the gazing Eyes,
And heighten'd by the Diamond's circling Rays,
On that Rapacious Hand for ever blaze?
Sooner shall Grass in Hide Park Circus grow,
And Wits take Lodgings in the Sound of Bow;
Sooner let Earth, Air, Sea, to Chaos fall,
Men, Monkies, Lap-dogs, Parrots, perish all!

She said; then raging to Sir Plume repairs,
And bids her Beau demand the precious Hairs:
(Sir Plume, of Amber Snuff-box justly vain,
And the nice Conduct of a clouded Cane)
With earnest Eyes, and round unthinking Face,

He first the Snuff-box open'd, then the Case,
And thus broke out— "My Lord, why, what the Devil?
"Z—ds! damn the Lock! 'fore Gad, you must be civil!
"Plague on't! 'tis past a Jest—nay prithee, Pox!
"Give her the Hair—he spoke, and rapp'd his Box.

It grieves me much (reply'd the Peer again)
Who speaks so well shou'd ever speak in vain.
But by this Lock, this sacred Lock I swear,
(Which never more shall join its parted Hair,
Which never more its Honours shall renew,
Clipt from the lovely Head where late it grew)
That while my Nostrils draw the vital Air,
This Hand, which won it, shall for ever wear.
He spoke, and speaking, in proud Triumph spread
The long-contended Honours of her Head.

But Umbriel, hateful Gnome! forbears not so;
He breaks the Vial whence the Sorrows flow.
Then see! the Nymph in beauteous Grief appears,
Her Eyes half languishing, half drown'd in Tears;
On her heav'd Bosom hung her drooping Head,
Which, with a Sigh, she rais'd; and thus she said.

For ever curs'd be this detested Day,
Which snatch'd my best, my fav'rite Curl away!
Happy! ah ten times happy, had I been,
If Hampton-Court these Eyes had never seen!
Yet am not I the first mistaken Maid,
By Love of Courts to num'rous Ills betray'd.
Oh had I rather un-admir'd remain'd
In some lone Isle, or distant Northern Land;
Where the gilt Chariot never marks the way,
Where none learn Ombre, none e'er taste Bohea!
There kept my Charms conceal'd from mortal Eye,
Like Roses that in Desarts bloom and die.
What mov'd my Mind with youthful Lords to rome?
O had I stay'd, and said my Pray'rs at home!
'Twas this, the Morning Omens seem'd to tell;
Thrice from my trembling hand the Patch-box fell;

The tott'ring China shook without a Wind,
Nay, Poll sate mute, and Shock was most Unkind!
A Sylph too warn'd me of the Threats of Fate,
In mystic Visions, now believ'd too late!
See the poor Remnants of these slighted Hairs!
My hands shall rend what ev'n thy Rapine spares:
These, in two sable Ringlets taught to break,

Once gave new Beauties to the snowie Neck.
The Sister-Lock now sits uncouth, alone,
And in its Fellow's Fate foresees its own;
Uncurl'd it hangs, the fatal Sheers demands;
And tempts once more thy sacrilegious Hands.
Oh hadst thou, Cruel! been content to seize
Hairs less in sight, or any Hairs but these!

Canto 5

SHE said: the pitying Audience melt in Tears,
But Fate and Jove had stopp'd the Baron's Ears.
In vain Thalestris with Reproach assails,
For who can move when fair Belinda fails?
Not half to fixt the Trojan cou'd remain,
While Anna begg'd and Dido rag'd in vain.
Then grave Clarissa graceful wav'd her Fan;
Silence ensu'd, and thus the Nymph began.

Say, why are Beauties prais'd and honour'd most,
The wise Man's Passion, and the vain Man's Toast?
Why deck'd with all that Land and Sea afford,
Why Angels call'd, and Angel-like ador'd?
Why round our Coaches crowd the white-glov'd Beaus,
Why bows the Side-box from its inmost Rows?
How vain are all these Glories, all our Pains,
Unless good Sense preserve what Beauty gains:
That Men may say, when we the Front-box grace,
Behold the first in Virtue, as in Face!
Oh! if to dance all Night, and dress all Day,
Charm'd the Small-pox, or chas'd old Age away;
Who would not scorn what Huswife's Cares produce,
Or who would learn one earthly Thing of Use?

To patch, nay ogle, might become a Saint,
Nor could it sure be such a Sin to paint.
But since, alas! frail Beauty must decay,
Curl'd or uncurl'd, since Locks will turn to grey,
Since paint'd, or not paint'd, all shall fade,
And she who scorns a Man, must die a Maid;
What then remains, but well our Pow'r to use,
And keep good Humour still whate'er we lose?
And trust me, Dear! good Humour can prevail,
When Airs, and Flights, and Screams, and Scolding fail.
Beauties in vain their pretty Eyes may roll;
Charms strike the Sight, but Merit wins the Soul.

So spake the Dame, but no Applause ensu'd;
Belinda frown'd, Thalestris call'd her Prude.
To Arms, to Arms! the fierce Virago cries,
And swift as Lightning to the Combate flies.
All side in Parties, and begin th' Attack;
Fans clap, Silks russle, and tough Whalebones crack;
Heroes and Heroins Shouts confus'dly rise,
And base, and treble Voices strike the Skies.
No common Weapons in their Hands are found,
Like Gods they fight, nor dread a mortal Wound.

So when bold Homer makes the Gods engage,
And heav'nly Breasts with human Passions rage;
'Gainst Pallas, Mars; Latona, Hermes arms;
And all Olympus rings with loud Alarms.
Jove's Thunder roars, Heav'n trembles all around;
Blue Neptune storms, the bellowing Deeps resound;
Earth shakes her nodding Tow'rs, the Ground gives way;
And the pale Ghosts start at the Flash of Day!

Triumphant Umbriel on a Sconce's Height
Clapt his glad Wings, and sate to view the Fight,
Propt on their Bodkin Spears, the Sprights survey
The growing Combat, or assist the Fray.

While thro' the Press enrag'd Thalestris flies,
And scatters Deaths around from both her Eyes,
A Beau and Witling perish'd in the Throng,

One dy'd in Metaphor, and one in Song.
O cruel Nymph! a living Death I bear,
Cry'd Dapperwit, and sunk beside his Chair.

A mournful Glance Sir Fopling upwards cast,
Those Eyes are made so killing—was his last:
Thus on Meander's flow'ry Margin lies
Th' expiring Swan, and as he sings he dies.

When bold Sir Plume had drawn Clarissa down,
Chloe stept in, and kill'd him with a Frown;
She smil'd to see the doughty Hero slain,
But at her Smile, the Beau reviv'd again.

Now Jove suspends his golden Scales in Air,
Weighs the Mens Wits against the Lady's Hair;
The doubtful Beam long nods from side to side;
At length the Wits mount up, the Hairs subside.
See fierce Belinda on the Baron flies,
With more than usual Lightning in her Eyes;
Nor fear'd the Chief th' unequal Fight to try,
Who sought no more than on his Foe to die.
But this bold Lord, with manly Strength indu'd,
She with one Finger and a Thumb subdu'd,
Just where the Breath of Life his Nostrils drew,
A Charge of Snuff the wily Virgin threw;
The Gnomes direct, to ev'ry Atome just,
The pungent Grains of titillating Dust.
Sudden, with starting Tears each Eye o'erflows,
And the high Dome re-ecchoes to his Nose.

Now meet thy Fate, incens'd Belinda cry'd,
And drew a deadly Bodkin from her Side.
(The same, his ancient Personage to deck,
Her great great Grandsire wore about his Neck
In three Seal-Rings which after, melted down,
Form'd a vast Buckle for his Widow's Gown:
Her infant Grandame's Whistle next it grew,
The Bells she gingled, and the Whistle blew;
Then in a Bodkin grac'd her Mother's Hairs,
Which long she wore, and now Belinda wears.)

Boast not my Fall (he cry'd) insulting Foe!
Thou by some other shalt be laid as low.
Nor think, to die dejects my lofty Mind;
All that I dread, is leaving you behind!
Rather than so, ah let me still survive,
And burn in Cupid's Flames,—but burn alive.

Restore the Lock! she cries; and all around
Restore the Lock! the vaulted Roofs rebound.
Not fierce Othello in so loud a Strain
Roar'd for the Handkerchief that caus'd his Pain.
But see how oft Ambitious Aims are cross'd,
And Chiefs contend 'till all the Prize is lost!
The Lock, obtain'd with Guilt, and kept with Pain,
In ev'ry place is sought, but sought in vain
With such a Prize no Mortal must be blest,
So Heav'n decrees! with Heav'n who can contest?

Some thought it mounted to the Lunar Sphere,
Since all things lost on Earth, are treasur'd there.
There Heroe's Wits are kept in pondrous Vases,
And Beau's in Snuff-boxes and Tweezer-Cases.
There broken Vows, and Death-bed Alms are found,
And Lovers Hearts with Ends of Riband bound;
The Courtiers Promises, and Sick Man's Pray'rs,
The Smiles of Harlots, and the Tears of Heirs,
Cages for Gnats, and Chains to Yoak a Flea;
Dry'd Butterflies, and Tomes of Casuistry.

But trust the Muse—she saw it upward rise,
Tho' mark'd by none but quick Poetic Eyes:
(So Rome's great Founder to the Heav'ns withdrew,
To Proculus alone confess'd in view.)
A sudden Star, it shot thro' liquid Air,
And drew behind a radiant Trail of Hair.
Not Berenice's Locks first rose so bright,
The heav'ns bespangling with dishevel'd light.

The Sylphs behold it kindling as it flies,
And pleas'd pursue its Progress thro' the Skies.

This the Beau-monde shall from the Mall survey,
And hail with Musick its propitious Ray.
This, the blest Lover shall for Venus take,
And send up Vows from Rosamonda's Lake.
This Partridge soon shall view in cloudless Skies,
When next he looks thro' Galilaeo's Eyes;
And hence th' Egregious Wizard shall foredoom
The Fate of Louis, and the Fall of Rome.

Then cease, bright Nymph! to mourn the ravish'd Hair
Which adds new Glory to the shining Sphere!
Not all the Tresses that fair Head can boast
Shall draw such Envy as the Lock you lost.
For, after all the Murders of your Eye,
When, after Millions slain, your self shall die;
When those fair Suns shall sett, as sett they must,
And all those Tresses shall be laid in Dust;
This Lock, the Muse shall consecrate to Fame,
And mid'st the Stars inscribe Belinda's Name!

Chapter 13

Analysis of the Poem

Plot Summary

Pope opens with a statement announcing the topic of his poem: A gentleman–a lord, in fact–has committed a terrible outrage against a gentlewoman, causing her to reject him. What was this offense? Why did it incite such anger in the lady?

The woman in question is named Belinda. She is sleeping late one day in her London home when a sylph–a dainty spirit that inhabits the air–warns her that "I saw, alas! some dread Event impend." The sylph, named Ariel, does not know what this event is or where or how it will manifest itself. But he does tell Belinda to be on guard against the machinations of men.

Belinda rises and prepares herself for a social gathering, sitting before a mirror and prettying herself with "puffs and powders" and scenting herself with "all Arabia." Afterward, she travels up the Thames River to the site of the social festivities, Hampton Court, the great palace on the north bank of the river that in earlier times was home to King Henry VIII. As she sits in the boat, "Fair Nymphs, and well-drest Youths around her shone, / But ev'ry Eye was fix'd on her alone." In other words, she was beautiful beyond measure. She smiled at everyone equally, and her eyes–bright suns–radiated goodwill. Especially endearing to anyone who looked upon her were her wondrous tresses:

This Nymph, to the Destruction of Mankind,
Nourish'd two Locks which graceful hung behind
In equal Curls, and well conspir'd to deck
With shining Ringlets the smooth Iv'ry Neck.

Among Belinda's admirers is a young baron at Hampton Court awaiting her arrival. He has resolved to snip off a lock of her hair as the trophy of trophies. Before dawn, before even the sun god Phoebus Apollo arose, the Baron had been planning the theft of a lock of Belinda's hair. To win the flavour of the gods, he had lighted an altar fire and, lying face down before it, prayed for success.

After Belinda arrives at Hampton Court with her company of friends, the partygoers play Ombre, a popular card game in which only 40 of the 52 cards are dealt—the eights, nines, and tens are held back. It appears that the Baron will win the game after his knave of diamonds captures her queen of hearts. However, Belinda yet has hope, even after the Baron plays an ace of hearts:

The King unseen
Lurk'd in her Hand, and mourn'd his captive Queen.
He springs to Vengeance with an eager Pace,
And falls like Thunder on the prostrate Ace
The Nymph exulting fills with Shouts the Sky;
The Walls, the Woods, and long Canals reply.

Belinda wins! Coffee is served, the vapours of which go to the Baron's brain and embolden him to carry out his assault on Belinda's hair. Clarissa, a lady who fancies the Baron, withdraws scissors from a case and arms him with the weapon. When he closes in behind Belinda, she bends over her coffee, exposing a magnificent lock. But a thousand sprites come to her aid, using their wings to blow hair over the lock. They also tug at one of her diamond earrings to alert her to the danger. Three times they warn her and three times she looks around. But all is for naught. The Baron opens wide his weapon, closes it around the lock, and cuts. The rape of her lock enrages Belinda:

Then flash'd the living Lightnings from her Eyes,
And Screams of Horror rend th' affrighted Skies.

Not louder Shrieks to pitying Heav'n are cast,
When Husbands, or when Lapdogs breathe their last,
Or when rich China Vessels, fal'n from high,
In glitt'ring Dust and painted Fragments lie!

A gnome named Umbriel descends to the Underworld on Belinda's behalf and obtains a bag of sighs and a vial of tears from the Queen of Spleen. With these magical gifts, he means to comfort poor Belinda. First, he empties the bag on her. A gentleman named Sir Plume—prompted by his belle, Thalestris, a friend of Belinda—then roundly scolds the Baron for his grave offense. But the Baron is unrepentant. Umbriel then empties the vial on Belinda. Grief overcomes her as her eyes half-drown in tears and her head droops upon her bosom. She says:

For ever curs'd be this detested Day,
Which snatch'd my best, my fav'rite Curl away!
Happy! ah ten times happy had I been,
If Hampton-Court these Eyes had never seen!

Clarissa tries to mollify Belinda in a long speech, but fails. A bit of a melee ensues when Belinda attempts to retrieve her lost lock. "Fans clap, Silks russle, and tough Whalebones crack." Belinda proves a fierce combatant. She attacks the Baron "with more than usual Lightning in her Eyes" and throws a handful of snuff from Sir Plume's box up his nose. But, alas, when the battle ends, the lock is nowhere to be found.

However, the poem ends on a happy note for Belinda, Pope says, because the trimmed lock of her golden hair has risen to the heavens, there to become a shining star.

Theme

The central theme of *The Rape of the Lock* is the fuss that high society makes over trifling matters, such as breaches of decorum. In the poem, a feud of epic proportions erupts after the Baron steals a lock of Belinda's hair. In the real-life incident on which Pope based his poem, the Peter and the Fermor families had a falling-out after Lord Petre snipped off one of

Arabella Fermor's locks. Other themes that Pope develops in the poem include human vanity and the importance of being able to laugh at life's little reversals. The latter motif is a kind of "moral to the story." Clarissa touches upon both of these themes when addressing tearful Belinda, shorn of her lock:

> But since, alas! frail Beauty must decay,
> Curl'd or uncurl'd, since Locks will turn to grey;
> Since painted, or not painted, all shall fade,
> And she who scorns a Man, must die a Maid,
> What then remains but well our Pow'r to use,
> And keep good Humour still whate'er we lose?

Climax

The climax of *The Rape of the Lock* occurs when the Baron snips away one of Belinda's locks.

Epic Conventions

Because a mock-epic parodies a classical epic, it uses the same conventions, or formulas, as the classical epic—but usually in a humourous way. For example, a convention of many classical epics is a sea voyage in which perils confront the hero at every turn. In *The Rape of the Lock,* the sea voyage is Belinda's boat trip up the Thames River. Her guardian sylph, Ariel, sees "black omens" that foretell disasters for Belinda even though the waves flow smoothly and the winds blow gently. Will she stain her dress? Lose her honor or her necklace? Miss a masquerade? Forget her prayers? So frightful are the omens that Ariel summons 50 of his companion spirits to guard Belinda's petticoat, as well as the ringlets of her hair. Following are examples of the epic conventions that Pope parodies:

- *Invocation of the Muse:* In ancient Greece and Rome, poets had always requested "the muse" to fire them with creative genius when they began long narrative poems, or epics, about godlike heroes and villains. In Greek mythology, there were nine muses, all sisters, who were believed to inspire poets, historians, flutists, dancers, singers, astronomers, philosophers, and other thinkers and artists. If one wanted to write a great poem, play a musical instrument with bravado, or develop a grand scientific or philosophical theory, he would ask for help from a muse. When a writer asked for help, he was said to be "invoking the muse." The muse of epic poetry was named Calliope [kuh LY uh pe]. In "The Rape of the Lock," Pope does not invoke a goddess; instead, he invokes his friend, John Caryll (spelled *CARYL* in the poem), who had asked Pope to write a literary work focusing on an event (the snipping of a lock of hair) that turned the members of two families—the Petres and the Fermors—into bitter enemies. Caryll thought that poking fun at the incident would reconcile the families by showing them how trivial the incident was.

- *Division of the Poem Into Books or Cantos:* The traditional epic is long, requiring several days several days of reading. Dante's *Divine Comedy*, for example, contains 34 cantos. When printed, the work consists of a book about two inches thick. Pope, of course, presents only five cantos containing a total of fewer than 600 lines. Such miniaturizing helps Pope demonstrate the smallness or pettiness of the behaviour exhibited by the main characters in the poem.
- *Descriptions of Soldiers Preparing for Battle:* In *The Iliad*, Homer describes in considerable detail the armor and weaponry of the great Achilles, as well as the battlefield trappings of other heroes. In *The Rape of the Lock*, Pope describes Belinda preparing herself with combs and pins–with "Puffs, Powders, Patches"–noting that "Now awful Beauty puts on all its Arms."
- *Descriptions of Heroic Deeds:* While Homer describes the exploits of his heroes during the Trojan War, Pope

describes the "exploits" of Belinda and the Baron during a card game called *Ombre,* which involves three players and a deck of 40 cards.

- *Account of a Great Sea Voyage:* In *The Odyssey,* Odysseus (also known as Ulysses) travels the seas between Troy and Greece, encountering many perils. In *The Aeneid,* Aeneas travels the seas between Troy and Rome, also encountering perils. In *The Rape of the Lock,* Belinda travels up the Thames in a boat.
- *Participation of Deities or Spirits in the Action:* In *The Rape of the Lock*—as in *The Iliad, The Odyssey, The Aeneid, The Divine Comedy,* and *Paradise Lost*—supernatural beings take part in the action.
- *Presentation of Scenes in the Underworld:* Like supernatural beings in classical epics, the gnome Umbriel visits the Underworld in *The Rape of the Lock.*

The Story behind the Poem

"The families concerned in the *Rape of the Lock*—the Fermors, Petres, and Carylls—were prominent members of that group of great intermarried Roman Catholic families owning land in the home counties, most of whom came within the circle of Pope's friends and acquaintances and to whom Pope considered his own family to belong. Some time before 21 March, 1712, when Pope sold his poem to Lintott, Robert, Lord Petre had cut off a lock of Arabella Fermor's hair, and John Caryll had suggested to Pope that he should write a poem to heal the estrangement that followed between the two families:

The stealing of Miss Belle Fermor's hair, was taken too seriously, and caused an estrangement between the two families, though they had lived so long in great friendship before. A common acquaintance and well-wisher to both, desired me to write a poem to make a jest of it, and laugh them together again. It was with this view that I wrote the Rape of the Lock.

The incident behind the poem has never been authoritatively tracked down to place and time. It is improbable, but possible, that it happened, as the poem states, at Hampton Court; and the counter-claims of the houses of the Fermors, Petres, or Carylls have never been substantiated." (Twickenham, Vol II, p. 83)

Was Belinda, as the poem hints, willing to marry the Baron? "Arabella may well have been considered as the possible bride for Lord Petre. The rape of the lock may well have been an incident in the period of circumspection—how thorough such circumspection was likely to be may be gathered from the correspondence of Caryll during 1710-11 when he was choosing a wife for his son. If two such families who 'had lived so long in friendship before' are estranged through a fairly trivial incident, it seems there is thunder in the air. All the fun of the poem read very differently when, less than two months before the poem was published, Lord Petre married Catherine Warmsley, a Lancashire heiress some seven or more years younger than Arabella and much richer." (Twickenham 93)

By the time Pope revised the poem in 1717, Lord Petre had died (of smallpox) and Arabella was married. Whatever the original purpose of the poem may have been, by the time Pope finished revising *The Rape of the Lock* the feud between the families was no longer particularly relevant

Chapter 14

Explanation of Cantos

Canto 1

Summary

The Rape of the Lock begins with a passage outlining the subject of the poem and invoking the aid of the muse. Then the sun ("Sol") appears to initiate the leisurely morning routines of a wealthy household. Lapdogs shake themselves awake, bells begin to ring, and although it is already noon, Belinda still sleeps. She has been dreaming, and we learn that the dream has been sent by "her guardian Sylph," Ariel. The dream is of a handsome youth who tells her that she is protected by "unnumber'd Spirits"—an army of supernatural beings who once lived on earth as human women. The youth explains that they are the invisible guardians of women's chastity, although the credit is usually mistakenly given to "Honour" rather than to their divine stewardship. Of these Spirits, one particular group—the Sylphs, who dwell in the air—serve as Belinda's personal guardians; they are devoted, lover-like, to any woman that "rejects mankind," and they understand and reward the vanities of an elegant and frivolous lady like Belinda. Ariel, the chief of all Belinda's puckish protectors, warns her in this dream that "some dread event" is going to befall her that day, though he can tell her nothing more specific than that she should "beware of Man!" Then Belinda awakes, to the licking tongue of her lapdog, Shock. Upon the delivery of a billet-doux, or love-letter, she forgets all about the dream. She then proceeds to her dressing table and goes through an elaborate ritual of dressing, in which her own image in the mirror is described as a "heavenly image," a "goddess." The Sylphs, unseen, assist their charge as she prepares herself for the day's activities.

Commentary

The opening of the poem establishes its mock-heroic style. Pope introduces the conventional epic subjects of love and war and includes an invocation to the muse and a dedication to the man (the historical John Caryll) who commissioned the poem. Yet the tone already indicates that the high seriousness of these traditional topics has suffered a diminishment. The second line confirms in explicit terms what the first line already suggests: the "am'rous causes" the poem describes are not comparable to the grand love of Greek heroes but rather represent a trivialized version of that emotion. The "contests" Pope alludes to will prove to be "mighty" only in an ironic sense. They are card-games and flirtatious tussles, not the great battles of epic tradition. Belinda is not, like Helen of Troy, "the face that launched a thousand ships" but rather a face that— although also beautiful— prompts a lot of foppish nonsense. The first two verse-paragraphs emphasize the comic inappropriateness of the epic style (and corresponding mind-set) to the subject at hand. Pope achieves this discrepancy at the level of the line and half-line; the reader is meant to dwell on the incompatibility between the two sides of his parallel formulations.

Thus, in this world, it is "little men" who in "tasks so bold... engage"; and "soft bosoms" are the dwelling-place for "mighty rage." In this startling juxtaposition of the petty and the grand, the former is real while the latter is ironic. In mock-epic, the high heroic style works not to dignify the subject but rather to expose and ridicule it. Therefore, the basic irony of the style supports the substance of the poem's satire, which attacks the misguided values of a society that takes small matters for serious ones while failing to attend to issues of genuine importance.

With Belinda's dream, Pope introduces the "machinery" of the poem—the supernatural powers that influence the action from behind the scenes. Here, the sprites that watch over Belinda are meant to mimic the gods of the Greek and Roman traditions, who are sometimes benevolent and sometimes malicious, but always intimately involved in earthly events. The scheme also makes use of other ancient hierarchies and systems of order. Ariel explains that women's spirits, when they die, return "to their first Elements." Each female personality type (these types correspond to the four humours) is converted into a particular kind of sprite. These gnomes, sylphs, salamanders, and nymphs, in turn, are associated with the four elements of earth, air, fire, and water. The airy sylphs are those who in their lifetimes were "light Coquettes"; they have a particular concern for Belinda because she is of this type, and this will be the aspect of feminine nature with which the poem is most concerned.

Indeed, Pope already begins to sketch this character of the "coquette" in this initial canto. He draws the portrait indirectly, through characteristics of the Sylphs rather than of Belinda herself. Their priorities reveal that the central concerns of womanhood, at least for women of Belinda's class, are social ones. Woman's "joy in gilded Chariots" indicates an obsession with pomp and superficial splendor, while "love of Ombre," a fashionable card game, suggests frivolity. The erotic charge of this social world in turn prompts another central concern: the protection of chastity. These are women who value above all the prospect marrying to advantage, and they have learned at an early age how to promote themselves and manipulate their suitors without compromising themselves. The Sylphs become an allegory for the mannered conventions that govern female social behaviour. Principles like honor and chastity have become no more than another part of conventional interaction. Pope makes it clear that these women are not conducting themselves on the basis of abstract moral principles, but are governed by an elaborate social mechanism—of which the Sylphs cut a fitting caricature. And while Pope's technique of employing supernatural machinery allows him to critique this situation, it also helps to keep the satire light and to exonerate individual women from too severe a judgment. If Belinda has all the typical female foibles, Pope wants us to recognize that it is partly because she has been educated and trained to act in this way.

The society as a whole is as much to blame as she is. Nor are men exempt from this judgment. The competition among the young lords for the attention of beautiful ladies is depicted as a battle of vanity, as "wigs with wigs, with sword-knots sword-knots strive." Pope's phrases here expose an absurd attention to exhibitions of pride and ostentation. He emphasizes the inanity of discriminating so closely between things and people that are essentially the same in all important (and even most unimportant) respects.

Pope's portrayal of Belinda at her dressing table introduces mock-heroic motifs that will run through the poem. The scene of her toilette is rendered first as a religious sacrament, in which Belinda herself is the priestess and her image in the looking glass is the Goddess she serves. This parody of the religious rites before a battle gives way, then, to another kind of mock-epic scene, that of the ritualized arming of the hero. Combs, pins, and cosmetics take the place of weapons as "awful Beauty puts on all its arms."

Canto 2

Summary

Belinda, rivaling the sun in her radiance, sets out by boat on the river Thames for Hampton Court Palace. She is accompanied by a party of glitzy ladies ("Nymphs") and gentlemen, but is far and away the most striking member of the group. Pope's description of her charms includes "the sparkling Cross she wore" on her "white breast," her "quick" eyes and "lively looks," and the easy grace with which she bestows her smiles and attentions evenly among all the adoring guests. Her crowning glories, though, are the two ringlets that dangle on her "iv'ry neck." These curls are described as love's labyrinths, specifically designed to ensnare any poor heart who might get entangled in them.

One of the young gentlemen on the boat, the Baron, particularly admires Belinda's locks, and has determined to steal them for himself. We read that he rose early that morning to build an altar to love and pray for success in this project. He sacrificed several tokens of his former affections, including garters, gloves, and billet-doux (love-letters). He then prostrated himself before a pyre built with "all the trophies of his former loves," fanning its flames with his "am'rous sighs." The gods listened to his prayer but decided to grant only half of it.

As the pleasure-boat continues on its way, everyone is carefree except Ariel, who remembers that some bad event has been foretold for the day. He summons an army of sylphs, who assemble around him in their iridescent beauty. He reminds them with great ceremony that one of their duties, after regulating celestial bodies and the weather and guarding the British monarch, is "to tend the Fair": to keep watch over ladies' powders, perfumes, curls, and clothing, and to "assist their blushes, and inspire their airs." Therefore, since "some dire disaster" threatens Belinda, Ariel assigns her an extensive troop of bodyguards. Brillante is to guard her earrings, Momentilla her watch, and Crispissa her locks. Ariel himself will protect Shock, the lapdog. A band of fifty Sylphs will guard the all-important petticoat. Ariel pronounces that any sylph who neglects his assigned duty will be severely punished. They disperse to their posts and wait for fate to unfold.

Commentary

From the first, Pope describes Belinda's beauty as something divine, an assessment which she herself corroborates in the first canto when she creates, at least metaphorically, an altar to her own image. This praise is certainly in some sense ironical, reflecting negatively on a system of public values in which external characteristics rank higher than moral or intellectual ones. But Pope also shows a real reverence for his heroine's physical and social charms, claiming in lines 17-18 that these are compelling enough to cause one to forget her "female errors." Certainly he has some interest in flattering Arabella Fermor, the real-life woman on whom Belinda is based; in order for his poem to achieve the desired reconciliation, it must not offend. Pope also exhibits his appreciation for the ways in which physical beauty is an art form: he recognizes, with a mixture of censure and awe, the fact that Belinda's legendary locks of hair, which appear so natural and spontaneous, are actually a carefully contrived effect. In this, the mysteries of the lady's dressing table are akin, perhaps, to Pope's own literary art, which he describes elsewhere as "nature to advantage dress'd."

If the secret mechanisms and techniques of female beauty get at least a passing nod of appreciation from the author, he nevertheless suggests that the general human readiness to worship beauty amounts to a kind of sacrilege. The cross that Belinda wears around her neck serves a more ornamental than symbolic or religious function. Because of this, he says, it can be adored by "Jews" and "Infidels" as readily as by Christians. And there is some ambiguity about whether any of the admirers are really valuing the cross itself, or the "white breast" on which it lies—or the felicitous effect of the whole. The Baron, of course, is the most significant of those who worship at the altar of Belinda's beauty. The ritual sacrifices he performs in the pre-dawn hours are another mock-heroic element of the poem, mimicking the epic tradition of sacrificing to the gods before an important battle or journey, and drapes his project with an absurdly grand import that actually only exposes its triviality. The fact that he discards all his other love tokens in these preparations reveals his capriciousness as a lover. Earnest prayer, in this parodic scene, is replaced by the self-indulgent sighs of the lover. By having the gods grant only half of what the Baron asks, Pope alludes to the epic convention by which the flavour of the gods is only a mixed blessing: in epic poems, to win the sponsorship of one god is to incur the wrath of another; divine gifts, such as immortality, can seem a blessing but become a curse. Yet in this poem, the ramifications of a prayer "half" granted are negligible rather than tragic; it merely means that he will manage to steal just one lock rather than both of them.

In the first canto, the religious imagery surrounding Belinda's grooming rituals gave way to a militaristic conceit. Here, the same pattern holds. Her curls are compared to a trap perfectly calibrated to ensnare the enemy. Yet the character of female coyness is such that it seeks simultaneously to attract and repel, so that the counterpart to the enticing ringlets is the formidable petticoat. This undergarment is described as a defensive armament comparable to the Shield of Achilles, and supported in its function of protecting the maiden's chastity by the invisible might of fifty Sylphs. The Sylphs, who are Belinda's protectors, are essentially charged to protect her not from failure but from too great a success in attracting men. This paradoxical situation dramatizes the contradictory values and motives implied in the era's sexual conventions.

In this canto, the sexual allegory of the poem begins to come into fuller view. The title of the poem already associates the cutting of Belinda's hair with a more explicit sexual conquest, and here Pope cultivates that suggestion. He multiplies his sexually metaphorical language for the incident, adding words like "ravish" and "betray" to the "rape" of the title. He also slips in some commentary on the implications of his society's sexual mores, as when he remarks that "when success a Lover's toil attends, / few ask, if fraud or force attain'd his ends." When Ariel speculates about the possible forms the "dire disaster" might take, he includes a breach of chastity ("Diana's law"), the breaking of china (another allusion to the loss of virginity), and the staining of honor or a gown (the two incommensurate events could happen equally easily and accidentally). He also mentions some pettier social "disasters" against which the Sylphs are equally prepared to fight, like missing a ball (here, as grave as missing prayers) or losing the lapdog. In the Sylphs' defensive efforts, Belinda's petticoat is the battlefield that requires the most extensive fortifications. This fact furthers the idea that the rape of the lock stands in for a literal rape, or at least represents a threat to her chastity more serious than just the mere theft of a curl.

Canto 3

Summary

The boat arrives at Hampton Court Palace, and the ladies and gentlemen disembark to their courtly amusements. After a pleasant round of chatting and gossip, Belinda sits down with two of the men to a game of cards. They play ombre, a three-handed game of tricks and trumps, somewhat like bridge, and it is described in terms of a heroic battle: the cards are troops combating on the "velvet plain" of the card-table. Belinda, under the watchful care of the Sylphs, begins flavourably. She declares spades as trumps and leads with her highest cards, sure of success. Soon, however, the hand takes a turn for the worse when "to the Baron fate inclines the field": he catches her king of clubs with his queen and then leads back with his high diamonds. Belinda is in danger of being beaten, but recovers in the last trick so as to just barely win back the amount she bid.

The next ritual amusement is the serving of coffee. The curling vapours of the steaming coffee remind the Baron of his intention to attempt Belinda's lock. Clarissa draws out her scissors for his use, as a lady would arm a knight in a romance. Taking up the scissors, he tries three times to clip the lock from behind without Belinda seeing. The Sylphs endeavor furiously to intervene, blowing the hair out of harm's way and tweaking her diamond earring to make her turn around. Ariel, in a last-minute effort, gains access to her brain, where he is surprised to find "an earthly lover lurking at her heart." He gives up protecting her then; the implication is that she secretly wants to be violated. Finally, the shears close on the curl. A daring sylph jumps in between the blades and is cut in two; but being a supernatural creature, he is quickly restored. The deed is done, and the Baron exults while Belinda's screams fill the air.

Commentary

This canto is full of classic examples of Pope's masterful use of the heroic couplet. In introducing Hampton Court Palace, he describes it as the place where Queen Anne "dost sometimes counsel take—and sometimes tea." This line employs a zeugma, a rhetorical device in which a word or phrase modifies two other words or phrases in a parallel construction, but modifies each in a different way or according to a different sense. Here, the modifying word is "take"; it applies to the paralleled terms "counsel" and "tea." But one does not "take" tea in the same way one takes counsel, and the effect of the zeugma is to show the royal residence as a place that houses both serious matters of state and frivolous social occasions. The reader is asked to contemplate that paradox and to reflect on the relative value and importance of these two different registers of activity. (For another example of this rhetorical technique, see lines 157-8: "Not louder shrieks to pitying heaven are cast, / when husbands, or when lapdogs breathe their last.") A similar point is made, in a less compact phrasing, in the second and third verse-paragraphs of this canto. Here, against the gossip and chatter of the young lords and ladies, Pope opens a window onto more serious matters that are occurring "meanwhile" and elsewhere, including criminal trials and executions, and economic exchange.

The rendering of the card game as a battle constitutes an amusing and deft narrative feat. By parodying the battle scenes of the great epic poems, Pope is suggesting that the energy and passion once applied to brave and serious purposes is now expended on such insignificant trials as games and gambling, which often become a mere front for flirtation. The structure of "the three attempts" by which the lock is cut is a convention of heroic challenges, particularly in the romance genre. The romance is further invoked in the image of Clarissa arming the Baron—not with a real weapon, however, but with a pair of sewing scissors. Belinda is not a real adversary, or course, and Pope makes it plain that her resistance—and, by implication, her subsequent distress—is to some degree an affectation. The melodrama of her screams is complemented by the ironic comparison of the Baron's feat to the conquest of nations.

Canto 4

Summary

Belinda's "anxious cares" and "secret passions" after the loss of her lock are equal to the emotions of all who have ever known "rage, resentment and despair." After the disappointed Sylphs withdraw, an earthy gnome called Umbriel flies down to the "Cave of Spleen." (The spleen, an organ that removes disease-causing agents from the bloodstream, was traditionally associated with the passions, particularly malaise; "spleen" is a synonym for "ill-temper.") In his descent he passes through Belinda's bedroom, where she lies prostrate with discomfiture and the headache. She is attended by "two handmaidens," Ill-Nature and Affectation. Umbriel passes safely through this melancholy chamber, holding a sprig of "spleenwort" before him as a charm. He addresses the "Goddess of Spleen," and returns with a bag of "sighs, sobs, and passions" and a vial of sorrow, grief, and tears. He unleashes the first bag on Belinda, fueling her ire and despair.

There to commiserate with Belinda is her friend Thalestris. (In Greek mythology, Thalestris is the name of one of the Amazons, a race of warrior women who excluded men from their society.) Thalestris delivers a speech calculated to further foment Belinda's indignation and urge her to avenge herself. She then goes to Sir Plume, "her beau," to ask him to demand that the Baron return the hair. Sir Plume makes a weak and slang-filled speech, to which the Baron disdainfully refuses to acquiesce. At this, Umbriel releases the contents of the remaining vial, throwing Belinda into a fit of sorrow and self-pity. With "beauteous grief" she bemoans her fate, regrets not having heeded the dream-warning, and laments the lonely, pitiful state of her sole remaining curl.

Commentary

The canto opens with a list of examples of "rage, resentment, and despair," comparing on an equal footing the pathos of kings imprisoned in battle, of women who become old maids, of evil-doers who die without being saved, and of a woman whose dress is disheveled. By placing such disparate sorts of aggravation in parallel, Pope accentuates the absolute necessity of assigning them to some rank of moral import. The effect is to chastise a social world that fails to make these distinctions.

Umbriel's journey to the Cave of Spleen mimics the journeys to the underworld made by both Odysseus and Aeneas. Pope uses psychological allegory (for the spleen was the seat of malaise or melancholy), as a way of exploring the sources and nature of Belinda's feelings. The presence of Ill-nature and Affectation as handmaidens serves to indicate that her grief is less than pure ("affected" or put-on), and that her display of temper has hidden motives. We learn that her sorrow is decorative in much the same way the curl was; it gives her the occasion, for example, to wear a new nightdress.

The speech of Thalestris invokes a courtly ethic. She encourages Belinda to think about the Baron's misdeed as an affront to her honor, and draws on ideals of chivalry in demanding that Sir Plume challenge the Baron in defence of Belinda's honor. He makes a muddle of the task, showing how far from courtly behaviour this generation of gentlemen has fallen. Sir Plume's speech is riddled with foppish slang and has none of the logical, moral, or oratorical power that a knight should properly wield.

This attention to questions of honor returns us to the sexual allegory of the poem. The real danger, Thalestris suggests, is that "the ravisher" might display the lock and make it a source of public humiliation to Belinda and, by association, to her friends. Thus the real question is a superficial one— public reputation—rather than the moral imperative to chastity. Belinda's own words at the close of the canto corroborate this suggestion; she exclaims, "Oh, hadst thou, cruel! been content to seize / Hairs less in sight, or any hairs but these!" (The "hairs less in sight" suggest her pubic hair). Pope is pointing out the degree to which she values outward appearance (whether beauty or reputation) above all else; she would rather suffer a breach to her integrity than a breach to her appearance.

Canto 5

The Baron remains impassive against all the ladies' tears and reproaches. Clarissa delivers a speech in which she questions why a society that so adores beauty in women does not also place a value on "good sense" and "good humour." Women are frequently called angels, she argues, but without reference to the moral qualities of these creatures. Especially since beauty is necessarily so short-lived, we must have something more substantial and permanent to fall back on. This sensible, moralizing speech falls on deaf ears, however, and Belinda, Thalestris and the rest ignore her and proceed to launch an all-out attack on the offending Baron. A chaotic tussle ensues, with the gnome Umbriel presiding in a posture of self- congratulation. The gentlemen are slain or revived according to the smiles and frowns of the fair ladies. Belinda and the Baron meet in combat and she emerges victorious by peppering him with snuff and drawing her bodkin. Having achieved a position of advantage, she again demands that he return the lock. But the ringlet has been lost in the chaos, and cannot be found. The poet avers that the lock has risen to the heavenly spheres to become a star; stargazers may admire it now for all eternity. In this way, the poet reasons, it will attract more envy than it ever could on earth.

Commentary

Readers have often interpreted Clarissa's speech as the voice of the poet expressing the moral of the story. Certainly, her oration's thesis aligns with Pope's professed task of putting the dispute between the two families into a more reasonable perspective. But Pope's position achieves more complexity than Clarissa's speech, since he has used the occasion of the poem as a vehicle to critically address a number of broader societal issues as well. And Clarissa's righteous stance loses authority in light of the fact that it was she who originally gave the Baron the scissors. Clarissa's failure to inspire a reconciliation proves that the quarrel is itself a kind of flirtatious game that all parties are enjoying. The description of the "battle" has a markedly erotic quality, as ladies and lords wallow in their mock-agonies. Sir Plume "draw[s] Clarissa down" in a sexual way, and Belinda "flies" on her foe with flashing eyes and an erotic ardor. When Pope informs us that the Baron fights on unafraid because he "sought no more than on his foe to die," the expression means that his goal all along was sexual consummation.

This final battle is the culmination of the long sequence of mock-heroic military actions. Pope invokes by name the Roman gods who were most active in warfare, and he alludes as well to the *Aeneid*, comparing the stoic Baron to Aeneas ("the Trojan"), who had to leave his love to become the founder of Rome. Belinda's tossing of the snuff makes a perfect turning point, ideally suited to the scale of this trivial battle. The snuff causes the Baron to sneeze, a comic and decidedly unheroic thing for a hero to do. The bodkin, too, serves nicely: here a bodkin is a decorative hairpin, not the weapon of ancient days (or even of Hamlet's time). Still, Pope gives the pin an elaborate history in accordance with the conventions of true epic.

The mock-heroic conclusion of the poem is designed to compliment the lady it alludes to (Arabella Fermor), while also giving the poet himself due credit for being the instrument of her immortality. This ending effectively indulges the heroine's vanity, even though the poem has functioned throughout as a critique of that vanity. And no real moral development has taken place: Belinda is asked to come to terms with her loss through a kind of bribe or distraction that reinforces her basically frivolous outlook. But even in its most mocking moments, this poem is a gentle one, in which Pope shows a basic sympathy with the social world in spite of its folly and foibles. The searing critiques of his later satires would be much more stringent and less forgiving.

Chapter 15

Pope's Explanation of the Poem

Written in 1715 by Pope (using the pseudonym Esdras Barnivelt), this humourous interpretation of *The Rape of the Lock* serves as a warning to critics not to take the poem too seriously. In the Key Pope exposes his own poem as a dangerous political allegory (Belinda represents Great Britain, the Lock represents the Barrier Treaty...). The Key also shows Pope trying to placate Sir George Brown (the original for Sir Plume, Sir George was none too happy with the role he played in the poem) by indicating there were at least two possible originals for Sir Plume.

A KEY TO THE LOCK

Or a Treatise proving, beyond all Contradiction, the dangerous Tendency of a late Poem entitled *The Rape of the Lock* to Government and Religion by Esdras Barnivelt, Apothecary.

THE EPISTLE DEDICATORY TO MR POPE

Though it may seem foreign to my Profession, which is that of making up and dispensing salutary Medicines to his Majesty's Subjects, (I might say my Fellow-Subjects, since I have had the Advantage of being naturalised) yet cannot I think it unbecoming me to furnish an Antidote against the Poyson which hath been so artfully distilled through your Quill, and conveyed to the World through the pleasing Vehicle of your Numbers. Nor is my Profession as an Apothecary so abhorrent from yours as a Poet, since the Ancients have thought fit to make the same God the Patron of Both. I have, not without some Pleasure, observ'd the mystical Arms of our Company, wherein is represented *Apollo* killing the fell Monster *Python;* this in some measure admonishes me of my Duty, to trample upon and destroy, as much as in me lies, that Dragon, or baneful Serpent, *Popery.*

I must take leave to make you my Patient, whether you will or no; though out of the Respect I have for you, I should rather Chuse to apply Lenitive than corrosive Medicines, happy, if they may prove an Emetic sufficient to make you cast up those Errors, which you have imbibed in your Education, and which, I hope, I shall never live to see this Nation digest.

Sir, I cannot but lament, that a Gentleman of your acute Wit, rectified Understanding, and sublimated Imagination, should misapply those Talents to raise ill Humours in the Constitution of the Body Politick, of which your self are a Member, and upon the Health whereof your Preservation depends. Give me leave to say, such Principles as yours would again reduce us to the fatal Necessity of the Phlebotomy of War, or the Causticks of Persecution.

In order to inform you of this, I have sought your Acquaintance and Conversation with the utmost Diligence; for I hoped in Person to persuade you to a publick Confession of your Fault, and a Recantation of these dangerous Tenets. But finding all my Endeavors ineffectual, and being satisfied with the Conscience of having done all that became a Man of an honest Heart and honourable Intention; I could no longer omit my Duty in opening the Eyes of the World by the Publication of this Discourse. It was indeed written some Months since, but seems not the less proper at this Juncture, when I find so universal an Encouragement given by both Parties to the Author of a libellous Work that is designed equally to prejudice them both. The uncommon Sale of this Book (for above 6000 of 'em have been already vended) was also a farther Progress, and to preserve his Majesty's Subjects, by exposing the whole Artifice of your Poem in Publick.

Sir, to address my self to so florid a Writer as you, without collecting the Flowers of Rhetorick, would be an unpardonable *Indecorum;* but when I speak to the World, as I do in the following Treatise, I must use a simple Stile, since it would be absurd to prescribe an universal Medicine, or *Catholicon,* in a Language not universally understood.

As I have always professed to have a particular Esteem for Men of Learning, and more especially for your self, nothing but the Love of Truth should have engaged me in a Design of this Nature. *Amicus Plato, Amicus Socrates, sed magis Amica Veritas.* I am

Your most
Sincere Friend, and Humble Servant,
E. Barnivelt.

A KEY TO THE LOCK

Since this unhappy Division of our Nation into Parties, it is not to be imagined how many Artifices have been made use of by Writers to obscure the Truth, and cover Designs, which may be detrimental to the Publick; in particular, it has been their Custom of late to vent their Political Spleen in Allegory and Fable. If an honest believing Nation is to be made a Jest of, we have a Story of *John Bull* and his Wife; if a Treasurer is to be glanced at, an *Ant* with a *white Straw* is introduced; if a Treaty of Commerce is to be ridiculed, 'tis immediately metamorphosed into a Tale of Count *Tariff.*

But if any of these Malevolents have never so small a Talent in Rhime, they principally delight to convey their Malice in that pleasing way, as it were, gilding the Pill, and concealing the Poyson under the Sweetness of Numbers. Who could imagine that an *Original Canto* of *Spencer* should contain a Satyr upon one Administration; or that *Yarhel's Kitchin,* or the *Dogs of Egypt,* should be a sarcasm upon another.

It is the Duty of every well designing Subject to prevent, as far as in him lies, the ill Consequences of such pernicious Treatises; and I hold it mine to warn the Publick of the late Poem, entituled, the *Rape of the Lock;* which I shall demonstrate to be of this nature. Many of these sort of Books have been bought by honest and well-meaning People purely for their Diversion, who have in the end found themselves insensibly led into the Violence of Party Spirit, and many domestick Quarrels have been occasioned by the different Application of these Books. The Wife of an eminent Citizen grew very noisy upon reading *Bob Hush; John Bull,* upon *Change,* was thought not only to concern the State, but to affront the City; and the Poem we are now treating of, has not only dissolved an agreeable Assembly of Beaus and Belles, but (as I am told) has set Relations at as great a distance, as if they were Married together.

It is a common and just Observation, that when the Meaning of any thing is dubious, one can no way better judge of the true Intent of it, than by considering who is the Author, what is his Character in general, and his Disposition in particular.

Now that the Author of this Poem is professedly a *Papist,* is well known; and that a Genius so capable of doing Service to that Cause, may have been corrupted in the Course of his Education by *Jesuits* of others, is justly very much to be suspected; notwithstanding that seeming *Coolness* and *Moderation,* which he has been (perhaps artfully) reproached with, by those of his own Profession. They are sensible that this Nation is secured with good and wholesome Laws, to prevent all evil Practices of the Church of *Rome*; particularly the Publication of Books, that may in any sort propagate that Doctrine: Their Authors are therefore obliged to couch their Designs the deeper; and tho' I cannot averr that the Intention of this Gentleman was directly to spread Popish Doctrines, yet it comes to the same Point, if he touch the Government: For the Court of *Rome* knows very well, that the Church at this time is so firmly founded on the State, that the only way to shake the one is by attacking the other.

What confirms me in this Opinion, is the accidental Discovery I made of a very artful Piece of Management among his Popish Friends and Abettors, to hide this whole Design upon the Government, by taking all the Characters upon themselves.

Upon the Day that this Poem was published, it was my Fortune to step into the *Cocoa Tree,* where a certain Gentleman was railing very liberally at the Author, with a Passion extremely well counterfeited, for having (as he said) reflected upon him in the Character of *Sir Plume.* Upon his going out, I enquired who he was, and they told me, *a Roman Catholick Knight.*

I was the same Evening at *Will's,* and saw a Circle round another Gentleman, who was railing in like manner, and shewing his Snuff-box and Cane, to prove he was satyrized in the same Character. I asked this Gentleman's Name, and was told, he was *a Roman Catholick Lord.*

A Day or two after I was sent for, upon a slight Indisposition, to the young Lady's to whom the Poem is dedicated. She also took up the Character of *Belinda* with much Frankness and good Humour, tho' the Author has given us a Key in his Dedication, that he meant something further. This Lady is also a *Roman Catholick.* At the same time others of the Characters were claim'd by some Persons in the Room; and all of them *Roman Catholicks.*

But to proceed to the Work itself.

In all things which are intricate, as Allegories in their own Nature are, and especially those that are industriously made so, it is not to be expected we should find the clue at first sight; but when once we have laid hold on that, we shall trace this our Author through all the Labyrinths, Doublings and Turnings of this intricate Composition.

First let it be observed, that in the most demonstrative Sciences, some *Postulata* are to be granted, upon which the rest is naturally founded. I shall desire no more than one *Postulatum* to render this obvious to the meanest Capacity; which being granted me, I shall not only shew the Intent of this Work in general, but also explain the very *Names,* and expose all his fictitious *Characters* in their true Light; and we shall find, that even his *Spirits* were not meerly contrived for the sake of *Machinary.*

The only Concession which I desire to be made me, is that by the *Lock* is meant

The Barrier Treaty

1. First then I shall discover, that BELINDA represents Great Britain, or (which is the same thing) her late MAJESTY. This is plainly seen in his Description of her.

   On her white Breast a sparkling Cross she bore.

   Alluding to the ancient Name of *Albion,* from her *white Cliffs,* and to the *Cross,* which is the Ensign of *England.*

2. The BARON, who cuts off the Lock, or Barrier Treaty, is the E[arl] of *O[xfor]d.*
3. CLARISSA, who lent the Scissars, my Lady *M[ashe]m.*
4. THALESTRIS, who provokes *Belinda* to resent the Loss of the Lock or Treaty, the D[uches]s of *M[arlborou]gh.*
5. SIR PLUME, who is mov'd by *Thalestris* to redemand it of *Great Britain,* P[rin]ce *Eu[ge]ne,* who came hither for that purpose.

There are other inferior Characters, which we shall observe upon afterwards; but I shall first explain the foregoing.

The first Part of the *Baron's* Character is his being *adventrous,* or enterprizing, which is the common Epithet given to the E[arl] of *O[xfor]d* by his Enemies. The Prize he aspires to is the T[reasur]y, in order to which he offers a Sacrifice.

——————————————an Altar built of twelve vast *French* Romances neatly gilt.

Our Author here takes occasion maliciously to insinuate this Statesman's *Love to France;* representing the Books he chiefly studies to be vast *French Romances.* These are the vast Prospects from the Friendship and Alliance of *France,* which he satyrically calls *Romances,* hinting thereby, that these Promises and Protestations were no more to be relied on than those idle Legends. Of these he is said to build an Altar; to intimate, that all the Foundation of his Schemes and Honours was fix'd upon the *French Romances* abovementioned.

A Fan, a Garter, Half a Pair of Gloves.

One of the Things he sacrifices is a *Fan,* which both for its *gaudy Show* and *perpetual Flutt'ring,* has been made the Emblem of *Woman.* This points at the Change of the *Ladies* of the *Bedchamber;* the *Garter* alludes to the Honours he conferr'd on some of his Friends; and we may without straining the Sense, call the Half Pair of Gloves, a *Gauntlet;* the Token of those Military Employments, which he is said to have sacrificed to his Designs. The Prize, as I said before, means the T[reasur]y, which he makes it his Prayers *soon to obtain,* and *long to possess.*

The Pow'rs gave ear, and granted half his Pray'r,
The rest the Winds dispers'd in empty Air.

In the first of these Lines he gives him the T[reasur]y, and in the last suggests that he should not long posses that Honour.

That *Thalestris* is the D[uches]s of *M[arlborou]gh,* appears both by her nearness to *Belinda,* and by this Author's malevolent Suggestion, that she is a Lover of War.

To Arms, to Arms, the bold *Thalestris* cries.

But more particlary in several Passages in her Speech to *Belinda,* upon the cutting off the Lock, or Treaty. Among other Things she says, *Was it for this you bound your Locks in Paper Durance?* Was it for this so much Paper has been spent to secure the Barrier Treaty?

Methinks already I your Tears survey,
Already hear the horrid Things they say;
Already see you a degraded Toast.

This describes the Aspersions under which that good Princess suffer'd, and the Repentance which must have followed the Dissolution of that Treaty, and particularly levels at the Refusal some People made to drink Her M[ajest]y's Health.

Sir Plume (a proper Name for a Soldier) has all the Circumstances that agree with P[rin]ce *Eu[ge]ne.*

Sir Plume of Amber Snuff-box justly vain,
And the nice Conduct of a clouded Cane,
With earnest Eyes.....

'Tis remarkable, this General is a great Taker of Snuff as well as Towns; his Conduct of the clouded Cane gives him the Honour which is so justly his due, of an exact Conduct in Battle, which is figured by his Truncheon, the Ensign of a General. His earnest Eye, or the Vivacity of his Look, is so particularly remarkable in him, that this Character could be mistaken for no other, had not this Author purposely obscur'd it by the fictitious Circumstance of a *round, unthinking Face.*

Having now explained the chief Characters of his *Human Persons* (for there are some others that will hereafter fall in by the by, in the Sequel of this Discourse) I shall next take in pieces his *Machinary,* wherein his Satyr is wholly confined to Ministers of State.

The Slyphs and Gnomes at first sight appeared to me to signify the two contending Parties of this Nation; for these being placed in the *Air,* and those on the *Earth,* I thought agreed very well with the common Denomination, High and Low. But as they are made to be the first Movers and Influencers of all that happens, 'tis plain they represent promiscuiosly the *Heads of Parties,* whom he makes to be the Authors of all those Changes in the State, which are generally imputed to the Levity and Instability of the *British* Nation.

This erring Mortals Levity may call,
Oh blind to Truth! The Sylphs contrive it all.

But of this he has given us a plain Demonstration; for speaking of these Spirits, he says in express Terms,

...The chief the Care of Nations own,

And guard with Arms Divine the British Throne.

And here let it not seem odd, if in this mysterious way of Writing, we find the same Person, who has before been represented by the *Baron,* again described in the Character of *Ariel;* it being a common way with Authors, in this fabulous Manner, to take such a Liberty. As for instance, I have read in the *English St. Evremont,* that all the different Characters in *Petronius* are but *Nero* in so many different Appearances. And in the Key to the curious Romance of *Barclay's Argenis,* that both *Polarchus* and *Archombrotus* mean only the *King* of *Navarre.*

We observe in the very Beginning of the Poem, that *Ariel* is possess'd of the Ear of *Belinda;* therefore it is absolutely necessary that this Person must be the Minister who was nearest the Queen. But whoever would be further convinc'd, that he meant the late T[reasure]r, may know him by his Ensigns in the following Line.

He rais'd his Azure Wand....

His sitting on the Mast of a Vessel shows his presiding over the *S[ou]th S[e]a* Tr[a]de. When *Ariel* assigns to his *Sylphs* all the Posts about *Belinda,* what is more clearly described, than the Tr[easure]r's disposing all the Places of the Kingdom, and particularly about her M[ajest]y? But let us hear the Lines.

...Ye Spirits to your Charge repair,
The flutt'ring Fan be Zephyretta's Care;
The Drops to thee, Brillant, we consign,
And, Momentilla, let the Watch be thine:
Do thou, Crispissa, tend her fav'rite Lock.

He has here particularized the Ladies and Women of the Bed-Chamber, the keeper of the Cabinet, and her M[ajest]y's Dresser, and impudently given Nicknames to each.

To put this Matter beyond all Dispute, the *Sylphs* are said to be *wond'rous fond of Place,* in the Canto following, where *Ariel* is perched uppermost, and all the rest take their Places subordinately under him.

Here again I cannot but observe, the excessive Malignity of this Author, who could not leave this Character of *Ariel* without the same invidious Stroke which he gave him in the Character of the *Baron* before.

Amaz'd, confus'd, he saw his Power expir'd,
Resign'd to Fate, and with a Sigh retir'd.

Being another Prophecy that he should resign his Place, which it is probable all Ministers do with a Sigh.

At the Head of the *Gnomes* he sets *Umbriel,* a dusky melancholy Spright, who makes it his Business to give *Belinda* the Spleen; a vile and malicious Suggestion against some grave and worthy Minister. The Vapours, Fantoms, Visions, and the like, are the Jealousies, Fears, and Cries of Danger, that have so often affrighted and alarm'd the Nation. Those who are described in the House of Spleen, under those several fantastical Forms, are the same whom their Ill-willers have so often called the *Whimsical.*

The two fore-going Spirits being the only considerable Characters of the Machinary, I shall but just mention the *Sylph* that is wounded with the Scissars at the Loss of the Lock, by whom is undoubtedly understood my L[ord] *To[wnshen]d,* who at that Time received a Wound in his Character for making the Barrier Treaty, and was cut of his Employment upon the Dissolution of it: But that Spirit reunites, and receives no Harm; to signify, that it came to nothing, and his L[o]rdsh[i]p had no real Hurt by it.

But I must not conclude this Head of the Characters, without observing, that our Author has run through every Stage of Beings in search of Topicks for Detraction; and as he has characteriz'd some Persons under Angels and Men, so he has represented an eminent Clergy-man as a Dog, and a noted Writer as a Tool. Let us examine the former.

.....But Shock, who thought she slept too long,
Leapt up, and wak'd his Mistress with his Tongue.
'Twas then, Belinda, if Report say true,
Thy Eyes first open'd on a Billet-doux.

By this *Shock,* it is manifest he has most audaciously and profanely reflected on Dr. *Sach[evere]ll,* who leap'd up, that is, into the Pulpit, and awaken'd *Great Britain* with his *Tongue,* that is, with his *Sermon.* which made so much *Noise;* and for which he has frequently been term'd by others of his Enemies, as well as by this Author, a Dog: Or perhaps, by his *Tongue,* may be more literally meant his *Speech* at his *Trial,* since immediately thereupon, our Author says, her Eyes open'd on a *Billet-doux; Billets-doux* being Addresses to Ladies from Lovers, may be aptly interpreted those Addresses of Loving Subjects to her M[ajest]y, which ensued that Trial.

The other Instance is at the End of the third Canto.

Steel did the Labours of the Gods destroy,
And strike to Dust th' Imperial Tow'rs of Troy.
Steel could the Works of mortal Pride confound,
And hew Triumphal Arches to the Ground.

Here he most impudently attributes the Demolition of *Dunkirk,* not to the Pleasure of her M[ajest]y, or her Ministry, but to the frequent Instigations of his Friend Mr. *Steel;* a very artful Pun to conceal his wicked Lampoonery!

Having now consider'd the general Intent and Scope of the Poem, and open'd the Characters, I shall next discover the Malice which is covered under the Episodes, and particular Passages of it.

The Game at *Ombre* is a mystical Representation of the late War, which is hinted by his making Spades the Trump; Spade in *Spanish* signifying a Sword, and being yet so painted in the Cards of that Nation; to which it is well known we owe the Original of our Cards. In this one Place indeed he has unawares paid a Compliment to the Queen, and her Success in the War; for *Belinda* gets the better of the two that play against her, the Kings of *France* and *Spain.*

I do not question but ev'ry particular Card has its Person and Character assign'd, which, no doubt, the Author has told his Friends in private; but I shall only instance the Description of the Disgrace under which the D[uke] of *M[arlborou]gh* then suffer'd, which is so apparent in these Verses.

Ev'n mighty Pam, that Kings and Queens o'erthrew,
And mow'd down Armies in the Fights of Lu,
Sad Chance of War! now destitute of Aid,
Falls undistinguish'd.....

That the Author here had an Eye to our modern Transactions, is very plain from an unguarded Stroke towards the End of this Game.

And now, as oft in some distemper'd State,
On one nice Trick depends the gen'ral Fate.

After the Conclusion of the War, the publick Rejoicings and*Thanksgivings* are ridiculed in the two following Lines.

The Nymph exulting, fills with Shouts the Sky,
The Walls, the Woods, and long Canals reply.

Immediately upon which there follows a malicious Insinuation, in the manner of a Prophecy, (which we have formerly observ'd this seditious Writer delights in) that the Peace should continue but a short Time, and that the Day should afterwards be curst which was then celebrated with so much Joy.

Sudden these Honours shall be snatch'd away,
And curst for ever this victorious Day.

As the Game at *Ombre* is a satyrical Representation of the late War; so is the Tea-Table that ensues, of the Council-Table and its Consultations after the Peace. By this he would hint, that all the Advantages we have gain'd by our late extended Commerce, are only Coffee and Tea, or Things of no greater Value. That he thought of the Trade in this Place, appears by the Passage where he represents the *Sylphs* particularly careful of the *rich Brocade;* it having been a frequent Complaint of our Mercers, that *French Brocades* were imported in too great Quantities. I will not say, he means those Presents of rich Gold Stuff Suits, which were said to be made for M[ajest]y by the K[ing] of *F[rance]*, tho' I cannot but suspect, that he glances at it.

Here this Author, as well as the scandalous *John Dunton,* represents the Mi[nist]ry in plain Terms taking frequent Cups.

And frequent Cups prolong the rich Repast.

Upon the whole, it is manifest he meant something more than common Coffee, by his calling it,

Coffee that makes the Politician wise.
And by telling us, it was this Coffee, that
Sent up in Vapours to the Baron's Brain
New Strategems...........

I shall only further observe, that 'twas at this Table the Lock was cut off; for where but at the Council Board should the Barrier Treaty be dissolved?

The ensuing Contentions of the Parties upon the Loss of that Treaty, are described in the Squabbles following the Rape of the Lock; and this he rashly expresses, without any disguise in the Words.

All sides in *Parties.....*

Here first you have a Gentleman who sinks beside his Chair: A plain Allusion to a Noble Lord, who lost his Chair of Pre[side]nt of the Co[unci]l.

I come next to the *Bodkin,* so dreadful in the Hand of *Belinda;* by which he intimates the *British Scepter,* so rever'd in the Hand of our late August Princess. His own Note upon this Place tells us he alludes to a Scepter and the Verses are so plain, the need no Remark.

The same (his ancient Personage to deck)
Her great great Grandsire wore about his Neck
In three Seal Rings, which, after melted down,
Form'd avast Buckle for his Widow's Gown;
Her Infant Grandame's Whistle next it grew,
The Bells she gingled, and the Whistle blew,
Then in a Bodkin grac'd her Mother's Hairs,s
Which long she wore, and now Belinda wears.

An open Satyr upon *Hereditary Right.* The three Seal Rings plainly allude to the three Kingdoms.

These are the chief Passages in the Battle, by which, as hath before been said, he means the Squabble of Parties. Upon this Occasion he could not end the Description of them, without testifying his malignant Joy at those Dissentions, from which he forms the Prospect that *both* should be disappointed, and cries out with Triumph, as if it were already accomplished.

Behold how oft ambitious Arms are crost,
And Chiefs contend till all the Prize is lost.

The Lock at length is turn'd into a *Star*, or the Old Barrier Treaty into a new and glorious *Peace;* this no doubt is what the Author, at the time he printed his Poem, would have been thought to mean, in hopes by that Complement to excape Punishment for the rest of his Piece. It puts me in mind of a Fellow, who concluded a bitter Lampoon upon the Prince and Court of his Days, with these Lines.

God save the King, the Commons, and the Peers,
And grant the Author long may wear his Ears.

Whatever this Author may think of that Peace, I imagine it the most *extraordinary Star* that ever appear'd in our Hemisphere. A Star that is to bring us all the Wealth and Gold of the *Indies;* and from whose Influence, not Mr. *John Partridge* alone, (whose worthy Labours this Writer so ungenerously ridicules) but all true *Britains* may, with no less Authority than he, prognosticate the Fall of *Lewis,* in the Restraint of the exorbitant Power of *France,* and the Fate of *Rome* in the triumphant Condition of the Church of *England.*

We have now considered this Poem in its Political View, wherein we have shewn that it hath two different Walks of Satyr, the one in the Story itself, which is a Ridicule on the late Transactions in general; the other in the Machinary, which is a Satyr on the Ministers of State in particular. I shall now show that the same Poem, taken in another Light, has a Tendency to Popery, which is secretly insinuated through the whole.

In the first place, he has conveyed to us the Doctrine of Guardian Angels and Patron Saints in the Machinary of his *Sylphs,* which being a Piece of Popish Superstition that hath been endeavoured to be exploded ever since the Reformation, he would here revive under this Disguise. Here are all the Particulars which they believe of those Beings, which I shall sum up in a few Heads.

1*st*. The Spirits are made to concern themselves with all human Acts in general.

2*dly*. A distinct Guardian Spirit of Patron is assigned to each Person in particular.

Of these am I, who thy Protection claim,
A watchful Sprite..........

3*dly*. They are made directly to inspire Dreams, Visions, and Revelations.

Her Guardian *Sylph* prolong'd her balmy Rest,
'Twas he had summon'd to her silent Bed
The Morning Dream....

4*thly*. They are made to be subordinate, in different degrees, some presiding over others, So *Ariel* hath his several Under-Officers at command.

Superior by the Head was *Ariel* plac'd.

5*thly*. They are employed in various Offices, and each hath his Office assigned him.

Some in the Fields of purest Aether play,
And bask and whiten in the Blaze of Day.
Some guide the Course, *&c.*

6*thly*. He hath given his Spirits the Charge of the several Parts of Dress; intimating thereby, that the Saints preside over the several Parts of Human Bodies. They have one Saint to cure the Tooth-ach, another cures the Gripes, and another the Gout,and so all the rest.

The flutt'ring Fan be Zephyretta's Care,
The drops to thee, Brillante, we consign, &c.
7thly. They are represented to know the Thoughts of Men.
As on the Nosegay in her Breast reclin'd,
He watch'd th' Ideas rising in her Mind.

8*thly*. They are made Protectors even to Animals and irrational Beings.

Ariel himself shall be the Guard of *Shock.*
So St. *Anthony* presides over Hogs, &c.

9thly. Others are made Patrons of whole Kingdoms and Provinces.

Of these the chief the Care of Nations own.

So St. *George* is imagined by the *Papists* to defend *England:* St. *Patrick, Ireland:* St. *James, Spain,* &c. Now what is the Consequence of all this? By granting that they have this Power, we must be brought back again to pray to them.

The *Toilette* is an artful Recommendation of the *Mass,* and pompous Ceremonies of the *Church of Rome.* The *unveiling* of the *Altar,* the *Silver Vases* upon it, being *rob'd* in *White,* as the Priests are upon the chief Festivals, and the *Head uncover'd,* are manifest Marks of this.

A heav'nly Image in the Glass appears,
To that she bends.....
Plainly denotes Image-Worship.

The *Goddess,* who is deck'd with *Treasures, Jewels,* and the *various Offerings of the World,* manifestly alludes to the Lady of *Loretto.* You have Perfumes breathing from the *Incense Pot* in the following Line.

And all *Arabia* breaths from yonder Box.

The Character of *Belinda,* as we take it in this third View. represents the Popish Religion, or the Whore of *Babylon;* who is described in the State this malevolent Author wishes for, coming forth in all her Glory upon the *Thames,* and overspreading the Nation with Ceremonies.

Not with more Glories in th' aetherial Plain,
The Sun first rises o'er the purple Main,
Than issuing forth the Rival of his Beams,
Launch'd on the Bosom of the Silver Thames.

She is dress'd with a *Cross* on her Breast, the Ensign of Popery, the *Adoration* of which is plainly recommended in the following Lines.

On her white Breast a sparkling Cross she wore,
Which Jews might kiss, and Infidels adore.

Next he represents her as the *Universal Church,* according to the Boasts of the Papists.

And like the Sun she shines on all alike.
After which he tells us,
If to her Share some Female Errors fall,
Look on her Face, and you'll forget them all.

Tho' it should be granted some Errors fall to her Share, look on the pompous Figure she makes throughout the World, and they are not worth regarding. In the Sacrifice following soon after, you have these two Lines.

For this, e'er *Phoebus* rose, he had implor'd
Propitious Heav'n, and en'ry Pow'r ador'd.

In the first of them, he plainly hints at their *Matins;* in the second, by adoring ev'ry Power, the *Invocation of Saints.*

Belinda's Visits are described with numerous *Waxlights,* which are always used in the Ceremonial Parts of the *Romish* Worship.

........Visits shall be paid on solemn Days,

When num'rous Wax-lights in bright Order blaze.

The *Lunar Sphere* he mentions, opens to us their *Purgatory,* which is seen in the following Line.

Since all Things lost on Earth are treasur'd there.

It is a Popish Doctrine, that scarce any Person quits this World, but he must touch at Purgatory in his Way to Heaven; and it is here also represented as the *Treasury* of the *Romish Church.* Nor is it much to be wonder'd at, that the *Moon* should be *Purgatory,* when a Learn'd Divine hath in a late Treatise proved *Hell* to be in the *Sun.*

I shall now before I conclude, desire the Reader to compare this Key with those upon any other Pieces, which are supposed to be secret Satyrs upon the State, either antient or modern; as with those upon *Petronius Arbiter, Lucian's* true History, *Barclay's Argenis,* or *Rablais's Garagantua;* and I doubt not he will do me the Justice to acknowledge, that the

Explanations here laid down, are deduced as naturally, and with as little Force, both from the general Scope and Bent of the Work, and from the several Particulars, and are every Way as consistent and undeniable as any of those; and ev'ry way as candid as any modern Interpretations of either Party, on the mysterious State Treatises of our Times.

To sum up my whole Charge against this Author in a few Words: He has ridiculed both the present Ministry and the last; abused great Statesmen and great Generals; nay the Treaties of whole Nations have not escaped him, nor has the Royal Dignity itself been omitted in the Progress of his Satyr; and all this he has done just at the Meeting of a new Parliament. I hope a proper Authority may be made use of to bring him to condign Punishment: In the mean while I doubt not, if the Persons most concern'd would but order Mr. *Bernard Lintott,* the Printer and Publisher of this dangerous Piece, to be taken into Custody, and examin'd; many further Discoveries might be made both of this Poet's and his Abettor's secret Designs, which are doubtless of the utmost Importance to the Government.

Canto I

Issuing forth the Rival of his Beams,
Launch'd on the Bosom of the Silver Thames.

She is dress'd with a Cross on her Breast, the Ensign of Popery, the Adoration of which is plainly recommended in the following Lines.

On her white Breast a sparkling Cross she wore,
Which Jews might kiss, and Infidels adore.

Next he represents her as the Universal Church, according to the Boasts of the Papists.

And like the Sun she shines on all alike.

After which he tells us,

If to her Share some Female Errors fall,
Look on her Face, and you'll forget them all.

Tho' it should be granted some Errors fall to her Share, look on the pompous Figure she makes throughout the World, and they are not worth regarding. In the Sacrifice following soon after, you have these two Lines.

> For this, e'er *Phoebus* rose, he had implor'd
> Propitious Heav'n, and en'ry Pow'r ador'd.

In the first of them, he plainly hints at their *Matins;* in the second, by adoring ev'ry Power, the *Invocation of Saints.*

Belinda's Visits are described with numerous *Waxlights,* which are always used in the Ceremonial Parts of the *Romish* Worship.

> ——————Visits shall be paid on solemn Days,
> When num'rous Wax-lights in bright Order blaze.

The *Lunar Sphere* he mentions, opens to us their *Purgatory,* which is seen in the following Line.

> Since all Things lost on Earth are treasur'd there.

It is a Popish Doctrine, that scarce any Person quits this World, but he must touch at Purgatory in his Way to Heaven; and it is here also represented as the *Treasury* of the *Romish Church.* Nor is it much to be wonder'd at, that the *Moon* should be *Purgatory,* when a Learn'd Divine hath in a late Treatise proved *Hell* to be in the *Sun.*

I shall now before I conclude, desire the Reader to compare this Key with those upon any other Pieces, which are supposed to be secret Satyrs upon the State, either antient or modern; as with those upon *Petronius Arbiter, Lucian's* true History, *Barclay's Argenis,* or *Rablais's Garagantua;* and I doubt not he will do me the Justice to acknowledge, that the Explanations here laid down, are deduced as naturally, and with as little Force, both from the general Scope and Bent of the Work, and from the several Particulars, and are every Way as consistent and undeniable as any of those; and ev'ry way as candid as any modern Interpretations of either Party, on the mysterious State Treatises of our Times.

To sum up my whole Charge against this Author in a few Words: He has ridiculed both the present Ministry and the last;

abused great Statesmen and great Generals; nay the Treaties of whole Nations have not escaped him, nor has the Royal Dignity itself been omitted in the Progress of his Satyr; and all this he has done just at the Meeting of a new Parliament. I hope a proper Authority may be made use of to bring him to condign Punishment: In the mean while I doubt not, if the Persons most concern'd would but order Mr. *Bernard Lintott*, the Printer and Publisher of this dangerous Piece, to be taken into Custody, and examin'd; many further Discoveries might be made both of this Poet's and his Abettor's secret Designs, which are doubtless of the utmost Importance to the Government.

Chapter 16

Complete Paraphrase

Canto I

What dire offence from am'rous causes springs,
What mighty contests rise from trivial things,
I sing—This verse to CARYL, Muse! is due:
This, ev'n Belinda may vouchsafe to view:
Slight is the subject, but not so the praise,
If She inspire, and He approve my lays.
Say what strange motive, Goddess! could compel
A well-bred Lord t' assault a gentle Belle?
O say what stranger cause, yet unexplor'd,
Could make a gentle Belle reject a Lord?

In tasks so bold, can little men engage,
And in soft bosoms dwells such mighty Rage?
Sol thro' white curtains shot a tim'rous ray,
And oped those eyes that must eclipse the day:
Now lap-dogs give themselves the rousing shake,

And sleepless lovers, just at twelve, awake:

Thrice rung the bell, the slipper knock'd the ground,
And the press'd watch return'd a silver sound.
Belinda still her downy pillow prest,
Her guardian
Sylph prolong'd the balmy rest:...........

'Twas He had summon'd to her silent bed
The morning-dream that hover'd o'er her head;

A Youth more glitt'ring than a
Birth-night Beau,
(That ev'n in slumber caus'd her cheek to glow)
Seem'd to her ear his winning lips to lay,.......

And thus in whispers said, or seem'd to say.

What . . . sing: I am writing (I sing) about a terrible offense resulting from an amorous cause.

CARYL, Muse: A friend of Pope, John Caryl, whom Pope addresses as the muse. An acquaintance of Caryl, Lord Petre, cut off a lock of hair of a young lady, Arabella Fermor. A quarrel erupted between the families. Caryl suggested that Pope write a poem to point up the silliness of the quarrel. Pope addresses Caryl as if he were a muse. For further information on "invoking the muse," see Epic Conventions, above.

Belinda: Arabella Fermor. Belinda is a poetic name associated with gentleness. For further information about Arabella Fermor, see Source, above.

Goddess: Another reference to Caryl as the muse.

Sol: the sun curtains: the curtains on Belinda's bed tim'rous: timorous, meaning *shy, timid* oped: opened must eclipse the day: Belinda's eyes are so bright that they rival the brightness of the sun.

lap-dogs: dogs small enough to be held in the lap

press'd watch: a kind of clock. Pressing a button on it caused a bell to sound the current hour or quarter hour.

Sylph: fairy, sprite

Birth-night: evening celebration of a royal person's birthday

Fairest of mortals, thou distinguish'd care
Of thousand bright Inhabitants of Air!
If e'er one vision touch'd thy infant thought,
Of all the Nurse and all the Priest have taught;.... .

Of airy Elves by moonlight shadows seen,
The silver token, and the circled green,

Or virgins visited by Angel-pow'rs,
With golden crowns and wreaths of heav'nly flow'rs;
Hear and believe! thy own importance know,.........

Nor bound thy narrow views to things below.
Some secret truths, from learned pride conceal'd,
To Maids alone and Children are reveal'd:
What tho' no credit doubting Wits may give?
The Fair and Innocent shall still believe.............

Know, then, unnumber'd Spirits round thee fly,
The light Militia of the lower sky:
These, tho' unseen, are ever on the wing,
Hang o'er the Box, and hover round the Ring.

Fairest . . . Air: The youth in her dream (Line 23) addresses Belinda as the fairest mortal, saying she is watched over by a thousand sprites inhabiting the air.

Silver token: coin left by a fairy as a gift for a favored mortal

Some . . . give: Certain secrets are revealed only to maidens like Belinda and to children, but not to highly educated people. Skeptics may doubt the truth of these secrets but Belinda and innocent children believe them.

Box, Ring: The spirits of the air hover around Belinda while she is in her theatre box or traveling in her carriage on a circular road (ring) in Hyde Park, a large park in the Westminster borough of London.

Think what an equipage thou hast in Air,......
And view with scorn two Pages and a Chair.
As now your own, our beings were of old,
And once inclos'd in Woman's beauteous mould;
Thence, by a soft transition, we repair
From earthly Vehicles to these of air.....................

Think not, when Woman's transient breath is fled
That all her vanities at once are dead;
Succeeding vanities she still regards,
And tho' she plays no more, o'erlooks the cards.
Her joy in gilded Chariots, when alive,........

And love of Ombre, after death survive.

For when the Fair in all their pride expire,

To their first Elements their Souls retire:

The Sprites of fiery Termagants in Flame

Mount up, and take a Salamander's name..............

Soft yielding minds to Water glide away,
And sip, with Nymphs, their elemental Tea.
The graver Prude sinks downward to a Gnome,
In search of mischief still on Earth to roam.
The light Coquettes in Sylphs aloft repair,............

And sport and flutter in the fields of Air.

Think . . .Chair: You now have an army of sprites to look after you, not just two pages

As . . . air: The sprites were once women with beauteous forms. After death, they became spirits of the air.

Think . . . dead: After a woman dies, she retains an interest in amusements.

Gilded Chariots: splendid carriages to ride in

Ombre: a popular card game for three players in which only 40 of the 52 cards are dealt—the eights, nines, and tens are held back.

Sprites . . . Termagants: The spirits of quarrelsome, overbearing women.

Salamander: in myth, a lizard-like reptile that lived in fire; a spirit in the alchemy of Paracelsus (1493-1541), a Swiss physician.

Soft yielding: Beginning here and continuing down to Line 66, the meaning is as follows: Other sprites live in water, keeping company with nymphs (minor goddess inhabiting the sea). Some sprites in the earth as gnomes (dwarflike creatures), and some of them live in the air.

"Know further yet; whoever fair and chaste
Rejects mankind, is by some Sylph embrac'd:

For Spirits, freed from mortal laws, with ease
Assume what sexes and what shapes they please.

What guards the purity of melting Maids,
In courtly balls, and midnight masquerades,
Safe from the treach'rous friend, the daring spark,
The glance by day, the whisper in the dark,
When kind occasion prompts their warm desires,.......

When music softens, and when dancing fires?
'Tis but their Sylph, the wise Celestials know,
Tho' Honour is the word with Men below.
Some nymphs there are, too conscious of their face,
For life predestin'd to the Gnomes' embrace..............

These swell their prospects and exalt their pride,
When offers are disdain'd, and love deny'd:
Then gay Ideas crowd the vacant brain,
While Peers, and Dukes, and all their sweeping train,
And Garters, Stars, and Coronets appear,................

And in soft sounds, Your Grace salutes their ear.
'Tis these that early taint the female soul,
Instruct the eyes of young Coquettes to roll,
Teach Infant-cheeks a bidden blush to know,
And little hearts to flutter at a Beau........................

What . . . Sylph: Sylphs (sprites) guard the purity of maidens from men who would take advantage of them.

Daring spark: a bold gentleman; an aggressive beau.

Some nymphs: From this phrase down to Line 90, the poem says that some sprites urge young ladies to be proud. In their vanity, these women refuse the offers of gentlemen.

Garters, Stars, and Coronets: the badges and other insignia of persons of high rank.

Your Grace: a member of the nobility. Although the phrase is in second-person point of view, it is to be read in third-person point of view as if it says, "His Grace."

Coquettes: flirtatious women

Teach . . . blush: Teach young ladies to wear rouge

Oft, when the world imagine women stray,
The Sylphs thro' mystic mazes guide their way,
Thro' all the giddy circle they pursue,
And old impertinence expel by new.
What tender maid but must a victim fall
To one man's treat, but for another's ball?
When Florio speaks what virgin could withstand,
If gentle Damon did not squeeze her hand?
With varying vanities, from ev'ry part,
They shift the moving Toyshop of their heart;

Where wigs with wigs, with sword-knots sword-knots strive,

Beaux banish beaux, and coaches coaches drive.
This erring mortals Levity may call;
Oh blind to truth! the Sylphs contrive it all.
Of these am I, who thy protection claim,
A watchful sprite, and Ariel is my name.
Late, as I rang'd the crystal wilds of air,
In the clear Mirror of thy ruling Star
I saw, alas! some dread event impend,
Ere to the main this morning sun descend,
But heav'n reveals not what, or how, or where:
Warn'd by the Sylph, oh pious maid, beware!
This to disclose is all thy guardian can:
Beware of all, but most beware of Man!"

Florio, Damon: Names commonly used in poetry in Pope's time the way we use Tom, Dick, and Harry—or John Doe—today. They do not refer to a specific person but to men in general.

Where . . . drive: The young gentlemen are vying for the attention of the young ladies.

Sword-knots: A sword knot was a loop of fabric or leather attached to the handle of a sword. A swordsman placed the loop around his wrist as a support for maintaining his grip.

Some sword knots were intended only as ornaments.

Beaux: plural of beau

This . . . all: Humans are wrong to think that young women are responsible for their frivolous and flirtatious behavior (levity). The truth is that sprites cause this behavior.

Of these: Beginning with this phrase and continuing down to Line 114, Belinda's guardian sprite introduces himself as Ariel, then discloses that a dreadful event is about to happen. He does not know what will occur, or how or where, but warns Belinda to beware.

Rang'd: ranged

He said; when Shock, who thought she slept too long,
Leap'd up, and wak'd his mistress with his tongue.
'Twas then, Belinda, if report say true,
Thy eyes first open'd on a Billet-doux;
Wounds, Charms, and Ardors were no sooner read,
But all the Vision vanish'd from thy head.
And now, unveil'd, the Toilet stands display'd,
Each silver Vase in mystic order laid.
First, rob'd in white, the Nymph intent adores,
With head uncover'd, the Cosmetic pow'rs.
A heav'nly image in the glass appears,
To that she bends, to that her eyes she rears;
Th' inferior Priestess, at her altar's side,
Trembling begins the sacred rites of Pride.
Unnumber'd treasures ope at once, and here
The various off'rings of the world appear;
From each she nicely culls with curious toil,
And decks the Goddess with the glitt'ring spoil.
This casket India's glowing gems unlocks,
And all Arabia breathes from yonder box.
The Tortoise here and Elephant unite,
Transformed to combs, the speckled, and the white.
Here files of pins extend their shining rows,
Puffs, Powders, Patches, Bibles, Billet-doux.

Now awful Beauty puts on all its arms;
The fair each moment rises in her charms,

Repairs her smiles, awakens ev'ry grace,
And calls forth all the wonders of her face;
Sees by degrees a purer blush arise,
And keener lightnings quicken in her eyes.
The busy Sylphs surround their darling care,

These set the head, and those divide the hair,

Some fold the sleeve, whilst others plait the gown:

And Betty's prais'd for labours not her own. Shock: Belinda's dog.

Billet-doux: love letter. From the French *billet* (*note, letter*) and *doux* (*sweet*). The French pronunciation is be yay DOO; the English pronunciation is BIL ay DOO.

Toilet: dressing table or dressing room.

Th' inferior Priestess: Servant, maid.

Decks . . . spoil: adorns Belinda with jewels and other ornaments.

Casket: box, case.

Tortoise: The shell of a tortoise was used in making combs.

Elephant: Reference to ivory.

Bibles: Small Bibles were fashionable accessories on ladies' dressing tables.

Now . . . arms: Here begins an epic convention, a warrior putting on his armor. In this case, of course, it is a woman putting on her clothes in preparation for vying in the battle of the sexes.

Canto II

Not with more glories, in th' ethereal plain,
The Sun first rises o'er the purpled main,
Than, issuing forth, the rival of his beams

Launch'd on the bosom of the silver Thames.
Fair Nymphs, and well-drest Youths around her shone...

But ev'ry eye was fix'd on her alone.
On her white breast a sparkling Cross she wore,
Which Jews might kiss, and Infidels adore.
Her lively looks a sprightly mind disclose,
Quick as her eyes, and as unfix'd as those:................

Favours to none, to all she smiles extends;
Oft she rejects, but never once offends.
Bright as the sun, her eyes the gazers strike,
And, like the sun, they shine on all alike.
Yet graceful ease, and sweetness void of pride,...........

Might hide her faults, if Belles had faults to hide:
If to her share some female errors fall,
Look on her face, and you'll forget 'em all.

Not . . . plain: Here begins an epic convention, the great voyage. In this case, Belinda is traveling in a boat on the Thames River with youths and guardian sprites. They all look so glorious that they rival the sunshine.

Which . . . kiss: An offensive line that is out of place in an otherwise delightful poem

This Nymph, to the destruction of mankind,
Nourish'd two Locks, which graceful hung behind....

In equal curls, and well conspir'd to deck
With shining ringlets the smooth iv'ry neck.
Love in these labyrinths his slaves detains,
And mighty hearts are held in slender chains.
With hairy springes we the birds betray,...............

Slight lines of hair surprise the finny prey,
Fair tresses man's imperial race ensnare,
And beauty draws us with a single hair.
Th' advent'rous Baron the bright locks admir'd;
He saw, he wish'd, and to the prize aspir'd.............

Resolv'd to win, he meditates the way,
By force to ravish, or by fraud betray;

For when success a Lover's toil attends,
Few ask, if fraud or force attain'd his ends.

Love . . . detains: Young men fall in love with her glorious curls (labyrinths) of hair, becoming slaves to her beauty.

With . . . ensnare: Just as we catch game birds in snares and fish ("finny prey") in nets, Belinda catches men with her hair.

Springes: traps, snares
Finny: having fins
For this, ere Phoebus rose, he had implor'd...........

Propitious heav'n, and ev'ry pow'r ador'd,
But chiefly Love—to Love an Altar built,
Of twelve vast French Romances, neatly gilt.
There lay three garters, half a pair of gloves;
And all the trophies of his former loves;............

With tender Billet-doux he lights the pyre,
And breathes three am'rous sighs to raise the fire.
Then prostrate falls, and begs with ardent eyes
Soon to obtain, and long possess the prize:
The pow'rs gave ear, and granted half his pray'r,.......

The rest, the winds dispers'd in empty air.

Phoebus: Apollo, the sun god. *Phoebus* means *bright one.* In Greek mythology, Phoebus Apollo became the sun, driving his golden chariot across the sky. Thus, *Phoebus* became a synonym for *sun.*

He: the baron (mentioned in Line 29).

To . . . built: From here down to Line 46, the poem says the baron places mementoes of young ladies of his acquaintance on an altar. Then he burns them in a "funeral" fire (pyre) fueled with love letters; he is offering a sacrifice that the gods may grant his wish to obtain locks of Belinda's hair.

But now secure the painted vessel glides,
The sun-beams trembling on the floating tides:

While melting music steals upon the sky,
And soften'd sounds along the waters die;

Smooth flow the waves, the Zephyrs gently play,
Belinda smil'd, and all the world was gay.
All but the Sylph—with careful thoughts opprest,
Th' impending woe sat heavy on his breast.
He summons strait his Denizens of air;

The lucid squadrons round the sails repair:
Soft o'er the shrouds aerial whispers breathe,
That seem'd but Zephyrs to the train beneath.
Some to the sun their insect-wings unfold,
Waft on the breeze, or sink in clouds of gold;

Transparent forms, too fine for mortal sight,
Their fluid bodies half dissolv'd in light,
Loose to the wind their airy garments flew,
Thin glitt'ring textures of the filmy dew,
Dipt in the richest tincture of the skies,

Where light disports in ever-mingling dyes,
While ev'ry beam new transient colours flings,
Colours that change whene'er they wave their wings.
Amid the circle, on the gilded mast,
Superior by the head, was Ariel plac'd;

His purple pinions op'ning to the sun,
He rais'd his azure wand, and thus begun.
Zephyrs: west winds or soft breezes.
Sylph: Ariel

He . . . repair: Ariel summons his helpers, and they gather around Belinda.

Shrouds: ropes or wires attached to a mast and secured on the sides of a ship. They keep the mast steady.

Light . . . flings: The light displays a variety of colors.

Disports: plays; amuses itself

Pinions: wings

Ye Sylphs and Sylphids, to your chief give ear!

Fays, Fairies, Genii, Elves, and Daemons, hear!

Ye know the spheres and various tasks assign'd

By laws eternal to th' aerial kind.
Some in the fields of purest Aether play,
And bask and whiten in the blaze of day.
Some guide the course of wand'ring orbs on high,
Or roll the planets thro' the boundless sky

Some less refin'd, beneath the moon's pale light
Pursue the stars that shoot athwart the night,
Or suck the mists in grosser air below,
Or dip their pinions in the painted bow,
Or brew fierce tempests on the wintry main,

Or o'er the glebe distil the kindly rain.
Others on earth o'er human race preside,
Watch all their ways, and all their actions guide:
Of these the chief the care of Nations own,
And guard with Arms divine the British Throne

Sylphids: Female sylphs, female sprites

Ye know: From this phrase down to Line 90, Ariel describes the tasks assigned to the various kinds of sprites.

Glebe: earth
Our humbler province is to tend the Fair,
Not a less pleasing, tho' less glorious care;
To save the powder from too rude a gale,
Nor let th' imprison'd-essences exhale;
To draw fresh colours from the vernal flow'rs;

To steal from rainbows e'er they drop in show'rs
A brighter wash; to curl their waving hairs,
Assist their blushes, and inspire their airs;
Nay oft, in dreams, invention we bestow,
To change a Flounce, or add a Furbelow

This day, black Omens threat the brightest Fair,
That e'er deserv'd a watchful spirit's care;
Some dire disaster, or by force, or slight;
But what, or where, the fates have wrapt in night.
Whether the nymph shall break Diana's law,

Or some frail China jar receive a flaw;
Or stain her honour or her new brocade;
Forget her pray'rs, or miss a masquerade;
Or lose her heart, or necklace, at a ball;
Or whether Heav'n has doom'd that Shock must fall..

Haste, then, ye spirits! to your charge repair:
The flutt'ring fan be Zephyretta's care;
The drops to thee, Brillante, we consign;
And, Momentilla, let the watch be thine;
Do thou, Crispissa, tend her fav'rite Lock;..........

Ariel himself shall be the guard of Shock.

Our humbler province: From this phrase down to Line 100, Ariel tells his sprites that one of their jobs is to tend to the needs of fair ladies—to keep their powders and perfumes in place, to curl their hair, to put color in their cheeks, etc.

Wash: skin lotion

Flounce: frill or ruffle

Furbelow: also a ruffle or any other ornament

Diana's law: the law of Diana (Greek name, *Artemis*), Apollo's twin sister and the virgin goddess of chastity. This law required young women to maintain their chastity.

Zephyretta: Sprite in charge of regulating the wind generated by a fan.

Drops: earrings.

Brillante: Sprite in charge of earrings

Momentilla: Sprite in charge of watching the time

Crispissa: Sprite in charge of guarding Belinda's favorite lock of hair.

Shock: Belinda's dog.
To fifty chosen Sylphs, of special note,
We trust th' important charge, the Petticoat:
Oft have we known that seven-fold fence to fail,
Tho' stiff with hoops, and arm'd with ribs of whale;...

Form a strong line about the silver bound,
And guard the wide circumference around.
Whatever spirit, careless of his charge,
His post neglects, or leaves the fair at large,
Shall feel sharp vengeance soon o'ertake his sins,

Be stopp'd in vials, or transfix'd with pins;
Or plung'd in lakes of bitter washes lie,
Or wedg'd whole ages in a bodkin's eye:
Gums and Pomatums shall his flight restrain,
While clogg'd he beats his silken wings in vain;

Or *Alum styptics with contracting pow'r*
Shrink his thin essence like a rivel'd flow'r:
Or, as Ixion fix'd, the wretch shall feel
The giddy motion of the whirling Mill,
In fumes of burning Chocolate shall glow,

And tremble at the sea that froths below!
He spoke; the spirits from the sails descend;
Some, orb in orb, around the nymph extend;
Some thrid the mazy ringlets of her hair;
Some hang upon the pendants of her ear:

With beating hearts the dire event they wait,
Anxious, and trembling for the birth of Fate.
Pomatums: ointments
Styptics: preparations that stop bleeding
Rivel'ed: shriveled, shrunken

Ixion: In Greek mythology, King of Lapithae, who dared to fall in love with Hera, queen of the gods and wife of Zeus. To punish him, Zeus had him tied in Hades to a wheel that revolved nonstop.

Mill: chocolate mill.

Thrid: threaded

Mazy: like a maze

Canto III

Close by those meads, for ever crown'd with flow'rs,
Where Thames with pride surveys his rising tow'rs,

There stands a structure of majestic frame,
Which from the neighb'ring Hampton takes its name.
Here Britain's statesmen oft the fall foredoom
Of foreign Tyrants and of Nymphs at home;
Here thou, great Anna! whom three realms obey.
Dost sometimes counsel take—and sometimes Tea.
Hither the heroes and the nymphs resort,
To taste awhile the pleasures of a Court;
In various talk th' instructive hours they past,
Who gave the ball, or paid the visit last;
One speaks the glory of the British Queen,
And one describes a charming Indian screen;
A third interprets motions, looks, and eyes;
At ev'ry word a reputation dies.
Snuff, or the fan, supply each pause of chat,
With singing, laughing, ogling, and _all that_.

Meads: meadows

Structure: the royal palace at Hampton Court

Anna . . . three: Anne (1665-1714), queen of England, Scotland, and Wales from 1702 to 1714.

At . . . dies: There was much gossip at the court.

Meanwhile, declining from the noon of day,
The sun obliquely shoots his burning ray;
The hungry Judges soon the sentence sign,
And wretches hang that jury-men may dine;
The merchant from th' Exchange returns in peace,
And the long labours of the Toilet cease.
Belinda now, whom thirst of fame invites,
Burns to encounter two advent'rous Knights,
At Ombre singly to decide their doom;
And swells her breast with conquests yet to come.
Straight the three bands prepare in arms to join,
Each band the number of the sacred nine.
Soon as she spreads her hand, th' aerial guard
Descend, and sit on each important card:
First Ariel perch'd upon a Matadore,

Then each, according to the rank they bore;
For Sylphs, yet mindful of their ancient race,...........

Are, as when women, wondrous fond of place.
Behold, four Kings in majesty rever'd,
With hoary whiskers and a forky beard;
And four fair Queens whose hands sustain a flow'r,
Th' expressive emblem of their softer pow'r;..........

Four Knaves in garbs succinct, a trusty band,
Caps on their heads, and halberts in their hand;
And particolour'd troops, a shining train,
Draw forth to combat on the velvet plain.

Two . . .Ombre: Ombre requires three players. Here, Belinda will vie with two gentlemen.

Straight . . . join: Here begins an epic convention, the battle.

Each . . . nine: In Greek mythology, the nine muses of Mount Olympus. The cards, dealt in groups, correspond in number to the nine muses in Greek mythology.

Matadore (also Matador): card of the highest value in ombre hoary whiskers: gray mustaches

Halberts (also *halberds* or *halbards*): A halbert was a weapon with a shaft five to six feet long topped by a pike, or spearhead, and below the pike an axe blade. A warrior could thrust with a halbert, as with a spear, or hack, as with a battle-axe.

The skillful Nymph reviews her force with care:........

Let Spades be trumps! she said, and trumps they were.
Now move to war her sable Matadores,
In show like leaders of the swarthy Moors.
Spadillo first, unconquerable Lord!
Led off two captive trumps, and swept the board........

As many more Manillo forc'd to yield,
And march'd a victor from the verdant field.

Him Basto follow'd, but his fate more hard
Gain'd but one trump and one Plebeian card.
With his broad sabre next, a chief in years,
The hoary Majesty of Spades appears,
Puts forth one manly leg, to sight reveal'd,
The rest, his many-colour'd robe conceal'd.
The rebel Knave, who dares his prince engage,
Proves the just victim of his royal rage.
Ev'n mighty Pam, that Kings and Queens o'erthrew
And mow'd down armies in the fights of Lu,
Sad chance of war! now destitute of aid,
Falls undistinguish'd by the victor spade!
Thus far both armies to Belinda yield;
Now to the Baron fate inclines the field.
His warlike Amazon her host invades,
Th' imperial consort of the crown of Spades.
The Club's black Tyrant first her victim dy'd,
Spite of his haughty mien, and barb'rous pride:
What boots the regal circle on his head,
His giant limbs, in state unwieldy spread;
That long behind he trails his pompous robe,
And, of all monarchs, only grasps the globe?

Spadillo: ace of spades

Manillo: two of spades, a card of high value

Basto: ace of clubs, card with third-highest value

Plebeian: card of little value

Knave: jack

Pam: jack of clubs

Lu: Loo, a card game in which the jack of clubs had the highest value

Mien: manner

What boots the regal circle: what good is the regal circle

Globe: golden ball which, along with a scepter, was an emblem of royal power

The Baron now his Diamonds pours apace;
Th' embroider'd King who shows but half his face,
And his refulgent Queen, with pow'rs combin'd
Of broken troops an easy conquest find.
Clubs, Diamonds, Hearts, in wild disorder seen,
With throngs promiscuous strow the level green.
Thus when dispers'd a routed army runs,
Of Asia's troops, and Afric's sable sons,
With like confusion different nations fly,
Of various habit, and of various dye,
The pierc'd battalions dis-united fall,
In heaps on heaps; one fate o'erwhelms them all.
The Knave of Diamonds tries his wily arts,
And wins (oh shameful chance!) the Queen of Hearts.
At this, the blood the virgin's cheek forsook,
A livid paleness spreads o'er all her look;
She sees, and trembles at th' approaching ill,
Just in the jaws of ruin, and Codille.
And now (as oft in some distemper'd State)
On one nice Trick depends the gen'ral fate.
An Ace of Hearts steps forth: The King unseen
Lurk'd in her hand, and mourn'd his captive Queen:
He springs to Vengeance with an eager pace,
And falls like thunder on the prostrate Ace.
The nymph exulting fills with shouts the sky;
The walls, the woods, and long canals reply.

Strow: archaic form of *strew*

Codille: A development in which the challenger failed to win the necessary cards. On the next play, Belinda wins the game.

Long canals: The canals on the grounds of Hampton Court
Oh thoughtless mortals! ever blind to fate,
Too soon dejected, and too soon elate.

Sudden, these honours shall be snatch'd away,
And curs'd for ever this victorious day.
For lo! the board with cups and spoons is crown'd,
The berries crackle, and the mill turns round;
On shining Altars of Japan they raise
The silver lamp; the fiery spirits blaze:
From silver spouts the grateful liquors glide,
While China's earth receives the smoking tide:
At once they gratify their scent and taste,
And frequent cups prolong the rich repast.
Straight hover round the Fair her airy band;
Some, as she sipp'd, the fuming liquor fann'd,
Some o'er her lap their careful plumes display'd,
Trembling, and conscious of the rich brocade.
Coffee, (which makes the politician wise,
And see thro' all things with his half-shut eyes)
Sent up in vapours to the Baron's brain
New Stratagems, the radiant Lock to gain.
Ah cease, rash youth! desist ere't is too late,
Fear the just Gods, and think of Scylla's Fate!
Chang'd to a bird, and sent to flit in air,
She dearly pays for Nisus' injur'd hair!

Berries crackle: The coffee beans crackle when roasted on the mill.

Altars of Japan: tables coated with varnish made from a substance of a Japanese tree of the cashew family.

China's . . . tide: The china coffee cups receive the steaming coffee.

Scylla's . . . hair: In Greek mythology, Scylla betrayed her father, Nisus, King of Megara, by cutting off a lock of his hair—a purple lock with magical powers that safeguarded him and his kingdom. Scylla did so because she was in love with her father's enemy, King Minos of Crete, who was attacking Megara. Nisus died and was changed into a sea eagle. Scylla later drowned and was changed into a sea bird that was chased by the eagle.

But when to mischief mortals bend their will,
How soon they find fit instruments of ill!
Just then, Clarissa drew with tempting grace
A two-edg'd weapon from her shining case:
So Ladies in Romance assist their Knight,
Present the spear, and arm him for the fight.
He takes the gift with rev'rence, and extends
The little engine on his fingers' ends;
This just behind Belinda's neck he spread,
As o'er the fragrant steams she bends her head.
Swift to the Lock a thousand Sprites repair,
A thousand wings, by turns, blow back the hair;
And thrice they twitch'd the diamond in her ear;
Thrice she look'd back, and thrice the foe drew near.
Just in that instant, anxious Ariel sought
The close recesses of the Virgin's thought;
As on the nosegay in her breast reclin'd,
He watch'd th' Ideas rising in her mind,
Sudden he view'd, in spite of all her art,
An earthly Lover lurking at her heart.
Amaz'd, confus'd, he found his pow'r expir'd,
Resign'd to fate, and with a sigh retir'd.

Fragrant steams: steam from the hot coffee
Weapon: scissors
Nosegay: small bouquet of flowers

The Peer now spreads the glitt'ring Forfex wide,
T' inclose the Lock; now joins it, to divide.
Ev'n then, before the fatal engine clos'd,
A wretched Sylph too fondly interpos'd;
Fate urg'd the shears, and cut the Sylph in twain,
(But airy substance soon unites again)
The meeting points the sacred hair dissever
From the fair head, for ever, and for ever!
Then flash'd the living lightning from her eyes,
And screams of horror rend th' affrighted skies.
Not louder shrieks to pitying heav'n are cast,

When husbands, or when lapdogs breathe their last;
Or when rich China vessels fall'n from high,
In glitt'ring dust and painted fragments lie!

Let wreaths of triumph now my temples twine
(The victor cry'd) the glorious Prize is mine!
While fish in streams, or birds delight in air,
Or in a coach and six the British Fair,
As long as Atalantis shall be read,
Or the small pillow grace a Lady's bed,
While visits shall be paid on solemn days,
When num'rous wax-lights in bright order blaze,
While nymphs take treats, or assignations give,
So long my honour, name, and praise shall live!
What Time would spare, from Steel receives its date,
And monuments, like men, submit to fate!
Steel could the labour of the Gods destroy,
And strike to dust th' imperial tow'rs of Troy;
Steel could the works of mortal pride confound,
And hew triumphal arches to the ground.
What wonder then, fair nymph! thy hairs should feel,
The conqu'ring force of unresisted steel?
The Peer: the baron
Forfex: Latin for scissors

Atalantis: Reference to *The New Atlantis*, a popular gossip novel by Mary de la Riviere Manley (1663-1724). It alluded to real-life scandals.

Steel receives: From this phrase down to Line 178, the poem tells of the power of steel to endure, to destroy the work of gods and men, and, of course, to trim a lock of hair.

Strike . . . Troy: In the Trojan War, the Greeks—using swords and spears of steel—slaughtered the Trojans and destroyed their city after gaining entry to the city inside a wooden horse.

Triumphal arches: arches built to honor and memorialize great men and heroes.

Canto IV

But anxious cares the pensive nymph oppress'd,
And secret passions labour'd in her breast.
Not youthful kings in battle seiz'd alive,
Not scornful virgins who their charms survive,
Not ardent lovers robb'd of all their bliss,
Not ancient ladies when refus'd a kiss,
Not tyrants fierce that unrepenting die,
Not Cynthia when her manteau's pinn'd awry,
E'er felt such rage, resentment, and despair,
As thou, sad Virgin! for thy ravish'd Hair.
For, that sad moment, when the Sylphs withdrew
And Ariel weeping from Belinda flew,
Umbriel, a dusky, melancholy sprite,
As ever sully'd the fair face of light,
Down to the central earth, his proper scene,
Repair'd to search the gloomy Cave of Spleen.

Not: Repeating a word at the beginning of successive clauses or phrases constitutes a figure of speech known as anaphora.

Cynthia: another name for the goddess Diana (Greek name, Artemis), Apollo's twin sister and the virgin goddess of chastity.

Cynthia is derived from the Greek word *Kynthia,* meaning *from or associated with Kynthos,* a mountain on the Greek island of Delos where Artemis and Apollo were born.

Cave of Spleen: Dwelling of the Queen of Spleen—that is, the queen of melancholy and low spirits.

Swift on his sooty pinions flits the Gnome,
And in a vapour reach'd the dismal dome.
No cheerful breeze this sullen region knows,
The dreaded East is all the wind that blows.
Here in a grotto, shelter'd close from air,
And screen'd in shades from day's detested glare,

She sighs for ever on her pensive bed,
Pain at her side, and Megrim at her head.
Two handmaids wait the throne: alike in place,
But diff'ring far in figure and in face.
Here stood Ill-nature like an ancient maid,
Her wrinkled form in black and white array'd;
With store of pray'rs, for mornings, nights, and noons,
Her hand is fill'd; her bosom with lampoons.
There Affectation, with a sickly mien,
Shows in her cheek the roses of eighteen,
Practis'd to lisp, and hang the head aside.
Faints into airs, and languishes with pride,
On the rich quilt sinks with becoming woe,
Wrapt in a gown, for sickness, and for show.
The fair ones feel such maladies as these,
When each new night-dress gives a new disease.
Grotto: cave
Megrim: melancholy, depression, low spirits; headache
A constant Vapour o'er the palace flies;
Strange phantoms rising as the mists arise;
Dreadful, as hermit's dreams in haunted shades,
Or bright, as visions of expiring maids.
Now glaring fiends, and snakes on rolling spires,
Pale spectres, gaping tombs, and purple fires:
Now lakes of liquid gold, Elysian scenes,
And crystal domes, and angels in machines.
Unnumber'd throngs on every side are seen,
Of bodies chang'd to various forms by Spleen.
Here living Tea-pots stand, one arm held out,
One bent; the handle this, and that the spout:
A Pipkin there, like Homer's Tripod walks;
Here sighs a Jar, and there a Goose-pie talks;
Men prove with child, as pow'rful fancy works,
And maids turn'd bottles, call aloud for corks.
Rolling spires: spirals

Elysian: heavenly

Bodies . . . chang'd: From this phrase down to Line 54, the poem describes people changed into objects by the Queen of Spleen. Victims of certain psychopathic disorders sometimes report that they have been changed into an object.

Pipkin: small pot or jar made of baked clay; small earthenware container

Homer's tripod: In Homer's Iliad, a tripod capable of moving itself.

Men . . . child: pregnant men

Safe past the Gnome thro' this fantastic band,
A branch of healing Spleenwort in his hand.
Then thus address'd the pow'r: "Hail, wayward Queen!
Who rule the sex to fifty from fifteen:
Parent of vapours and of female wit,
Who give th' hysteric, or poetic fit,
On various tempers act by various ways,
Make some take physic, others scribble plays;
Who cause the proud their visits to delay,
And send the godly in a pet to pray.
A nymph there is, that all thy pow'r disdains,
And thousands more in equal mirth maintains.
But oh! if e'er thy Gnome could spoil a grace,
Or raise a pimple on a beauteous face,
Like Citron-waters matrons cheeks inflame,
Or change complexions at a losing game;
If e'er with airy horns I planted heads,
Or rumpled petticoats, or tumbled beds,
Or caus'd suspicion when no soul was rude,
Or discompos'd the head-dress of a Prude,
Or e'er to costive lap-dog gave disease,
Which not the tears of brightest eyes could ease:
Hear me, and touch Belinda with chagrin,
That single act gives half the world the spleen."

Safe past: safely passed

Spleenwort: type of fern with healing powers. The reference to it is an allusion to Vergil's *Aeneid,* in which the hero, Aeneas, passes safely into the underworld because he is carrying a magical golden bough.

Who . . . way: The Queen of Spleen can influence the behavior of young ladies in various ways.

Make . . . plays: Some young ladies under the influence of a fit caused by the Queen of Spleen may take medicine. Others may scribble (plays, notes, love letters, drawings).

pet: in a bad mood

Citron-waters: an alcoholic beverage distilled from the rinds of the lemon and citron (a yellow, thick-skinned fruit that resembles the lemon but is larger and less acidic)

If . . . heads: If I have ever planted horns in the heads of men. This clause is an allusion to an old tale saying that men would grow horns if their wives were unfaithful.

Costive . . . disease: gave a scolding to a slow-moving or constipated pet dog

The Goddess with a discontented air

Seems to reject him, tho' she grants his pray'r.

A wond'rous Bag with both her hands she binds,
Like that where once Ulysses held the winds;
There she collects the force of female lungs,
Sighs, sobs, and passions, and the war of tongues.
A Vial next she fills with fainting fears,

Soft sorrows, melting griefs, and flowing tears.
The Gnome rejoicing bears her gifts away,
Spreads his black wings, and slowly mounts to day.
Sunk in Thalestris' arms the nymph he found,
Her eyes dejected and her hair unbound.

Full o'er their heads the swelling bag he rent,
And all the Furies issu'd at the vent.
Belinda burns with more than mortal ire,
And fierce Thalestris fans the rising fire.
"O wretched maid!" she spread her hands, and cry'd,

(While Hampton's echoes, "Wretched maid!" reply'd)
"Was it for this you took such constant care
The bodkin, comb, and essence to prepare?
For this your locks in paper durance bound,
For this with tort'ring irons wreath'd around?
For this with fillets strain'd your tender head,
And bravely bore the double loads of lead?
Gods! shall the ravisher display your hair,
While the Fops envy, and the Ladies stare!
Honour forbid! at whose unrivall'd shrine
Ease, pleasure, virtue, all our sex resign.
Methinks already I your tears survey,
Already hear the horrid things they say,
Already see you a degraded toast,
And all your honour in a whisper lost!
How shall I, then, your helpless fame defend?
'Twill then be infamy to seem your friend!
And shall this prize, th' inestimable prize,
Expos'd thro' crystal to the gazing eyes,
And heighten'd by the diamond's circling rays,
On that rapacious hand for ever blaze?
Sooner shall grass in Hyde-park Circus grow,
And wits take lodgings in the sound of Bow;
Sooner let earth, air, sea, to Chaos fall,
Men, monkeys, lap-dogs, parrots, perish all!"
She said; then raging to Sir Plume repairs,
And bids her Beau demand the precious hairs;
(Sir Plume of amber snuff-box justly vain,
And the nice conduct of a clouded cane)
With earnest eyes, and round unthinking face,
He first the snuff-box open'd, then the case,
And thus broke out—"My Lord, why, what the devil?
"Z—ds! damn the lock! 'fore Gad, you must be civil!
Plague on't!'t is past a jest—nay prithee, pox!

Give her the hair"—he spoke, and rapp'd his box.

A wond'rous . . . winds: In Homer's *Odyssey*, Ulysses (Greek name, Odysseus) received a bag of winds from Aeolus, the god of the winds. When opened, the bag would release winds favorable to Ulysses on his sea voyage home.

Thalestris: See characters, above.

The swelling . . . rent: The gnome ripped the bag open.

Bodkin: hairpin

Paper durance: confinement in paper. Belinda had apparently had her locks wrapped in paper while receiving a permanent.

Tort'ring: torturing

Fillets: bands of ribbon worn to keep hair in place

Loads of lead: leaden ends of paper wraps encircling curls. The curls were wrapped in paper before treatment of them with chemicals that created a "permanent wave." The lead on the ends of the paper made it easy to attach one end of the paper to the other.

Fops: Vain men who pay undue attention to their clothes and manners.

Degraded toast: a woman who has been toasted for her beauty but then degraded or embarrassed by some event

And shall . . . blaze: Belinda worries that the baron will display the prize (the lock of hair) in a diamond ring he will wear.

Hyde-park Circus: The circular road in Hyde Park where Londoners drove their carriages.

Sound of Bow: Bow was a commercial district of London. It was unlikely that a fashionable person would want to live amid the hubbub there.

Clouded cane: Sir Plume carries a cane, or walking stick, made of wood with dark (clouded) grain

Z—ds: zounds (pronounced ZOONS), a mild oath. *Zounds* is a corruption of *by His wounds*, meaning the wounds of Christ. When spoken quickly, *by His wounds* becomes *zounds*.

"It grieves me much" (reply'd the Peer again)
"Who speaks so well should ever speak in vain.
But by this Lock, this sacred Lock I swear,
(Which never more shall join its parted hair;
Which never more its honours shall renew,
Clipp'd from the lovely head where late it grew)
That while my nostrils draw the vital air,
This hand, which won it, shall for ever wear."
He spoke, and speaking, in proud triumph spread
The long-contended honours of her head.

In this passage, the baron says that pleas for him to return the lock of hair are in vain, for he means to keep and display it.

But Umbriel, hateful Gnome! forbears not so;
He breaks the Vial whence the sorrows flow.
Then see! the nymph in beauteous grief appears,
Her eyes half-languishing, half-drown'd in tears;
On her heav'd bosom hung her drooping head,
Which, with a sigh, she rais'd; and thus she said.
"For ever curs'd be this detested day,
Which snatch'd my best, my fav'rite curl away!
Happy! ah ten times happy had I been,
If Hampton-Court these eyes had never seen!
Yet am not I the first mistaken maid,
By love of Courts to num'rous ills betray'd.
Oh had I rather un-admir'd remain'd
In some lone isle, or distant Northern land;
Where the gilt Chariot never marks the way,
Where none learn Ombre, none e'er taste Bohea!
There kept my charms conceal'd from mortal eye,
Like roses, that in deserts bloom and die.
What mov'd my mind with youthful Lords to roam?
Oh had I stay'd, and said my pray'rs at home!

'Twas this, the morning omens seem'd to tell,
Thrice from my trembling hand the patch-box fell;
The tott'ring China shook without a wind.
Nay, Poll sat mute, and Shock was most unkind!
A Sylph too warn'd me of the threats of fate,

In mystic visions, now believ'd too late!
See the poor remnants of these slighted hairs!
My hands shall rend what ev'n thy rapine spares:
These in two sable ringlets taught to break,
Once gave new beauties to the snowy neck;

The sister-lock now sits uncouth, alone,
And in its fellow's fate foresees its own;
Uncurl'd it hangs, the fatal shears demands,
And tempts once more thy sacrilegious hands.
Oh hadst thou, cruel! been content to seize

Hairs less in sight, or any hairs but these!"

But Umbriel: From this phrase down to Line 145, the poem says Umbriel breaks the vial of tears he obtained from the Queen of Spleen, enabling Belinda to vent her sorrow in a storm of tears.

Bohea: type of black tea grown in a mountain region of China patch-box: box containing a preparation for making beauty marks

Poll: pet parrot

Shock: the dog

Rend: tear out

Sable: black

Canto V

She said: the pitying audience melt in tears.
But Fate and Jove had stopp'd the Baron's ears.
In vain Thalestris with reproach assails,
For who can move when fair Belinda fails?
Not half so fix'd the Trojan could remain,

While Anna begg'd and Dido rag'd in vain.
Then grave Clarissa graceful wav'd her fan;
Silence ensu'd, and thus the nymph began.
"Say why are Beauties prais'd and honour'd most,
The wise man's passion, and the vain man's toast?
Why deck'd with all that land and sea afford,
Why Angels call'd, and Angel-like ador'd?
Why round our coaches crowd the white-glov'd Beaux,
Why bows the side-box from its inmost rows;
How vain are all these glories, all our pains,
Unless good sense preserve what beauty gains:
That men may say, when we the front-box grace:
'Behold the first in virtue as in face!'
Oh! if to dance all night, and dress all day,
Charm'd the small-pox, or chas'd old-age away;
Who would not scorn what housewife's cares produce,
Or who would learn one earthly thing of use?
To patch, nay ogle, might become a Saint,
Nor could it sure be such a sin to paint.
But since, alas! frail beauty must decay,
Curl'd or uncurl'd, since Locks will turn to grey;
Since painted, or not painted, all shall fade,
And she who scorns a man, must die a maid;
What then remains but well our pow'r to use,
And keep good-humour still whate'er we lose?
And trust me, dear! good-humour can prevail,
When airs, and flights, and screams, and scolding fail.
Beauties in vain their pretty eyes may roll;
Charms strike the sight, but merit wins the soul."

Jove: Jupiter, Roman name for Zeus, the king of the gods in Greek mythology.

The Trojan: . . . vain: allusion to Aeneas, the hero of Vergil's *Aeneid*. While sojourning in Carthage, Aeneas became the lover of Carthage's queen, Dido. Although Dido and her sister, Anna, pleaded for him to remain in Carthage, Aeneas abruptly left her to continue his sea voyage to Italy. There, according to Roman mythology, he founded a colony that would blossom into Roman civilization.

Side box, front-box: In the theatre, young ladies preferred the front boxes, facing the stage. Young men sat in the side boxes

So spoke the Dame, but no applause ensu'd;

Belinda frown'd, Thalestris call'd her Prude.
"To arms, to arms!" the fierce Virago cries,
And swift as lightning to the combat flies.
All side in parties, and begin th' attack;
Fans clap, silks rustle, and tough whalebones crack;

Heroes' and Heroines' shouts confus'dly rise,
And bass, and treble voices strike the skies.
No common weapons in their hands are found,
Like Gods they fight, nor dread a mortal wound.
So when bold Homer makes the Gods engage,

And heav'nly breasts with human passions rage;
'Gainst Pallas, Mars; Latona, Hermes arms;
And all Olympus rings with loud alarms:
Jove's thunder roars, heav'n trembles all around,
Blue Neptune storms, the bellowing deeps resound:

Earth shakes her nodding tow'rs, the ground gives way.
And the pale ghosts start at the flash of day!
Triumphant Umbriel on a sconce's height
Clapp'd his glad wings, and sate to view the fight:
Propp'd on the bodkin spears, the Sprites survey

The growing combat, or assist the fray.
While thro' the press enrag'd Thalestris flies,
And scatters death around from both her eyes,
A Beau and Witling perish'd in the throng,
One died in metaphor, and one in song.

"O cruel nymph! a living death I bear,"
Cry'd Dapperwit, and sunk beside his chair.
A mournful glance Sir Fopling upwards cast,
"Those eyes are made so killing"—was his last.
Thus on Maeander's flow'ry margin lies

Th' expiring Swan, and as he sings he dies.

Whalebones: horny plates in the jaws of baleen whales that catch plankton. Tough and flexible, they were used to stiffen women's corsets.

Pallas: Another name for Athena (Roman name, Minerva), goddess of wisdom and war

Mars: god of war (Greek name, Ares)

Latona: mother of Apollo and Artemis (Diana). Her Greek name was Leto.

Hermes: messenger of the Olympian gods (Roman name, Mercury)

Neptune: god of the sea (Greek name, Poseidon)

Sconce: bracket on a wall for holding a candle or a torch; candlestick holder affixed to a wall plaque.

Bodkin spears: pins

Witling: a person who tries to be witty

Dapperwit: character in the comedy *Love in a Wood; or St. James Park* (1671), by playwright William Wycherley (1640-1716)

Sir Fopling: character in the comedy *The Man of Mode, or, Sir Fopling Flutter* (1676), by George Etherege (1635-1691)

Those . . . killing: words from an opera

Maeander: winding river in Western Turkey. The modern name for this river is Menderes.

When bold Sir Plume had drawn Clarissa down,
Chloe stepp'd in, and kill'd him with a frown;
She smil'd to see the doughty hero slain,
But, at her smile, the Beau reviv'd again.

Now Jove suspends his golden scales in air,
Weighs the Men's wits against the Lady's hair;
The doubtful beam long nods from side to side;
At length the wits mount up, the hairs subside.
See, fierce Belinda on the Baron flies,

With more than usual lightning in her eyes:
Nor fear'd the Chief th' unequal fight to try,
Who sought no more than on his foe to die.
But this bold Lord with manly strength endu'd,
She with one finger and a thumb subdu'd:

Just where the breath of life his nostrils drew,
A charge of Snuff the wily virgin threw;
The Gnomes direct, to ev'ry atom just,
The pungent grains of titillating dust.
Sudden, with starting tears each eye o'erflows,

And the high dome re-echoes to his nose.
Now meet thy fate, incens'd Belinda cry'd,
And drew a deadly bodkin from her side.
(The same, his ancient personage to deck,
Her great great grandsire wore about his neck,

In three seal-rings; which after, melted down,
Form'd a vast buckle for his widow's gown:
Her infant grandame's whistle next it grew,
The bells she jingled, and the whistle blew;
Then in a bodkin grac'd her mother's hairs,

Which long she wore, and now Belinda wears.)

Jove: King of the gods (Greek name, Zeus)

Endu'd: *endued*, meaning *endowed*

Snuff: tobacco reduced to a powder. It is inhaled through the nose, rubbed on the gums, or chewed.

Bodkin: dagger of her great-great grandfather. It was melted down to form a buckle, then a whistle. Part of it eventually became a pin (another meaning of *bodkin*).

"Boast not my fall" (he cry'd) "insulting foe!
Thou by some other shalt be laid as low,
Nor think, to die dejects my lofty mind:
All that I dread is leaving you behind!

Rather than so, ah let me still survive,
And burn in Cupid's flames—but burn alive."

"Restore the Lock!" she cries; and all around
"Restore the Lock!" the vaulted roofs rebound.
Not fierce Othello in so loud a strain
Roar'd for the handkerchief that caus'd his pain.
But see how oft ambitious aims are cross'd,
And chiefs contend 'till all the prize is lost!
The Lock, obtain'd with guilt, and kept with pain,
In ev'ry place is sought, but sought in vain:
With such a prize no mortal must be blest,
So heav'n decrees! with heav'n who can contest?
Some thought it mounted to the Lunar sphere,
Since all things lost on earth are treasur'd there.
There Hero's wits are kept in pond'rous vases
And beau's in snuff-boxes and tweezer-cases.
There broken vows and death-bed alms are found,
And lovers' hearts with ends of riband bound,
The courtier's promises, and sick man's pray'rs,
The smiles of harlots, and the tears of heirs,
Cages for gnats, and chains to yoke a flea,
Dry'd butterflies, and tomes of casuistry.
Cupid: god of love (Greek name: Eros)

Othello: In Shakespeare's play of the same name, Othello wrongly believes his wife has been unfaithful because her handkerchief was found in the possession of another man. He shouts condemnations at her. Click here for the Othello Study Guide if you wish additional information.

Hero: priestess of Aphrodite. She commits suicide after her lover, Leander, drowns. This word may also refer to a character in Ludovico Ariosto's epic poem *Orlando Furioso* (1516), in which the title character loses his wits. They are thought to be on the moon.

Riband: ribbon

Tomes: books

Casuistry: (1) system that attempted to answer moral questions by applying the principles of ethics and theology to specific cases; (2) method of attempting to justify a seemingly sinful act as moral through the application of deceptive reasoning.

But trust the Muse—she saw it upward rise,
Tho' mark'd by none but quick, poetic eyes:
(So Rome's great founder to the heav'ns withdrew,
To Proculus alone confess'd in view)
A sudden Star, it shot thro' liquid air,
And drew behind a radiant trail of hair.
Not Berenice's Locks first rose so bright,
The heav'ns bespangling with dishevell'd light.
The Sylphs behold it kindling as it flies,
And pleas'd pursue its progress thro' the skies.
This the Beau monde shall from the Mall survey,
And hail with music its propitious ray.
This the blest Lover shall for Venus take,
And send up vows from Rosamonda's lake.
This Partridge soon shall view in cloudless skies,
When next he looks thro' Galileo's eyes;
And hence th' egregious wizard shall foredoom
The fate of Louis, and the fall of Rome.
Then cease, bright Nymph! to mourn thy ravish'd hair,
Which adds new glory to the shining sphere!
Not all the tresses that fair head can boast,
Shall draw such envy as the Lock you lost.
For, after all the murders of your eye
When, after millions slain, yourself shall die:
When those fair suns shall set, as set they must,
And all those tresses shall be laid in dust,
This Lock, the Muse shall consecrate to fame,
And 'midst the stars inscribe Belinda's name

Rome's great founder. Romulus. According to Roman mythology, he and his brother, Remus, founded Rome. Romulus became the city's first king. After he died in a storm, the Romans assumed he was carried into the heavens, and they worshipped him as the god Quirinus.

Proculus: Roman senator. After Romulus died, Proculus had a vision in which Romulus said Rome was destined for greatness.

Berenice: Reference to Berenice's Hair, a star group that astronomers call *Coma Berenices*. This northern constellation is between the constellations Boötes and Leo and north of the constellation Virgo. Berenice herself was the wife of Egypt's Ptolemy III Euergetes. When he went off on a dangerous mission to Syria, Berenice cut off a lock of her hair as a votive offering in praying for his safe return. Legend says that it was taken into the heavens to form a new constellation.

Beau monde: French for fashionable society

Mall: avenue in the St. James district of London's Westminster borough. It is near St. James's Palace, the royal residence after fire destroyed Whitehall Palace in 1698. The Mall was a popular walkway for the well-to-do residents of St. James.

Venus: goddess of love (in Greek mythology, Aphrodite).

Romsamonda's lake: lake in St. James's Park.

Partridge: allusion to John Partridge, an astrologer who made unfounded predictions in almanacs

Galileo's eyes: lenses of a telescope

fate of Louis: fate of the King of France

Chapter 17

Study Questions

Q.1. Critically analyse the Poem the Rape of the Lock.

Or

Q. Discuss the Rape of the Lock critically

Or

Q. Discuss the poetical elements in the Rape Of the Lock.

Critical debate about Pope has frequently been acrimonious. In his lifetime, Pope himself was often to blame. As he wrote in 1733: 'Fools rush into my head, and so I write' (Satire II.i, l.4). Unsurprisingly, the fools in question wrote back, and much of the early comment on his work is marked by the desire for revenge rather than for justice. By the end of the century, however, critics were asking the more radical question, whether satire could really be poetry at all. William Bowles, the editor of Pope's Works, argued that true poetry was marked by a poetical subject, such as the beauty of nature, whereas writing focussed on the ordinary activities of men and women in polite society was inevitably as artificial as its subject matter. Over the next few years an increasing number of poets and critics sniped at Pope as a mere versifier rather than a true poet.

The strongest defence of Pope came from Byron. If there were a general wreck of English literature, he wrote to his publisher, the English would rush to save Shakespeare and Milton, but the rest of the world would save Pope's work first, because Pope was 'the moral poet of all civilisation'. Byron was ready to defend Pope against all comers, and pretty much on any grounds — as a poet of imagination and invention, as well as the poet of good sense — but in particular he insisted that what others called Pope's artificiality was in truth his 'faultlessness'. The underlying claim in Byron's defence of Pope is that the moral authority of the verse is implicit in, bound up with, its executive efficiency. I want to begin by exploring Byron's sense that a well-made couplet is a moral act.

Certainly Pope would have accepted this line of argument. Take this example, from the 'Epistle to a Lady', published in 1735:

> See Sin in State, majestically drunk,
> Proud as a Peeress, prouder as a Punk;
> Chaste to her Husband, frank to all beside,
> A teeming Mistress, but a barren Bride.
> ('Epistle to a Lady', ll.69-72)

The verse here draws attention to its own efficiency. The four lines are held together by the pattern of a triple alliteration in the first half-line, and again in the last. In the first couplet, the characteristic Popean imperative, 'See', introduces a suitably firm half-line of four monosyllables, leading to the tottering imbalance of 'majestically', which needs all five syllables, as if groping to find the extra step, missing it, and collapsing on the word 'drunk'. The seemingly innocuous 'Proud as a Peeress' moves on through 'prouder', suggesting a rise, and then falls back on 'Punk'. The emphatic rhyme of drunk and Punk locks the two lines into a single unit, as the adjective and noun are allowed to find their appropriate partners.

The four half-lines of the second couplet are organized to underline the mad logic which governs the world Pope describes: the paradox of a woman who is chaste to her husband because she denies him and not because she is faithful to him, the clash of this chastity with her availability to everybody else, and the predictable but morally incoherent consequence of her fertility as a mistress and her sterility as a bride.

As often in Pope's work, the significant action takes place in the smaller units of the verse, within rather than between the couplets. Here the four half-lines are formed as a double chiasmus, the ABBA pattern serving at once to highlight and to resist the confusion:

> *[A] Chaste / Husband and [B] frank / all,*
> *[B] Mistress / teeming and [A] Bride / barren.*

The conspicuous orderliness of the verse is played against the disorder of the world to which it directs our gaze, setting up the two-way or binary opposition so typical of formal verse satire: the precise voice of the satirist, and the mere noise of the external scene. The attempt to clarify, to make sense of the chaos, is the characteristic action of Pope's satire.

The discriminating power of the satirist's voice is typically pointed enough to make explicit moral commentary redundant:

> *Here Files of Pins extend their shining Rows,*
> *Puffs, Powders, Patches, Bibles, Billet-doux.*
> *(The Rape of the Lock, I, ll.137-8)*

Logically these lines can be read in either of two ways, as a mere statement of things to be found on Belinda's dressing-table, or as a list which invites us to 'see' competing levels of value. Clearly, if we are to recognize that the list registers Belinda's lack of discrimination, we must ourselves order the items: distinguish between religious and secular love, for example, or identify puffs, powders and patches as the means, billet-doux as the ends. The lines only act as verse, rather than inventory, if we implicitly side with Pope in separating out what Belinda has confused. Precisely the same responsibility is left with the reader elsewhere in the poem, where Pope uses zeugma:

> *Or stain her Honour, or her new Brocade,*
> *Forget her Pray'rs, or miss a Masquerade,*
> *Or lose her Heart, or Necklace, at a Ball...*
> *(The Rape of the Lock, II, ll.107-109)*

Belinda may fail to recognize the difference between a literal outer stain and a metaphorical inner one, but the line has no poetic energy if the reader is unable to do so. In this instance, the most heterogeneous ideas are yoked together not by the poet's violence but by Belinda's moral feebleness. The wit resides in the insinuated need to distinguish them.

It is in the use of rhyme that Pope shows himself most resourceful in alerting the reader to an order forgotten or violated or, more rarely, defended. Thus, in passage 7 on the sheets, Wharton's moral instability is underlined by the rhyming of words which morally don't 'rhyme': adores and whores. The lines describing Cloe in the 'Epistle to a Lady' offer a more elaborate example:

She, while her Lover pants upon her breast,
Can mark the figures on an Indian chest;
And when she sees her Friend in deep despair,
Observes how much a Chintz exceeds Mohair.

('Epistle to a Lady', ll.167-170)

The breast/chest rhyme seems at first too routinely an echo to be interesting, but this suspicion is briefly interrupted by the thought that the warm human breast of the woman isn't, after all, equivalent to the carved wooden chest which catches her attention. But then we realise that it has to be re-admitted because Cloe has just been described as lacking a heart. The chime makes its own satirical point; Cloe's breast, with its merely external beauty, is indeed properly rhymed with chest.

The other pairing, despair/mohair, works well enough, but is a less subtle reworking of a similar rhyme in Canto IV of The Rape of the Lock, where Pope uses rhyme with supreme inventiveness:

But anxious Cares the pensive Nymph oppress'd,
And secret Passions labour'd in her Breast.
Not youthful Kings in Battel seiz'd alive,
Not scornful Virgins who their Charms survive,
Not ardent Lovers robb'd of all their Bliss,
Not ancient Ladies when refus'd a Kiss,
Not Tyrants fierce that unrelenting die,

Not Cynthia when her Manteau's pinn'd awry,
E'er felt such Rage, Resentment and Despair,
As Thou, sad Virgin! for thy ravish'd Hair.

(The Rape of the Lock, Canto IV, ll.1-10)

The first four couplets here employ what Hugh Kenner calls 'reasonable' rhymes; it is no surprise to find alive rhymed with survive, or bliss with kiss. The wit lies in the way the naturalness of the rhymes is undermined by the imbalance between the first and second lines of each couplet, setting up parallels which themselves go 'awry', between kings who didn't want to be captured and virgins who did, or between lovers who wish to give and ladies who demand to be given a kiss. The word 'awry', carefully placed as the sense of imbalance mounts to a climax, allows Pope to close the paragraph with the unreasonable rhyme, of despair/hair, that governs the whole poem.

What all these devices — the use of chiasmus, lists, zeugma, rhyme, puns — have in common is that they depend for their effect on the reader's recognizing them, and identifying and correcting the element of moral blindness they are intended to mimic. It is necessary, in other words, that however subtle it might be, Pope's art should not be concealed; its aim is to invite the reader to duplicate its clarity, and to weigh that against the external disorder. Pope's verse accordingly offers two sources of interest: the reasonableness of its form, and the unreason of the world it represents. Typically, the sharper the tension between these two, the more satisfying the verse. Borrowing terms used by Sir Philip Sidney at the end of the sixteenth century, we can say that we are offered two kinds of pleasure: delight in the harmony and order offered by the artist's skill in representing the world, and laughter at the disharmony of the world represented. Sidney's distinction interestingly anticipates the tension between the reasonable form and the disorderly content in Pope's verse satires.

But there are other terms in which to describe the reason/disorder distinction, which better serve to explain the urgency it generates, especially in the later writings. The point can be made by reference to some important passages in Locke's Essay Concerning Human Understanding. (1690). Locke argues that we have no direct access to reality. The human mind comes by 'the materials of reason and knowledge' only from 'experience': that is, by means of 'our observation employed either about external sensible objects, or about the internal operations of our minds perceived and reflected on by ourselves'. The 'understanding is not much unlike a closet wholly shut from light, with only some little opening left, to let in external visible resemblances, or ideas of things without'; the only significant difference is that the mind can remember and order its materials.

One can stress here either the vulnerability of the mind, its proneness to what Locke politely calls 'Wrong Assent', because it depends on the evidence of faculties which it cannot check, or one can stress the mind's efficiency, its ability to construct essays on human understanding, or the laws of motion in the universe. But even in Locke's generally optimistic account, there is enough warrant for the satirist who wants to place man at the wrong end of the telescope. We are in Locke's view the prisoners of the material world, endlessly obtruded on:

> These simple ideas, when offered to the mind, the understanding can no more refuse to have, nor alter when they are imprinted, nor blot them out and make new ones itself, than a mirror can refuse, alter, or obliterate the images or ideas which the objects set before it do therein produce.
>
> (Essay Concerning Human Understanding, p.98)

Understandably, then, the poet concerned to resist 'Wrong Assent' is anxious to control the flood of images into his mind, which once entered can never be removed. The moral incoherence of the behaviour of those around him must be noted instantly, the judgment filed alongside the observation. It becomes the endless task of the mind to edit what is imprinted on it, and to separate what has been wrongly associated — to distinguish between the items cluttered together on Belinda's dressing-table, or the values confused in her mind. Such is the inconstancy in the external world, however, that the poet is obliged to repeat, in couplet after couplet, these acts of discrimination and definition:

Life's stream for Observation will not stay,
It hurries all too fast to mark their way.
In vain sedate reflections we would make,
When half our knowledge we must snatch, not take.
('Epistle to Cobham', ll.31-4)

The couplet can be seen as a 'snatch' at knowledge, a moment's purchase on the world, in which confusion is simultaneously admitted (the content) and mastered (the form). Thus the only unity many of Pope's poems have is the unity of repetition, as moment succeeds to moment, couplet to couplet. The story Pope tells in the 'Epistle to Bathurst', of Sir Balaam's rise and fall, moves at breakneck speed as Balaam loses touch with reality. As his fortune grows, and with it his self-conceit, his life becomes grotesquely mechanical:

A Nymph of quality admires our Knight;
He marries, bows at Court, and grows polite:...
First, for his Son a gay Commission buys,
Who drinks, whores, fights, and in a duel dies;
His daughter flaunts a Viscount's tawdry wife;
She bears a Coronet and P-x for life
('Epistle to Bathurst', ll.385-92)

Increasingly the couplets scramble to keep pace with the life-stories of figures moving with Lilliputian absurdity, and at the last break into fragments:

My Lady falls to play; so bad her chance,
He must repair it; takes a bribe from France;
The House impeach him; Coningsby harangues;
The Court forsake him, and Sir Balaam hangs.
('Epistle to Bathurst', ll.395-8)

The comedy here is of the kind defined by Henri Bergson, of would-be free and autonomous figures surrendering their freedom, like so many marbles dropping down a flight of stairs. Only the couplets, neatly catching the movements, live fully.

The binary pattern described here is central to the strategy of Pope's later writings. It's not of course the whole story; occasionally he will allow a moment of sympathy to cross the dividing line:

> *'Odious! in woollen! 'twould a Saint provoke,*
> *(Were the last words that poor Narcissa spoke)*
> *No, let a charming Chintz, and Brussels lace*
> *Wrap my cold limbs, and shade my lifeless face:*
> *One would not, sure, be frightful when one's dead —*
> *And — Betty — give this Cheek a little Red.'*
> *('Epistle to Cobham', ll.242-7)*

The satire is directed at the faults implicit in Narcissa's name, far from saintly in her protests against the laws introduced to protect home industries by making it illegal to bury the dead in anything other than woollens. But she is still 'poor Narcissa', anxious to warm limbs beginning to feel the chill of death, to shade a face that will never again see the light, and to observe the courtesies of not being 'frightful' even as she prepares for the grave.

The one major poem in which Pope chose to undermine rather than to insist on the binary structure, and which for that reason stands somewhat apart from the rest of his work, is The Rape of the Lock.. The felt difference in tone between the Rape and later poems has been often perceived as simply that: a matter of tone — charm, lightness, vivacity — rather than of structure and poetic strategy. This does less than justice to the subtlety of the poem. The essential purpose of mock- epic, as the name implies, is to point up the contrast between the true epic values celebrated by Homer and Virgil, and the false or at least less admirable codes followed by contemporary society.

Here Pope uses the epic tradition to accuse his society of being unable to distinguish between appearance and reality. That the theft of a lock of hair can be confused with the violation of the heroine's body is only the most obvious sign of a larger confusion between the name and reality of honour, brought to its comic climax in Belinda's cry: 'Oh hadst thou, Cruel! been content to seize / Hairs less in sight, or any hairs but these!' Such lines could only be spoken in a world which can't distinguish — as Pope can, and we must — between the real world and the arena of fashionable play, which is revealed as merely a mock-world, where in the final battle all that happens is that Beaus and Witlings die in metaphor and song.

The bringing together of the epic idiom and social observation provides the immediate humour of the poem, sharpened by Pope's own interest in translating Homer:

But when the Sun the Height of Heaven ascends,
The Sire of Gods his golden Scales suspends,
With equal Hand: in these explored the Fate
Of Greece and Troy, and poised the mighty Weight:
Press'd with its Load, the Grecian Balance lies
Low sunk on Earth, the Trojan strikes the Skies.
(Iliad, VIII, ll.87-92)

Now Jove suspends his golden Scales in Air,
Weighs the Men's Wits against the Lady's Hair;
The doubtful Beam long nods from side to side;
At length the Wits mount up, the Hairs subside.
(Canto V, ll.71-4)

These are the familiar devices of mock-epic, and the triviality of Belinda's world is easily demonstrated. But the comparison of epic and social worlds is made to work in both directions: better the rape of a lock than the abduction of Helen. The text demands to be read lightly, as it were in the mood of the sylphs, as well as severely, in the gnomic mood. Take as an example Pope's version of the Homeric feast:

For lo! the Board with Cups and Spoons is crown'd,
The Berries crackle, and the Mill turns round.
On shining Altars of Japan they raise
The silver Lamp; the fiery Spirits blaze.

From silver Spouts the grateful Liquors glide,
While China's Earth receives the smoking Tyde.

(*Canto III, ll.105-110*)

There is here a fragile sylphic consciousness, which sees in porcelain cups the solidity of 'China's Earth', and toys with the thought that the 'fiery Spirits' may indeed be spirits, since we have already heard of the 'Sprights of fiery Termagants in Flame'. This is played against the severer view, in which the reference to coffee, China and Japan forms part of the poem's continuing critique of the way the world has been plundered and diminished to amuse a belle: 'all Arabia breathes' from a box on Belinda's dressing-table, while the Tortoise and the Elephant — to Hindus an emblem of the world — are reduced to combs, and all the 'glitt'ring Spoil' of the East is laid out to prepare for her toilette.

But the dressing table passage is itself richly multivalent (the obvious contrast is with Swift's accounts of female beauty); Indian glows, Arabia breathes, even the pins assemble into a miniature army, while the Tortoise and Elephant 'unite', caught for a moment in a fantastic act of love, before they are 'Transform'd to Combs, the speckled and the white'. In laying claim to the 'various Off'rings' of the world, Belinda has at the same time enchanted and eroticised them.

Belinda's errors are manifest: her adoration of cosmetic rather than cosmic powers, her indulgence in 'the sacred Rites of Pride', the reverence she bestows on her own 'heav'nly Image' in the mirror. In the mock-epic scheme the episode alludes to the arming of the hero before battle ('Now awful Beauty puts on all its Arms'), which throws the emphasis on the unreality of her actions; she is, precisely, 'making-up' as she 'Repairs her smiles':

Sees by Degrees a purer Blush arise,
And keener Lightnings quicken in her Eyes.
(*Canto I, ll.143-4*)

But the 'purer Blush' — the third blush in this Canto — suggests another level of the poem. Ariel comments on the 'bidden blush' of the young coquette at l.89; his appearance in Belinda's dream, in the guise of 'a Birth-night Beau', has already 'caus'd her Cheek to glow' (ll.24-5). The blush she puts on with rouge is certainly false, and in that sense not pure; but just because it is only painted on, it is 'purer' than the one aroused by her erotic dream. The true blush carries a hint of shame, and the wish not to be observed; the painted one is a non-blush, designed to attract attention, a work of art which Belinda constructs almost dispassionately, 'intent' as she is on the 'heav'nly Image' which 'appears' in her mirror.

It is her task as 'Priestess' to create the beauty who at the beginning of Canto II sallies forth on the Thames in the guise of a 'Goddess', outdoing the sun in glory, and in whose light 'Fair Nymphs, and well-drest Youths around her shone', reflecting back her own radiance. The figure thus created seems invulnerable, like the sun:

Favours to none, to all she Smiles extends,
Oft she rejects, yet never once offends.
Bright as the Sun, her Eyes the Gazers strike,
And, like the Sun, they shine on all alike.

There is brilliancy as well as charm in this portrait; Belinda's eyes 'strike' as well as 'shine', and the rhyme with 'alike' suggests her aloofness. The imagery is developed from the early hint in Canto I that the sun (like the Baron) is both an admirer and a victim of Belinda's beauty:

Sol thro' white Curtains shot a tim'rous Ray,
And op'd those Eyes that must eclipse the Day

The sun's action is an attempt at male mastering (a 'shot') which becomes a defeat, Belinda's a female yielding which is also a victory ('eclipse the day'). But in Canto II the presence of the sylphs undermines the idea of Belinda as Goddess. They float above the barge, 'Their fluid Bodies half dissolv'd in Light', their 'airy Garments' flying 'Loose to the Wind', and alert us to all that is softening in Belinda's experience:

But now secure the painted Vessel glides,
The Sun-beams trembling on the floating Tydes,

While melting Musick steals upon the Sky,
And soften'd sounds along the Waters die.
(Canto II, ll.47-50)

Belinda, who might also be decribed as a 'painted Vessel', is not 'secure' in this world of trembling sun-beams and music with a dying fall. The carefully manufactured Belinda doesn't alienate us, because we see behind the beauty created at the make-up table not just to her pride —which the satirist will naturally want to mock — but also to her vulnerability — which Pope, acting here as something else as well as a satirist, surely invites us to forgive. The disproportion between the goddess and the girl, the gap which opens up between the image and the reality, allows room for our compassion as well as for satirical laughter

That this gaps exists may, of course, simply compound the charge to be made against Belinda. In her parody of the arming of the Homeric warrior she has revealed herself unconscious of the dignity of the epic world; now she shows herself unaware of the world of biological fact which lies beneath the social forms she embraces so willingly. Cleanth Brooks drew attention long ago to the pervasive sexual reference of the poem: Belinda's 'any Hairs but these!', her excitement as she prepares to 'encounter two adventrous Knights' in the game of Ombre (literally, 'man'), her 'livid paleness' as she finds herself 'Just in the Jaws of Ruin, and Codille', and the 'Earthly Lover lurking at her Heart' whose appearance weakens Ariel's power to protect her. Belinda's locks have, after all, been 'Nourish'd' to 'the Destruction of Mankind', they 'conspire' to deck her beauty, and are compared to 'Sprindges' and 'Chains', designed to catch and hold their prey. On this account, she not only falls short of the epic standards which ought to guide her conduct, she also fails to recognise the nature of the sexual imperatives which in fact direct her actions.

To see Belinda as the sexual aggressor as well as the victim might seem to go half- way towards excusing the Baron's theft of the lock: as if an elegant coiffure could be interpreted as contributory negligence. (In British courts in the twentieth century, it probably would...) But the point is worth pursuing. Ariel spells out the life the sylphs are protecting for Belinda:

> *Know farther yet; Whoever fair and chaste*
> *Rejects Mankind, is by some Sylph embrac'd*
>
> *(Canto I, ll.67-8)*

The witty (and utterly unreasonable) rhyme of chaste and embrac'd suggests both what is tempting and what is sterile about the life of a coquette: neither genuinely chaste nor fully sexual, but caught instead in morning dreams about glittering youths which lead on to the erotic play before her own image at the dressing-table. Belinda is about to embark on a life given over to pride and the denial of love, until she is left with nothing to do except to instruct the next generation of coquettes to roll their eyes and blush to order (Canto I, ll.79-90). From this, at least, the Baron interrupts her.

But the Baron's action remains a violation. Belinda's unawareness, while a fault, is also a necessary one. It is one of the paradoxes of sexual flirtation that those involved must both know and not know the rules by which they play. Every move has to be at once a coded message which each partner can understand, and a contentless gesture which commits neither to any further move, or even to the acknowledgment that a move has been made. The Baron's assault makes explicit meanings which Belinda fails to see, and in doing so puts an end to the exploratory value of the game.

This point can be made by reference to Jane Austen, who was like Pope a subtle observer of the due decorums of sexual engagement (though also a more anxious one). Austen shows in Pride and Prejudice how easily the social rules can be disturbed. In Chapter 11 Miss Bingley proposes to Elizabeth Bennett that they should take a turn about the room. Mr Darcy rudely declines to join them: 'you are conscious that your figures show to the greatest advantage in walking... I can admire you so much better as I sit by the fire.' Miss Bingley has played her hand unskilfully; unlike Belinda she knows what she is about, but she has left herself no room for dignified retreat. But while Darcy reads her motives correctly, in exposing them so bluntly he is in danger of denying his society its various means of exploring, or playing with, sexual feeling (he has already announced his objection to cards and to dancing). His contempt for the play of flirtation is as unwise as Miss Bingley's conduct is immodest, and he receives his due punishment when his proposal of marriage to Elizabeth catches her unprepared, and unsym-pathetic. Elizabeth Bennett, meanwhile — this is perhaps the only way in which she resembles Belinda -- has failed to realise that her behaviour will inevitably be interpreted, or misinterpreted, by those around her; her prejudice allows her to believe that she can act simply as a free individual. But we live in societies; and as Maynard Mack has pointed out, eighteenth century society was given to games, and expected its members to handle its codes carefully, and to understand what was at stake if they failed to do so.

What ensues in The Rape of the Lock is the journey to the Cave of Spleen, Belinda's grief, and Clarissa's attempt to restore her to 'good Humour' (Canto V, ll.9-34). Clarissa's speech was added to the poem in 1717, with a note explaining that it was intended 'to open more clearly the MORAL of the poem'. Critical response has perhaps been too trusting of this note. Clarissa's arguments are a parody of Sarpedon's speech to Glaucus in the twelfth book of the Iliad (XII, ll.371-96. Sarpedon requires that 'great acts superior Merit prove', that is, that the wealth and respect he and Glaucus enjoy must be justified by their courage in war.

Clarissa requires that 'good Sense preserve what Beauty gains', that is, that the attention won by beauty must be maintained — not justified — by good humour in social life. She goes on to deploy a number of the key terms in the moral vocabulary of Augustan society — 'good Humour', 'Virtue', 'Merit' — but these too are defined as resources to be used when beauty begins to fade. They are forms of 'pow'r', or ways to 'prevail', and more precious because they are more effective than 'Airs, and Flights, and Screams, and Scolding'. At the centre of Sarpedon's speech is a distinction: since all men must die, it is better then to 'give' one's life bravely in the front line of battle, than to 'pay' the death we 'owe' to nature in a cowardly fashion. Clarissa, however, confounds distinctions; her conclusion, 'Charms strike the Sight, but Merit wins the Soul', means only that Charm is a woman's first line of attack, and Merit her second: all that matters in her account is that the woman who miscalculates her strategies in the marriage game will 'die a Maid'.

If the Baron's real fault is not the damage done to Belinda's coiffure but his blundering treatment of a necessary social and sexual code, Clarissa is hardly less guilty. (Appropriately, she and the Baron are seen to act as allies; it is Clarissa who provides the scissors in Canto III.) Each, like the satirist, draws attention to the way what are presented as ends — the charm of Belinda's toilette, the merit of good humour — are in fact employed as means of sexual pursuit. But what the poem also tells us is that the deception and self-deception this involves are not only allowable, but indispensable. This seems at odds with the idea of satirical writing as a form of attack. The truths betrayed by Clarissa and the Baron, about human sexual motivation, are of course known to the satirist, and the reader is expected to understand them. Yet to reveal these truths is impolite, even disabling. Once you have agreed explicitly that an invitation to 'come up for a cup of coffee' is the first stage in a courtship game, it's difficult either to make or to accept the invitation... ? If the real life Arabella Fermor had read The Rape of the Lock as, say, Cleanth Brooks has read it, she could hardly have sat down again at her dressing-table, still less to a game of Ombre. The poem at once reveals and declines to press home its understanding.

Accordingly, the conclusion is not an exhortation to honesty and right con-duct, but a graceful fiction, with Pope's account of the apotheosis of the lock. The final couplets play with wonderful subtlety on the uses of rhyme:

For, after all the Murders of your Eye,
When, after Millions slain, your self shall die;
When those fair Suns shall sett, as sett they must,
And all those tresses shall be laid in Dust;

This Lock, the Muse shall consecrate to Fame,
And 'midst the Stars inscribe Belinda's Name!

(Canto V, ll.145-50)

Pope moves daringly from flattery to realism, from mock-deaths to real death; no rhyme could be more reasonable, more certain, than that of must and Dust. Measured against that inevitablity, the rhyme of Fame and Name seems to hollow out the substance of both words, reminding us that identity and reputation are both but a breath. But these rhymes also include the poet, who too must die, and who too must hope that his name will survive through the fame of the poem. Wiser than those he writes about, the satirist shares their mortality, and here, at least, is content to join the world he has exposed.

Q.2. What is Pope's Ideology of Violation in the Rape of the Lock.

Or

Q. How does Pope include the reader to the rhetoric of misogyny.

Or

Q. Dscuss the position of women as discussed in the Rape of The Lock.

Pope's "The Rape of the Lock" creates a dilemma for readers and critics alike. While it is an enduring work of art, encompassing mastery of the heroic couplet with humour and insight, it nonetheless inscribes an ideology of violation. Pope's masterpiece, while on one level sympathetic toward the lack of women's opportunities in a patriarchal society, on the other, perpetuates the commodification of women and, in doing so, violates the reader as well, by including the reader as an implied accomplice to the rhetoric of misogyny.

"The Rape of the Lock" has traditionally been read as a mock heroic criticism of the superficiality inherent within Pope's culture of the time. Pope is intent upon exposing the absurdity of the often superficial context of Augustan era lives. He is aware of the culturally limited parameters placed around women and is, in one sense, sympathetic. He is aware that "she who scorns a Man, must die a Maid" (v.28). Indeed, men are not treated especially well in the poem: the Baron is most surely "barren" and Sir Plume is an idiot. Yet, women in the text seem to remain the object of both ridicule and criticism. Readers continue to think of Belinda in terms of suffering from a type of "fall"; Donald B. Clark argues that Belinda "cannot transcend her own prudishness," and as a result, "she 'falls'"

Further, as Kate Beaird Meyers relates, "when the 'hero' 'rapes' the lock of the egotistical Belinda, he figuratively exposes-castrates an already emasculated ("effeminate") social group. Belinda is the butt of the joke". If both men and women are "guilty" and worthy of criticism, and if Pope is conscious of woman's limited opportunity within the dominant power structure, why does both Pope write Belinda into the text as the butt of a joke and the reader often find so much humour in Belinda's situation?

Even though initially Pope attempts to approach Belinda sympathetically, he trivializes and mocks her and thus, implicitly, all women. Laura Brown shows that Pope trivializes Belinda "throughout the ironic juxtaposition of her [insignificant] story with classical epic". Further, the heroic material of the epic style Pope emulates also trivializes Belinda. "Her trivial, commodified and amoral world is castrated," as Brown notes, "with grandeur of epic, a world of gods and goddesses, of heroes larger than life, where history is made and great nations find their identity".

Pope's patronizing tone is evident even before the "official" poem begins in his letter to Arabella Fermor. Pope "apologizes" to her before the text of the poem begins by stating that the poem "was intended only to divert a few young Ladies, who have good Sense and good Humour enough, to laugh not only at their Sex's little unguarded Follies, but at their own". Pope's misogynistic "apology" subverts his stated intention. As Meyers illustrates, "the choice of 'divert' is perfect: Pope hopes to divert attention away from his act of misogynous judgement and focus it on what he calls the 'folly' of female nature".

Women are, for Pope, laughable creatures in need of appraisal as to their faults. Women are thus both object and subject of ridicule and are even extended the invitation of joining in and enjoying the humour at their own expense.

Pope also views women, as later exemplified in his portrayal of Belinda, as trivial and ignorant beings: "For the ancient Poets are in one respect like many modern Ladies; Let an Action be never so trivial in it self, they always make it appear of the utmost Importance". Pope goes on to explain that he is aware that women are not capable of understanding difficult language, so he will "explain two or three difficult Terms" (217). Pope, however, is overtly "ridiculing women for a lack [of knowledge] created by the patriarchal society he represents and inviting all his readers to join in his misogyny". Moreover, the poem is intended for John Caryll and the educated men who will comprise his audience and, as Meyers explains, "Pope's humour illustrates the fact that women did not know the esoteric terminology of epic machinery because they were denied the opportunity to learn it".

As a result of Pope's false premises, his qualitative preface rings untrue. Furthermore, as Meyers (in discussing Susan Schibanoff's contentions concerning the subject) relates, the "letter actually makes the poem more offensive":

Authorial apologies to the female reader for anti-feminist texts are... something other than heart-felt laments. They are attempts both to intimidate her and... to immasculate her.

They warn her that the written traditions of antifeminism have contemporary custodians who will not allow these texts to disappear.

Pope employs terminology throughout the poem which heightens the view of women as commodified object, necessarily reliant upon and subject to men. While men are "Peers," women are often either "coquettes" or "Prudes." Women suffer from "faults" and "fem ale errors." Women are "degraded," men "The Victor." Men have "Wits" which are measured against "the Lady's Hair," but as women's brains are "vacant," there is little surprise that the "Wits mount up, the Hairs subside". Pope's rhetoric is a discourse of violation in which women become the signified and the reader remains outside of the text, yet serves as privileged insider to the ideology of the patriarchal cultural elite. Pope's Everywoman, Belinda, is, as Ellen Pollak articulates, "an empty vessel laden down with a cargo of disembodied object" and the reader is invited to join in Pope's criticism of her materialistic superficiality.

Admittedly, Pope is critical of more than just Belinda, but as Pollak explains, though Pope criticizes the sterility of a world in which the signs of things have actually become substitutes for the things themselves, where virtue has been reduced to reputation and men themselves to swordknots, where in effect people live in a materialistic and metonymic void, he never does controvert the premise that female sexuality is a material property over which man has a natural claim.

Female sexuality is equated with commodities in "The Rape of the Lock," and Belinda's dressing scene in the first canto serves as evidence. Women are valued for their beauty, yet must resort, as Belinda does, to a type of external self-construction in order to attain peak performance. With the help of "Cosmetic Pow'rs," "a heav'nly Image...appears" (i.124-5). Belinda appropriates the "various Off'rings of the world" (i.130), and as "awful Beauty puts on all it Arms" (i.139) with the aid of combs, pins, "Puffs, Powders, Patches, Bibles, Billet-doux," (i.138) "the Fair each moment rises in her Charmes" (i.140). Pope convincingly makes the point that Belinda, at least in the eyes of men, is not "naturally" beautiful. This scene in the poem bears striking similarity to Swift's "The Lady's Dressing Room," in its cataloguing and its cosmetic emphasis. Like Celia, Belinda is now a type of elaborately contrived monster. As Laura Claridge relates, "Belinda, as an object embodying Pope's fears of woman, enacts the position of woman as potential monster, a 'power less transcendent of nature than her male counterpart' and therefore more treacherous in her artifice". The result of this passage is that, as Brown contends.

> Belinda's beauty can only be seen through the commodities that she wears.... The poem identifies her in terms of products of mercantilist expansion; and it begins to develop a rhetoric of the commodity through which she and her culture can be described – a language of commodity fetishism where objects become the only reality.

Belinda's "Labours" result in a "purer Blush," (i.143) yet this natural blush is tenuous at best, as it is simply a cosmetic aid to enhance her "natural" blush. However, for Pope, even this false blush signals danger. "Belinda's art," as Claridge assert s, "is so dangerous that her artfully constructed face can cause us to 'forget' 'Female Errors' (ii.17,18); in fact, this face conduces to the 'Destruction of Mankind' (ii.19). She is a trap". This is why, as Meyers shows,

> Pope must stress such points as the artificiality of Belinda's "purer" blushes, created by rouge, not by Nature (i.143). It is crucial that woman be separated from Nature — kept in her place, threatened with ostracism, convinced of her ignorance, denied knowledge of her strength beyond cultural forms.

Belinda, as a commodity herself solely because of her gender, heightens the inscription of her own marginalization unknowingly. By taking on, literally, the characteristics of mercantile imperialism which she then hides behind, by painting herself into a socially prescribed and acceptable text, she implicitly endorses commodity fetishism and the inscription of the marginalization of women and becomes, both literally and symbolically, a walking commodity. Thus, "woman's display of beauty" through Belinda, as Pollak explains, can be identified with man's display of booty.... While according to rational analysis Pope's coquette is "masculinized" female, by symbolic accretion she is a complex manifestation of male prowess itself — its inspiration, its conquered object, its result.

Pope further encodes an ideology of violation through the device of the Sylphs. While critics such as Elizabeth Gurr argue that "the function of the sylphs is to define the bounds of acceptable behaviour", the fact remains that the Sylphs are the spirits of dead coquettes and, as such, are pale mirror images (and ineffectual at that) of women. The Sylphs rally to Belinda's aid, guard and watch over her, and attempt to ensure that she will stay within the acceptable parameters of chastity. Yet the Sylphs are textual non-entities. They are mere wisps of what women "should be"; as soon as Belinda recognizes (consciously or no) alleged sexual longing, the Sylphs are forced to retire.

The Sylphs' very inability to resist perpetuates Pope's literature of violation. Those women who behave "coquettishly" will maintain ghost-like lives of deprivation, unable to achieve anything. The reader, again, is entrusted with Pope's dark moral and implicitly encouraged to agree and condone. Pope, as Meyers contends, pushes an agenda of "'the cult of passive womanhood'":

> His linking of Belinda to the Sylphs can be read as a warning to all women that they will only enjoy the protection of male society as long as they co-operate in the "inviolable preservation" of their chastity. The woman who strays loses the protection of the same society that led her astray in the first place.

The final irony, however, surrounding the Sylphs is, as C.E. Nicholson maintains, that they "cannot protect Belinda herself. The elaborate fiction of their particularized domain collapses when she succumbs, 'in spite of her Art,' to the natural occurrence of sexual desire". Finally, as Claridge submits, the Sylphs "remind us of the ways in which women function as transparent signifiers who transport meaning for others: they wait upon meaning, whether to be filled with child or penis or pen". Pope's use of the Sylphs as a textual device, then, furthers the patronizing "moral" he alludes to throughout the text and, in the process, further marginalizes women. Pope's reliance upon the reader, moreover, to share in his discourse assumes:

1. The reader is male and therefore intelligent enough to appreciate the dynamics of gender-based power structures,

2. The reader is female and in need of his moral," or 3) the reader is a sympathizer, regardless of gender.

Pope's willingness to participate in and endorse the commodifcation of women, and his desire to include the reader in his "joke," is further illuminated in the final two cantos. After Belinda has been "raped," we are exposed to the Cave of Spleen episode. We see surreal Freudian examples of quite possibly Belinda (and perhaps all women) in the state of "degraded Toast" (iv.109). In a scene reminiscent of William Burroughs,

Unnumber'd Throngs on ev'ry side are seen
Of Bodies chang'd to various Forms by Spleen.
Here living Teapots stand, one Arm held out,
One bent; the Handle this, and that the Spout:
Pipkin there like Homer's Tripod walks;
Here prove with Child, as pow'rful Fancy works,
and maids turn'd Bottels, call aloud for Corks.

(iv.47-54)

Women are receptacles, waiting to be filled by male corks. While both genders are assigned commodity status, it is the woman who is reliant upon others (men): corks provide closure; bottles (as vessels) require the aid of corks in order to be (ful)filled and marketable.

Pope's exploration of Belinda's psycho-sexual longings seems suspicious. The implication that Belinda is a waiting vessel, anticipating the Baron's immanent (sexual) arrival is disturbing. Belinda is the victim of a rape, however symbolic it may appear: she is the violated. Yet, Pope very patronizingly dwells on the sexuality which is overrunning HER. Pope's hintings at Belinda's unconscious desire of sexual fulfillment, presumably at the baron's hands, strikes one as perhaps too closely resembling the rhetoric of the "Blame the Victim" syndrome (my term): the idea that the Baron should be exonerated because Belinda must have wanted it. Yet, Belinda is the one violated by a man incapable of controlling excess emotion.

Pope's use of the word, "steel," helps further the idea of blaming Belinda. Pope quite clearly states at the end of canto iii that Belinda has been shorn by "unresisted Steel" (178; emphasis added). The steel is unresisted because, as Claridge illustrat es, "the hair offers no resistance.... But, more problematic, the steel may be 'unresisted' because the hair wants to be cut". Moreover, "while Pope uses this implication to seduce Belinda-Arabella into assuming her proper social role as wife and commodity," a larger issue is at stake:

> This is the attempted theft of femaleness, a power that far exceeds the literal state of the hymen.... Paradoxically, we could even suggest that, rather than stealing Belinda's virginity, the Baron seeks her fertility — to castrate her into being a virgin.

Pope's insistence that Belinda "wanted it" might be further clarified in her astonishing statement: "Oh hadst thou, Cruel! been content to seize/Hairs less in sight, or any Hairs but these!" (iv.175-6). The fact that she publicly acknowledges the Baron's rape of her virginity as a viable option, indeed preference, seems to indicate Pope's thoughts on the subject. Yet, even though Pope seems to implicate Belinda as an active participant in the rape, the dynamics of her thought process might be more complex than Pope realises. Belinda, whose locks give her a great deal of power in their phallic symbolism, is, as Myers explains, "figuratively castrated," and in the process, "the 'hero' regains control of his society". Belinda has been taught her lesson (by Pope?) and is not actually willing to give up her virginity in order to regain her power.

As Belinda as a character is meant to be ridiculed, Pope offers both Belinda and the reader a model of the "appropriate" form of woman in the character of Clarissa. Clarissa tells Belinda that "she who scorns a Man, must die a Maid," (v.28) and advocates "good Humour" and, implicitly, marriage, since "frail Beauty must decay" (v.25). Clarissa's "pragmatic" solution to Belinda's image/identity/sexual "problems" serves to perpetuate Pope's view of the cultural status quo.

Clarissa's speech advocates the sublimation of feminine consciousness as a pragmatic method of survival. As Howard D. Weinbrot writes, Clarissa's speech, then, is the moral centre of The Rape of the Lock. It rejects spleen, girlhood, hostility, isolation, powerlessness, inutility, folly and frustration in favour of good humour, womanliness, affection, community, power, use and virtue.

Weinbrot's comments comprise the very point Pope wants us to think: marriage and rote mindless acceptance will result in "true" womanliness, use and virtue!

The logical problem with Clarissa, as Claridge points out, is the question: "is she a mouthpiece of the author's, conveying the moral message, or a prude, or a jealous would-be object of the Baron's affection?". More importantly, Clarissa is [actually] a man, in gender, of course, not in sex .... [She] reads as a male in this text because she is too simple, in the world and context which Pope creates, to be female.... Thus marriage, which is what Clarissa really urges ... allows for the kind of control and heroic closure to chaotic desire that Belinda... represent[s]: marriage defines a hero's endeavors by conferring meaning upon the chaos of sexual energy.

As Pollak notes, then, for "Belinda, the passage from girlhood to womanhood – from the simply 'female' to the truly 'feminine'— must involve not merely a giving up of sexual independence, but all other forms of independence as well".

The poem's ending, in which the lock rises into the air, reminds us of Pope's moral. In the end, the woman is unable to regain/retain the power available to her and she remains the butt of the joke. Within the paradigms of gender consciousness, she is seen as a clownish object, cosmetically enhanced, reeking of commodification. As Meyers relates, intended to remind women of Belinda's heavenly reprimand,the astro-lock becomes... a symbol of the lengths to which the guardians of a phallocentric culture will go to retain control.

.... [Finally] the uppity woman is put in her place; the status quo is restored.

Pope attempts to placate both Belinda and women in general by telling Belinda that he will write her into textual immortality. However, as Claridge shows, he simply "reappropriates generative power through his anxious claim to superiority over the female.... He will contain the female by inscribing her".

Pope's inscription of women through the vehicle of his poem inscribes the reader as well, through an ideology of non-attainment and containment. Pope's discourse maintains a privileged agenda; we are exposed to the rhetoric Pope values. Pope's objectification exposes within us a type of awareness deprivation in which we are forced to acknowledge gaps in the text; we ourselves are held hostage to Pope's implicit ideology of violation.

Pope, in utilizing the mock-heroic as a device, further displays the dialectics of commodity fetishism. Pope mirrors imperialist mercantilism in stealing (styles, phrases, archetypes, et cetera) from his predecessors, requisitioning their materials and taking them for his own. This act further perpetuates commodity fetishism and violates the reader in the process by making the reader an implied accomplice. In the very act of reading, the reader acts as a symbolic receiver of appropriated property and t akes on the mantle of victim.

Finally, The Rape of the Lock can be read as a Reader Response text which perpetuates an ideology of violation. Pope seeks to stimulate the reader's task by offering a variance of signified and signifiers and asking the reader to respond. Pope's sympathy toward female plight is likely well meant; nonetheless, the fact remains that both Belinda and the reader are well aware that Belinda has three options: she can die a Maid, become a degraded Toast, or get married. Belinda, the object of Pope'e encoded patriarchy, remains essentially option-less and the subject of patronizing humour.

Pope's poem is, whatever literary qualities it may possess, an argument for and product of a patriarchal commodified polemic which rapes both Belinda and the reader in its defence of traditionally male values.

Q.3. Discuss Pope's portrayal of Belinda and her societyin *The Rape of the Lock*

Or

Q. Discuss 'beau-monde'in The Rape of The Lock

Or

Q. Analyse Pope's satirical attack on the faishonable society

In 'The Rape of the Lock' Alexander Pope (1688-1744) employs a mock-epic style to satirise the 'beau-monde' (fashionable world, society of the elite) of eighteenth century England. The richness of the poem, however, reveals more than a straightforward satirical attack. Alongside the criticism we can detect Pope's fascination with, and perhaps admiration for, Belinda and the society in which she moves. Pope himself was not part of the 'beau-monde'. He knew the families on which the poem is based but his own parents, though probably comfortably off, were not so rich or of the class one would have to be in to move in Belinda's circle. He associated with learned men and poets, and there can have been little common ground between the company he kept at Will's Coffee House and those who frequented Hampton Court.

The incident at the centre of the poem is the Baron's theft of a lock of hair and the ensuing estrangement of two families. The opening lines of the poem introduce the reader to the satirical stance he is taking towards the society portrayed in the poem.

What dire Offence from am'rous Causes springs,
What mighty Contests rise from trivial Things, [I.1-2]

Pope suggests that they are taking a trivial incident too seriously, displaying an exaggerated sense of their own importance. Throughout the poem Pope continues to make this point through his use of the mock-epic style, which itself takes a trivial incident too seriously, and uses disproportionately grand language to describe an unworthy subject.

Belinda is belittled early in the poem by the revelation of Ariel [l.27-114], who tells her that part of her will survive after her death.

Think not, when Woman's transient Breath is fled,
That all her Vanities at once are dead:
Succeeding Vanities she still regards,
And tho' she plays no more, o'erloks the Cards.
Her Joy in gilded Chariots, when alive,
And Love of Ombre, after Death survive.
For when the Fair in all their Pride expire,
To their first Elements their Souls retire: [l.51-9]

We might expect this part, the deepest and most essential part of her being, the 'first Elements', to be her soul, but in Belinda's case it is her 'Vanities', her 'Joy in gilded Chariots' and her 'Love of *Ombre*', suggesting that her soul consists of nothing more that vanity and a love of pleasure.

Belinda's vanity is seem to take the form of religious devotion in the passage describing her morning toilette.

And now, unveil'd, the Toilet stands display'd,
Each Silver Vase in mystic Order laid.
First, rob'd in White, the Nymph intent adores
With Head uncover'd, the Cosmetic Pow'rs.
A heav'nly Image in the Glass appears,
To that she bends, to that her Eyes she rears; [l.121-6]

The ironic transposition of 'cosmic powers' in '*Cosmetic* Pow'rs' indicates the excessive value she attributes to her make-up, and bowing to her own image shows her devotion to her religion of narcissism. The passage is a mock version of the arming of the epic hero, her weaponry of cosmetics being ridiculed by the implicit comparison with the swords and shields of the epic hero. The passage includes a mock catalogue.

Here Files of Pins extend their shining Rows,
Puffs, Powders, Patches, Bibles, Billet-doux. [l.137-8]

This catalogue, echoing the catalogue of troops and weaponry found in epics, is one of the many indications of the jumbled values to be found in Belinda's society. The Bible is seen as a trinket for the adornment of her dressing table, along with the puffs and powders.

The main force of this passage is satire, but alongside the satire Pope reveals a hint of fascination with the charm and delicacy of Belinda and her cosmetic devotion.

From each she nicely culls with curious Toil,
And decks the Goddess with the glitt'ring Spoil,
This Casket India's glowing Gems unlocks,
And all Arabia breathes from yonder Box. [l.131-4]

The rich imaginative vision in a passage such as this shows more than a desire to deprecate; it suggests that he too is at least partly fascinated by glitter. Pope appreciates the cosmetics in terms of the wider context of their origins and purpose, which Belinda could not do, and his tone reveals an attitude of amused, detached, fascination rather than straightforward disapproval.

In the second Canto Pope turns his mocking attention to the Baron. Pope's ridicule of the Baron is more severe, and the hint of admiration detected in his treatment of Belinda is absent. In *The Aeneid* when Aeneas builds an altar Virgil is reminding us of his piety; his humility before divine powers.

The Baron's worship is presented in terms of ridiculous excess. His altar is made from the profane escapist literature of romance, and his trophies, 'three Garters, half a Pair of Gloves' [ll.39] are ridiculous in comparison with the booty collected by conquering armies.

There is a parallel between the passages describing Belinda's toilette and the Baron's worship, each revealing the idealised image he/she holds of him/her self - Belinda as a goddess and the Baron as a hero - and it is through the absurdity of these ideals taken to extremes that Pope deflates them. Pope mocks the Baron not only as a poor parody of an epic hero but also for adopting an affected stance as a traditional courtly lover.

With tender Billet-doux he lights the Pyre,
And breathes three am'rous Sighs to raise the Fire,
Then prostrate falls, and begs with ardent Eyes
Soon to obtain, and long possess the Prize: [ll.41-4]

Pope is showing us a profane world in which a man worships the woman, and the woman worships herself.

The ridicule achieved by the comparison between the struggle between Belinda and the Baron and an epic battle reaches its peak in the battles of Cantos 3 and 5. In Canto 3 the glory and excitement of epic warfare is evoked, but the warriors are mere cards in a game of ombre. In Canto 5 the belle and the Baron tussle with the weapons of a snuff box and a bodkin, and Pope evokes scenes of farce and slapstick.

A Charge of Snuff the wily Virgin threw;
The Gnomes direct, to ev'ry Atome just,
The pungent Grains of titillating Dust.
Sudden, with starting Tears each Eye o'erflows,
And the high Dome re-echoes to his Nose.
Now meet thy Fate incens'd Belinda cry'd,
And drew a deadly Bodkin from her Side. [V.82-8]

In this dramatic scene we see supposedly civilised and sophisticated people behaving like squabbling children, and the violent emotions which can lurk under the dignified surface of the 'beau-monde' are revealed. One of the effects of the whole poem is to show that the glitter and refinement of this world can be a veneer to cover the basest human motives.

Pope also shows us, in a mock version of the heroic underworld, the human casualties of the 'beau-monde'.

There Affectation with a sickly Mien
Shows in her Cheek the Roses of Eighteen,

Practis'd to Lisp, and hang the Head aside,
Faints into Airs, and languishes with Pride; [IV.31-4]

This is harsh criticism, but since we see these people in a context of suffering the response Pope demands seems to include as much pity as laughter. Although condemning the 'beau-monde' for its triviality and lack of proper moral values, Pope is sensitive to the plight of the human beings caught up in its 'rat-race'.

Behind the ridicule which Pope achieves through his satire, we detect a depth of understanding in his attitude towards Belinda's predicament. Belinda's honour is very important for her future, even if in a broader context her idea of 'honour' is seen to mean little more than 'reputation'. Belinda has to steer a difficult path on which she has to attract prospective husbands yet not get a reputation as a coquette. The words of Thalestris represent a very real danger if she should veer too far on one direction.

Methinks already I your Tears survey,
Already hear the horrid things they say,
Already see you a degraded Toast,
And all your Honour in a Whisper lost! [IV.107-10]

The words of Clarissa show the danger of the other extreme:

Since painted, or not painted, all shall fade,
And she who scorns a Man, must die a Maid; [V.27-8]

This understanding and sympathy renders the poem more likely to be accepted by Mrs Arabella Fermor, to whom it is addressed, and more likely to achieve its intended aim of reconciling the Fermor and Petre families.

Behind the comparisons between the epic world and the 'beau-monde' Pope also looks at the contrast between the ideals and the reality of the 'beau-monde' itself. The opening lines of the second paragraph introduce this theme:

Say what strange Motive, Goddess! cou'd compel
A well-bred Lord t'assault a gentle Belle?
Oh say what stranger Cause, yet unexplor'd,
Cou'd make a gentle Belle reject a Lord? [I.7-10]

The 'motives' and 'causes' are as basic as human motives and causes anywhere. Sexual passion, for example, would hardly be openly admitted in polite society, yet it always lurks just below the surface. One example of this is in the title of the poem, for the act of cutting off a lock of hair can be seen, even if only as a joke, as sublimated rape. Sexuality is also implicit in this couplet:

On her white Breast a sparkling Cross she wore,
Which Jews might kiss, and Infidels adore. [ll.7-8]

Here we have an obvious double meaning which not only exposes the trivialising of a Christian symbol but also reveals the underlying purpose of Belinda's meticulous attention to her appearance. The Sylphs, the guardian spirits of 'beau-monde' belles, are well aware of the possible outcome of sophisticated pleasantries with lords:

To Fifty chosen Sylphs, of special Note,
We trust th'important Charge, the Petticoat:
Oft have we known that sev'nfold Fence to fail,

Tho' stiff with Hoops, and arm'd with Ribs of Whale. [ll.117-20]

If we look for an explicit moral message in the poem we must look to Clarissa's speech [V.7-34], which Pope included specifically for that purpose. This is the most sobre passage in the poem and it embodies Pope's message to the 'beau-monde', and in particular to the Fermor and Petre families. It is a plea for maturity and good sense, for virtue and care of the soul; all the things which the satire has shown to be lacking. By asking them to see their lives in a wider context he hopes to persuade them to adopt a more rational sense of proportion. By laughing at the mock-epic style they will have to admit that they are laughing at themselves, and Pope hopes this will inculcate a spirit of good humour and reconciliation.

Although not himself of the 'beau-monde' Pope was part of the same era. The finesse and delicacy of 'beau-monde' manners is matched by Pope's style, and the good humour, wit, and charm which characterises Pope's manner must represent an expression of the same ideals pursued by the Baron and other courtly men of the age. An affinity between them is revealed by Pope's empathy, fine judgements, and carefully aimed criticisms, and Pope must have been at least a little fascinated by the 'beau-monde' to apply his talents to this poem which, in an ironic way, celebrates Belinda and her world and, as Pope himself suggests in the final couplet of the poem, has preserved them for posterity.

This Lock, the Muse shall consecrate to Fame,

And mid'st the Stars inscribe *Belinda's* Name! [V.149-50]

Q.4. Discuss Mock Epic elements and HorationInfluence in The Rape of theLock

Or

Q. Discuss Epic conventions and Horace's satire in the Rape of the Lock

Clearly, Pope demonstrates two quite separate influences in *The Rape of the Lock*: mock epic and Horation satire. But since these two are quite antipodal—at least in terms of style and conventions—we shall examine not only instances of their presence, but the manner in which they are combined.

Just as history provides the most suitable material for the epic poem, Pope's use of a *contemporary* history—necessarily of lesser import—is equally befitting the mock epic. Accordingly, rather than depicting kings or majestic men and their distinguished deeds, intending to provoke our admiration, with perfect irony, Pope takes for his mock epic a vain female as hero, displaying her lowly trials and provoking our scorn. Here then we find our first common element, for Horace also is concerned with contemporary issues, though he certainly chooses an entirely different form for its exposition. Indeed, When Trebatius warns him away from satire, suggesting, "... if such great love of writing grips you, think big;/sing about unbeaten Caesar's deeds, and be rewarded," which certainly smacks of contemporary epic, Horace politely declines: "I'm insufficient; we all can't write of battle lines." Another instance in which *The Rape of the Lock* makes use of epic convention and differs from Horace's Satires, is the introductory invocation of the Muse. Though this has no parallel in the Satires,

Horace does begin the first epistle, in Book I of Epistles with: "My very first Muse sang of you." It's inclusion, by Pope, is not only necessitated by the mock epic form, but also by the ending of the work: Belinda wins immortality by means of the poem itself—muse related—as well as by the lock rising to form a new heavenly body: "But trust the Muse—she saw it upward rise,/Tho' mark'd by none but quick Poetic Eyes," which is essentially saying the same thing: her immortality is owing to poetry.

Even Horace himself acknowledges, also in the Epistles: "It is the Muse who gives immortality."

Pope also uses the initial reference to the Muse to establish the presence of the supernatural, though instead of the classical gods providing the machinery, inciting to battle and protecting the mortal hero—as would be the case in epic convention—we find the Sylphs of Rosicrucian Philosophy. The Sylphs, of course, proved a perfect choice, for not only do the lack the reverence of classical gods, thus proving more suitable protectorates of our unworthy hero, but they also brought with them a literary connection with erotica, particularly in *Le Comte de* The foulness of language, in *Book I Satire* is in no way indicative of Horace's other satires, but it does, nevertheless, demonstrate by exaggeration—just as Book II teaches by exaggeration—that the language of Horace is the language of the street: "... my things are more like conversation," as well as "... talk is all it is." This is Horace himself speaking, in *Book I*, of his own work. In the final Satire of that book, written at a later date, this idea had been slightly modified:

The work must be concise...

The language should be grave at times, but often funny, sometimes rhetorical and poetic, sometimes urbanely smooth.

Here we see something slightly more reminiscent of *The Rape of the Lock*, but nevertheless, the style of language found in Horace's *Satires*—even in the most poetic instance, is far below that of Pope's mock epic.

Comedy and the latter Greek Epic. If there is no similarity in diction, the low, mundane content described by that diction, in *The Rape of the Lock*, is certainly reminiscent of Horace.

We might now turn to Belinda. We have already said that she is a character whose heroic propensities are a belittlement of the epic hero, and thus ideal for the mock epic, but now we shall examine her thematic importance.

"Still, false desires fool a large proportion of mankind,/ they'll tell you, 'Nothing's enough. What we own we are.'" Although here Horace refers to money, it seems wholly appropriate to see this as applicable to Belinda, for her lock represents not only her vanity, but the vanity of women, and so "what we own we are" clearly explains the importance of the theft. And yet, since that importance is but shallowness, the reader is witness to the irony of the affair. Likewise, those guilty of the numerous foibles exposed by Horace are often ignorant not only of their guilt but of the foibles themselves. It is this *exposure* which is key to Horace's method, and which we find also in *The Rape of the Lock.*

Certainly, Belinda—and the general woman she represents—is as much ignorant of her own guilt as of the crime itself.

Indeed, the stand Pope seems to be taking is one which can be seen all through both books of Horace's *Satires,* namely that happiness comes not from external but internal sources—and only then when the doctrine of *moderation* is present: "Eating's highest pleasure lies in you,/not in the flavour of your food." In fact, the "simple life," (moderation in all things) take on great thematic importance for it unifies all eight satires of *Book II.* And it is Belinda vanity, her concern with the pleasures of the external world which ties, thematically, *The Rape of the Lock* with the *Satires* of Horace.

Another connection which Belinda brings to mind between *The Rape of the Lock* and the *Satires* is the idea that bad example teaches. This is essential to both Pope and Horace.

Because of the implicit nature of the lesson in *The Rape of the Lock,* the poem itself must stand as testament to the above maxim. Horace though, in typical conversational and autobiographical clarity, declares:

... if perhaps I laugh too much at people, grant me my right and your indulgence. The best of father's made me this way.

By the use of bad examples he taught me how to live.

We should also bear in mind that Belinda is young, and that Pope, in the introductory letter to Mrs. Arabella Fermor—the real life Belinda—says of his poem:... it was intended only to divert a few young ladies, who have good sense and good humour enough to laugh not only at their sex's unguarded follies, but at their own.

Certainly, Pope is being extremely diplomatic here, for if the young ladies had good sense, then the source of *The Rape of the Lock* would never have existed. The point though is that Pope speaks of "*young* ladies,". This satire not only targets the young as its subject, but also the young as its audience, who should learn from the work. This too is reminiscent of Horace: "if someone now decreed the tastiness of roasted gull,/Rome's youth, docile students of debauchery, would obey."

Here Horace not only depicts the young as being impressionable, but logically, because of that impressionability, they are in most need of moral lesson; and Horation satire—with its aim not so much to attack vice but to present vice and thus the lesson, as well as the absence of causticity—is the perfect vehicle for that lesson, as well as for that group of people.

As we have seen, even though style and conventions separate mock epic from Horace's satires, Pope has managed, in *The Rape of the Lock,* to fuse the two. From epic we have high language, supernatural machinery, battle and war, the journey to the underworld and all the rest, transported down to the level of mock epic and becoming, there, high language-low content, Sylphs, drawing room wars of the sexes and a battle of frowns, snuff and a bodkin, and a journey to the Cave of Spleen.

From Horace we have the exposing of folly not with malice or anger, but with an authorial smile: "But tell me, what law is violated if someone laughs/while speaking truth?" Secondly, though *Book I* of *Satires* is almost obtuse in it directness, *Book II*, representing a more artistically mature Horace—and so best exemplifying his style, demonstrates a more indirect and more comic method of teaching. This is achieved by exaggerating the moral instruction, and by using comic sometimes absurd characters to voice those lessons.

We might conclude, at risk of oversimplification, that *The Rape of the Lock* is composed of mock epic *elements* and *style* and the Horatian *attitude.*

Q.5. Discuss The Moral of the Rape of the Lock

Or

Q. Analyse the importance of moral in an epic with reference to the Rape of the Lock

Or

Q. Critically analyse Clarissa's speech

The Rape Of The Lock is a page torn from petty, pleasure-seeking life of a fashionable beauty. Some of Pope's contemporaries, like John Dennis found The Rape Of The Lock immoral and distasteful. According to them it lacked true wit and judgement. Dennis's remarks on Mr. Pope's Rape Of The Lock(1728) severely criticizes the poem for deviating from the rules of the Epics. His charge was that Pope dealt in trifles, without morals in his mock Epic. However, most critics feel that Clarissa's speech at the opening of Canto V sets the moral tone. As Warburton put it, Pope introduced Clarissa's speech " to open more clearly more clearly the moral of the poem". Pope knew that a moral was thought as an important aspect in an Epic. From the very beginning, The Rape Of The Lock has moral motive, though it remains hidden for some time. His aim was to teach the lesson of "Concord" and good humour between two quarrelling families. But Satire in Pope is so finely chiseled by wit, that it is rarefied into pure humour. Thus, in such a scheme of poetry there is not much scope for serious moral lessons. Even the moral lesson that is there in Clarissa's speech is one more facet of Pope's consummate wit and humour. Even so what can we call these lines of Clarissa but setting a strict moral standard for the 18th century ladies:

"But since, alas frail beauty must decay,
Curled or uncurled, since locks will turn to grey;
Since painted, or not painted, all shall fade,
And she who scorns a man, must die a maid:
What then remains but our power to use,
And keep good humour still, whatever we lose?" (Ll. 669-674)

It would not be wrong then to say that Pope did have a moral preoccupation, even if it is covered in a veneer of wit and humour.

Satirical tone implies moral tone:

A true satire is purposive and instructive. In fact, the real end of satire is 'the amendment of vices by correction'. The Rape Of The Lock is a perfect specimen of satiric literature, and its moral tone is quite patent. Here comes the element of the criticism of life in Pope's mock-Heroic satire. The Rape Of The Lock contains a good deal of the poet's critical evaluation of the English social life of the eighteenth century. Pope's subject of study here is the showy, artificial and frivolous life of the aristocratic, fashionable society of his own time. He ruthlessly exposes here the gay and thoughtless belles and the idle and vain beaux of the time. He misses no chance to hit hard at all that characterizes that shallow, artificial age — its affectation and vanity, its coquetry and frivolity, its gay foppery and spineless morality.

A particular incident in the battle scene of canto V shows Pope's mastery in reducing to size the pompous men and women of his age. It is the scene where Belinda vanquishes the Baron with a pinch of snuff:

"Just where the breath of life his nostrils drew,
A charge of snuff the wily virgin threw" (LI. 725-726)
"Sudden, with starting tears each eye O'erflows,
And the high dome re-echoes to his nose". (LI. 729-730)

What a sorry figure the Baron cuts! And what scandalous behaviour on the part of an aristocratic lady! In one stroke Pope has demolished the pompousness of his vainglorious characters.

Pope's moralizing tone on Belinda's toilet and the Baron:

Pope's pointed and critical survey of his age is amply evident in his descriptions of the toilet of Belinda, the strange altar raised by the proud Baron and the 'nice conduct' of Sir Plume and his 'clouded cane'. Belinda's long and labourious toilet clearly demonstrates her vanity and pride which are certainly unfortunate sins. Pope brings out forcefully the obdurate female pride as well as vanity of his age through his portrait of Belinda and her conduct.

"And now, unveiled the toilet stands displayed,
Each silver vase in mystic order laid.
First, robbed in white, the nymph intent adores,
With head uncovered the cosmetic poweres.
A heavenly image in the glass appears,
To that she blends, to that her eyes she rears
The inferior priestess, at her altar's side
Trembling begins the sacred rites of pride,(LI. 121-128)

And how ridiculous the Baron looks when he,
"But chiefly Love-to-Love an altar built,
Of twelve vast French romances neatly gilt.
They lay three garters, half apair og gloves;
And all the trophies to his former loves;
With tender billets-doux he lights the pyre,
And breathes three amorous sighs to raise the fire.
Then prostate falls and begs with ardent eyes
Soon to obtain, and long possess the prize" (LI.185-192)

The Baron's too is, indicative of the moral depravity of the age. Sir Plume stands for the shallow lazy punctilio of the age that has no strength of character or force of morality.

Moralising Tone of Clarissa

But Pope's criticism is not negative. He strikes mightily with his sweeping banter. But he instructs and advices, too, for the cure of the moral degeneration of his age. The poem has a moral purpose, and this constitutes the constructive aspect of Pope's criticism of life. The long speech, given to Clarissa, at the beginning of Canto V chiefly contains his unambiguous instruction to his age, particularly to the ladies of fashion and rank of his time.

Through his lecture, Pope tries to enlighten and rectify the frivolous society of his time.He gives his wise counsel here to the gay and silly pursuers of pleasures and vanities, about the transience of all fashions and show, and the triumph of the quality of character. After all, beauty, with all its charms and allurements, must pass away ere long, and can gain nothing, in the ultimate analysis without the virtue of heart. All the female charms of a lovely belle would sem meaningless, unless a good and loving husband brings out the best in her:

"And trust me dear: good humour can prevail,
When airs, and flights, and screams, and scolding fail
Beauties in vain their pretty eyes may roll,

Charms strike the sight, but merit wins the soul." (LI. 675-678)

It's this 'merit' - the 'good humour' which wins the soul; that Pope wants his ladies to imbibe and not merely the 'charms' that only 'strike the sight'. And all through this mock-epic poem Pope sets himself to poke fun at this terrible and excessive obsession with one's beauty. The women spend most of their time with their 'toilet' and in reading letters and the men with writing these obnoxious love letters replete with conventional Romantic phraseology.

But Clarissa is not at all prude as the lines quoted above might convey. Hers is the one same voice advocating a sense of good humour so as to preserve all the achievement of the beauty and charm of her sex. Even in her view beautification is not undesirable.

"Say, why are beauties praised and honoured most,
The wise man's passion and the vain man's toast?
Why decked with all that land and sea afford,
Why angels called, and angel like adored?" (LI.653-656)

To her even the amorous supplication of the fashionable ,outh is highly desirable:

"Why round our coaches crowd the white-glove beaux?
Why bows the side box from its inmost rows?" (LI. 657-658)

But she cannot resist from giving a warning and stating the disadvantages of shunning morality:

"How vain are all these glories, all our pains,
Unless good sense preserve what beauty gains:
That men may say, when we the front-box grace:
Behold the first in virtue as in face" (LI.659-662)

In fact, Pope cannot resist revealing Clarissa's hypocricy either. Even Clarissa forgets her sense of morality and perhaps out of envy towards Belinda or simply out of goodwill towards the baron aids him in his heinous crime of 'raping' the lock of Belinda.

"But when to mischief mortals bend their will,
How soon they find fit instruments of ill!" (LI. 415-416)

Even Clarissa is tempted towards evil and she aids the Baron in his evil designs:

"Just then, Clarissa drew with tempting graces,
A two-edged weapon from her shinning case:
So ladies in Romance assist their knight,
Present the spear, and arm him for the fight." (LI.417-420)

Pope's attitude is impersonal in "The Rape Of The Lock"

The Rape Of The Lock is a triumph of English satire, although it is not a personal satire, like The Dunciad or Mac Flecknoe. Its moral purpose is directed not to any individual in particular, but to society, specially the polished society of Pope's age. In his Dedicatory Epistle to Miss fermor, Pope writes of the purpose of his poem: "It was intended only to divert a few young ladies who have good sense and good humour enough to laugh not only at their sex's little unguarded follies, but at their own". The poem, indeed, is a refined, playful satire on the universal follies andf foibles of the fasionable people of all ages, particularly those of England of the 18th century. The superiority of the poem as a satire is patent, in no less measure, in the moral aspect.

Conclusion:

Actually Popes satire is a double-edged sword; it cuts both way. At the very moment when he is using Clarissa, a sort of mouthpiece of his, to lay down the moral tenets for his age(itself of a flimsy nature as is the subject of his mock-epic) he is making a fun of her and revealing her weakness and hypocricy. He leaves none unscathed. So strong is the vanity and the deep-rooted rottenness of their nature that their shortcomings stick with them even after their death:

"Think not, when women's transient breath is fled,
That all her vanities at ince are dead:
Succeeding vanities she still regards,
And though she plays no more O'erlooks the cards,

Her joy in gilded Chariots, when alive,
And love of ombre after death survive.
For when the fair in all their pride expire,
To their first elements their souls retire." (Ll. 51-58)

Even the men turn to gnomes after death, with all their vices. But of course Pope does all this 'beating' in good humour and tries to laugh off the vices in men.

In the opinion of Matthew Arnold, poetry is at bottom a criticism of life. This criticism, however, should not be merely critical. It must be constructive and instructive too. It must imply a contrast between what life is and what life ought to have been. Judged from this criterion The Rape Of The Lock is a satisfactory work by Pope. It is not merely a scathing satire but a criticism of life in the true sense of the term and it is a style which is witty and humourous.

Q.6. "The Rape of the Lock" is a courageous attack upon eighteenth century society.Dicuss

Or

Q. What elements in the poem make the poem a n attack on 18 th Century society.

To criticize canonized literature is a difficult task. To pick apart the work of a literary authority demands a great deal of careful thought and solicitude for we are dealing with a delicate subject: the accepted works of an established poet. However, with the passage of time, our notion of what is acceptable will inevitably vary. Are we to readily embrace all historical works as acceptable in today's society? Certainly not. One must acknowledge change.

The particular poet to which this essay refers is none other than Alexander Pope, fittingly known as the master of satire. The specific poem in question is one of his most celebrated works: "The Rape of the Lock. " Although a timeless piece of literature, "The Rape of the Lock" is somewhat of a controversial poem. The subject matter, although greatly enhanced through the use of exaggeration and hyperbole, represents a very dark side of human nature. Being the most prevalent of the mock epics, this poem employs all the devices of the standard epic in attaining a comic effect. Yet is this comic approach suitable in mocking the manifestation of this social mishap? Was Pope trivializing the assault upon a woman? There are several lines in this mock epic, however, that seem particularly disturbing, specifically the Baron's premeditated assault:

He saw, he wished, and to the prize aspired. Resolved to win, he meditates the way, By force to ravish, or by fraud betray.

(Lines 3032, Canto 2)

In addition to this possessive aspiration was his relentless gloating following the actual "rape of the lock." Making this accomplishment public seemed to be of utmost importance to the Baron:

"Let the wreaths oftriumph now my temples twine," The victor cried, "the glorious prize is mine."

(Lines 16162, Canto 3)

The "glorious prize: " one woman's virtue. If one were to imagine such ranting and raving spewing forth from the mouth of a sexual offender, this epic might in fact be eliminated from the canon. For truly, literature perpetrating such immorality cannot be acceptable for study in school and higher learning institutions. Be that as it may, these words are protected by a thin veil: comedy.

The poem is known for its exaggerating nature, and so all actions, whether they are comical or insolent, are justified and taken in the appropriate manner. Yet does this veil truly justify the intensity of the crime? Whether an offender robs a woman of a lock of hair or her chastity is not necessarily the issue, for in both cases the woman is robbed of her pride and humility.

In the 1 700's, women were not often credited with anything more than beauty, therefore physical attractiveness was considered the essence of a woman. Her reputation relied on her ability to remain silent and chaste, and this reputation was crucial to her credibility as a woman. To mar a woman's countenance in such a society would devastate her entire character. Moreover, to publicize this violation in a mock epic could only serve to add insult to injury. A woman's merit was shattered before society, and a man had the audacity to say she was overreacting.

With Belinda being the main female .character, it is insulting to women for this character to surface as a purely superficial being. The nature of Belinda is not the silent and demure figure idealized by eighteenth century society. Her reaction to the Baron's assault was both boisterous and inane, fueled by fury. Her insistence for him to "Restore the Lock! " are proof of her blind rage, and reveal that her primary concern is her appearance. These actions reveal massive amounts of vanity and foolishness, and little else. The application of cosmetics is another exaggerated method of exposing her immeasurable vanity:

A heavenly image in the glass appears; To that she bends, to that her eyes she rears. The inferior priestess, at her altar's side, Trembling begins the sacred rites of Pride.

(Lines 124128, Canto 1)

This revelation of her vanity further adds to her seemingly shallow nature. Despite its comic disposition, this poem alludes to Belinda's invariable egotism. The sniveling remarks that Pope assigns to this woeful character do little to validate her temperament:

"Forever cursed be this detested day, Which snatched my best, my flavourite curl away! "

(Lines 14748, Canto 4)

Bearing the plight of womankind at heart, one might read "The Rape of the Lock" with predetermined conviction. This refers to the underlying fact that although the crime involves a lock of hair, the somber parallel to this violation is of a deeply serious nature, and to make light of such a situation is an abomination. Of course, things are not always as they seem; the surface matter is not necessarily the essence of poetry.

Attempting to abandon all personal bias, this author read "The Rape of the Lock" once more. Perhaps indignation can temporarily blind a reader, for this poem, in retrospect, has much more to offer than criticism of women alone.

First and foremost, Arabella Fermor permitted this poem to be published. Pope, after all, had the respect and courtesy to request her permission. The fact that she allowed the publication of the poem grants this work credibility. This showed that Pope was appreciative of her ability to reason, and decide whether or not such an intrepid composition should be published. In vehement defence of the "weaker" sex, one may fail to empower this woman with a sense of humour. Miss Fermor might have felt that the publication of Pope's work would succeed in soothing the situation, and thus resolved upon admitting the publication. Furthermore, Alexander Pope was aware that women had much more to offer than physical charm.

Some secret truths, from learned pride concealed, To maids alone and children are revealed.

(Lines 13738, Canto 1)

Pope gently asserted that a woman's intelligence and grace were only available to those who were willing to hear. Vanity was learned, acquired early in life and encouraged through the course of one's existence. Consequently, many were held responsible for this feature for it has become part of human nature. Vanity played a large role for either sex in this epic; it was the element behind Belinda's rage, and the force behind the Baron's bravado. One might defiantly assume that Belinda was the sole bearer of vanity, when in truth few of these characters could be classified as demure. Take, for instance, the Baron:

Steel could the labour of the Gods destroy, And strike to dust the imperial towers of Troy... What wonder then, fair nymph! thy hairs should feel, The conquering force of unresisted steel?"

(Lines 1734, 1778, Canto 3)

Did this man dare to equate his dastardly deed to the labour of Gods? Evidently so. The ego of this man surpassed that of the fair damsel by far. It is the Baron, perchance, who ends up receiving the bulk of Pope's criticism. So was Alexander Pope trivializing an assault upon a woman? Indeed he was. However, this trivialization was neutralized as Pope then proceeded to mock the behaviour of the entire group, including the men. This makes his beguiling comments towards Belinda less concerning, for no sex was being entirely isolated from the situation; no gender was free from ridicule. In fact, Pope's observations of men were even less appealing:

With earnest eyes, and round unthinking face, He first the snuffbox opened, then the case, And thus broke out "My Lord, why, what the devil! Z_ds! damn the lock! 'fore Gad, you must be civil! "

(Lines 12528, Canto 4)

This grand performance revealed nothing more of Sir Plume aside from his vast knowledge of curses. Furthermore, the presence of a lady failed to encourage this man to restrict his use of harsh language. This impudent fellow possessed no more intelligence than the woman by his side. This reveals that Pope not only mocked the vanity of women, but also the l arrogance of men. Essentially, the pretentious nature of the elite became i the object of ridicule. It seems that the comic veil Pope used successfully conveyed his assessment of the supercilious temper of his society. Coupled with Miss Fermor's permission to publish, the inclusion of both sexes validates Pope's work. The poet was not implicating a particular gender in this epic, but rather the diminutive occurrences that tend to be blown out of proportion with regards to the society of the time. The word "rape" though, does carry a dismal connotation by today's standards, so with this word headlining the poem, the literature may be implicated as being suggestive.

The definition of rape is "to take by force;" the modern definition adds "forcible sexual intercourse imposed on a woman." The former interpretation, however, asserts that rape is not only restricted to a brutal sexual act, but to the devastation of values, property, or emotion. The "rape of the lock" troubles human nature to this very day. The lock of truth, the lock of justice, the lock of virtue these are violated daily at any given moment. As in the poem, the "glorious prize" will not ever be attained, for power is fleeting. It is not a tangible thing one can seize and maintain forever. Perhaps this is what Alexander Pope attempted to convey in the lock's ascension into the "shining sphere."

A sudden star, it shot through liquid air, And drew behind a radiant trail of hair.

(Lines 12728, Canto 5)

The lines concluding this poem leave the reader with a sense of closure, and in keeping with the tone of the poem, remain perfectly preposterous. Yet the poem maintains its serious value through the course of hundreds of years. For a piece of work to be held within the canon, it must be given credibility in itself without question. The Rape of the Lock is certainly worthy of admiration, if not for its significant messages, then for its pure wit and charm.

The time honoured nature of this poem lies in its undeniable truth. At the time of the poem's composition, Pope may or may not have been conscious of the change yet to come; alongside the progression of society lies the increasing awareness of women as individual beings. The women of today may have trouble, then, when asked to swallow the words of men from the past. Although these words remain exquisite in their complexity, they may not remain true to modern day society. Again, one must acknowledge change. Conversely, preconceived bias is a disagreeable notion to carry into any form of literature. It may be most advantageous for the reader to remain completely impartial in order to assimilate the intended message of the poem. Indeed, it is often literature that makes us aware of our own biases. Through careful examination, it is easy to see that the content of "The Rape of the Lock" distributes criticism rather equitably.

To the poet's credit, "The Rape of the Lock" is a courageous attack upon eighteenth century society. Alexander Pope managed to deliver this attack in a lighthearted and carefree manner, making the criticism easy to endure. So is the comic approach suitable in mocking the manifestation of this social mishap? It may be, for the most amusing feature of this mock epic is the poet's ability to mask the sobriety of his words in such a facetious manner. Yet while Pope's most obvious criticism dealt with unnecessary quarreling, he also offered an observation regarding the role of men and women in society. He emanated a sense of empathy towards the female gender in his otherwise witty presentation:

Hear and believe! thy own importance know, Nor bound thy narrow views to things below.

(Lines 13536, Canto 1)

"The Rape of the Lock" requires the reader to have the ability to differentiate between the obvious and the subliminal. However, there is no piece of literature, art, or music that is the same to any two people, so to acknowledge change one must acknowledge variety in interpretation. Alexander Pope may have been ahead of his time in recognizing the inner beauty of women, yet his words demand much of the reader's patience and insight, for beneath a witty facade of outrageous comedy lie some observations of truth that somehow have a distinct resemblance to the society of today.

Q.7. Discuss the Motif of Mercantilism in Alexander Pope's The Rape of the Lock

Or

Q. Critically analyse the role of Supernatural Machinery in the Rape of the Lock

Or

Q. Discuss the importance of supernatural element in the Rape of the Lock

One of the essential features of an Epic as laid down by Aristotle is the use of "Machinery", the supernatural characters. God and other Supernatural beings take part in the action taking place in the Epic. The supernatural agents are called the "Machinery". Thus we find Gods and other supernatural agents taking as an active role in the Epics of Homer, Milton, Virgil, and Tasso. From the constructional point of view it's importance is well brought out in the bantering words of Pope himself: "The use of these machines is evident: since no epic poem can possibly subsist without them, the wisest way is to reserve them for your greater necessities: when you cannot extricate your hero by any human means, or yourself by your own wit, seek relief from heaven, and gods will do your business very readily." Dryden while defending the supernatural machinery in the Epic stated, "I am of opinion that neither Homer, Virgil, Statius, Aristo, nor our English Spencer could have formed their poems half so beautiful without those gods and those spirits, and those enthusiastic poets of poetry which compose the most noble part of their writing."

The original version of The Rape Of The Lock, one of the most poised and artful poems in Western Literature, was made up only of two cantos. It was meant to bring about a happy reconciliation between the two families of the Fermors and the Petres. This version was not meant to be published and was intended for private circulation only. Impressed by its runaway success Pope thought of expanding the poem to five cantos and giving it a mock Heroic shape. When Pope thought of expanding the poem, there were two possibilities before him him. He could have used materials either from Christian or Greek classics or could have made the moral qualities personified to preside over the action of the poem.

The use of Christian machinery was not considered suitable for the mock Epic poem, because being a Catholic he could not have taken the Christian stories so light heartedly. The other alternative was the Greek classics but Pope shared Dr.Johnson's dislike of combining old mythology with modern poetry. While he was thus fumbling for a way out he happened to read a book called "Le Comte De Gabalis", by a French author called Abb-de-Villars, containing an account of the Rosicrucian doctrine of the spirits. Pope has described about this book in his dedicatory letter to Miss Arabells Fermor-"The machinery madam, is a term invented by the critics, to signify that part which the Deities, Angels, or Daemons are made to act in a poem ; ...These machines I determin'd to raise on a very new and odd foundation, the Rosicrucian Doctrine of Spirits. The Rosicrucians are people I must bring you acquainted with. The best account of them is in a French book called Le Comte de Gabalis.... According to these gentlemen, the four elements are inhabited by spirits, which they call sylphs, Gnomes, Nymphs and Salamanders. "Pope also referred to another book called Pluralite de Mondes. Pope's sylphs are, of course, more vividly realised than those of de Villars, and in the same way that he rifles other systems to enrich the Rosicrucian mythology, he rifles earlier English poets to enrich the sylphs themselves.

Besides supplying an essential requirement of Epic poetry, the spirits in The Rape Of The Lock serves another purpose also. In the dedication of the poem, Pope claims that 'Human persons in this poem, are as fictitious as the airy ones.' By introducing the fictitious machinery, therefore, Pope made the poem more impersonal and thereby substantiated the claim. The erotic quality of the Rosicrucian spirits determined the poem's guiding motive.

According to Rosicrucian mythology the four elements are inhabited by the spirits, which are called spirits(air), gnomes(earth), nymphs(water) and salamanders(fire). The gnomes or spirits of earth, delight in mischief, but the sylphs, which dwell in air, are the best conditioned creatures imaginable. The Gomes or spirits of earth, delight in mischief sylphs, which dwell in air, are the best conditioned creatures imaginable. Two of these kinds — sylphs and gnomes predominated in The Rape of the Lock. As to their origin Pope referred to Ovid's Metamorphosis and to the doctrine of the transformation of the soul.

These aerial spirits of Rosicrucian mythology writing, light beings, which would exactly suit his mock- heroic poem. The spirits can change their sex at will and their bodies are invulnerable, since if their bodies are divided they can, in the words of burton, 'with admirable celerity ... come together again'. The gods and Goddesses of Homer would not do for his flimsy poem, nor would the angels of Milton's Paradise Lost. The pigmy beings, like the sylphs and the gnomes, are suited to the theme and atmosphere of the poem and they are as artificial as the society depicted in The Rape Of The Lock.

The fairies of the Midsummers Nights Dream are also tiny creatures, but they are different in nature and spirit from the sylphs, and gnomes of The Rpe Of The Lock. The former are gay, delightful spirits, wandering about in moonlight; they embody all the beauty and freshness of nature and bestowed with supernatural powers plays pretty cool pranks on human beings. The 'light militia of the lower sky' represented in The Rape Of The Lock are very different characters. They are artificial spirits and they all the vanity and superficiality which they had when they were "enclosed in woman's beauteous mould". The artificial mythology of the sylphs harmonizes with the artificial story. It is full of fanciful wit.

The Arial spirits in The Rape Of The Lock performs quite a few important functions. With the sylphs arrival in 1714 Belinda's living beauty is realised to the full as, surrounded by them at her dressing table, laying artifice upon artifice, she grows lovelier while we watch. Nor is that loveliness mere daubing, as Dennis protested in his bad tempered 'Remarks on Mr.Pope's Rape Of The Lock', 1728. Belinda, assisted by these celestials in painting a "purer" blush on her cheeks is practicing no fraud on nature, but bringing forth what nature is capable of, in an ideal world.

Repairs her smiles, awakens ev'ry grace,
And calls forth all the wonders of her Face.

Ariel is the head of the spirits guarding Belinda. Ariel has a premonition that some calamity is in wait for Belinda. Thus to protect her, Ariel assigns different functions to the spirits under his control. One was given the charge of Belinda's fan, another was to take care of her earrings, the third was to look her watch, and the fourth was to guard her flavourite lock. Ariel himself took charge of the dog. The important duty of guarding the petticoat was given to fifty chosen sylphs against any sort of negligence in their duty. Severe punishments like shutting up in small bottles, to be pierced with pins, to be held fast in the eye of Bodkin or to be stuck up in gums, was to be awarded to those who failed to discharge their duties. In spite of all the careful vigilance of the spirits, the 'lock' is raped. The spirits fail to do anything. They neither prevent the changes nor retard it. Though the episode of Umberiel visiting the cave of Spleen gives an opportunity to the poet to satirize the evil nature and affectation of the leaders and gentleman of his society. It also serves the action of the poem, for Belinda becomes alternatively angry and sad as Umbriel empties the bag of passions and the vial of sorrows over her head. In The Rape Of The Lock the part played by the spirits are entirely complemented with the trivial subject and the foppish characters of the poem.

The sylphs are the shimmering, helpless, half-dissolved guardians of a moral order as flimsy as their own ariel forms. Once such creatures enter the verse, no fixed morality could remain. The human view point, the sylphic, the epic sense of things, all play into and out of one another, the limitations of each suggested by the presence alongside it of those contrary possible worlds. The machinery helped Pope to mock the 18th century aristocratic conventions and the prevailing morality. It is through these spirits that Pope satirizes the vanity and fickleness of the ladies of the day:

'Tis these that early taint the female soul,
Instruct the eyes of young Coquettes to roll,
Teach infant cheeks a hidden blush to know,
And little hearts to flutter at a beau.'
Again Pope tells how the spirits help the females:
'With varying vanities from every part
They shift the moving toyshop of their heart'

The toilet of the ladies is also satirized through these spirits Ariel says:

'Our humbler province is to tend the fair,
Not a less pleasing, though less glorious care,
To save the powder from too rude a gale,
Nor let the imprison'd essences exhale'

Society is the very arena in which the sylphs desire her to shine. Epic needs a tyrant. Like Satan in Paradise Lost, the sylphs here with their tiny size holds a new kind of terror and plays the role of tyrant for they go on increasing the vanity of Belinda and misguides her. They provide her with a false sense of security. Cleanth Brook says," It is Pope's treatment of the sylphs which allows him to develop with the most delicate modulation his whole attitude towards Belinda and the special world which she graces". Through the use of the sylphs Pope managed to point out satirically woman's excessive fondness for rank and pomp. And if they could have their way, they would maintain it even after their death.

By inventing the sylphs Pope solved the almost impossible problems that the theorists set for the heroic poet. He is almost certainly the only modern poet to create a company of believable deities which are not simply the ancient classical divinities in modern dress, and which are not offensive to a Christian audience. G.Holden points out, "It is Pope's use of this machinery, moreover, which more than any single feature made the poem the single success that it is." Wilson Knight points out that the machinery increases the dramatic suspense and therefore story-depth,, since they foreknow and warn of the central disaster and help to universalize semi-humourously the whole action, forming, indeed, the binding symbolism of the little drama; are related to certain paradisal and, in Umbriel's journey, hellish colourings touching Dante, Shakespeare, and Milton; and finally reflect the implied belief of poetic art forms in General that humanity and its sensible world do not exhaust the total of the comprehensive statement. They are of a race that lives in the pure upper light, that guides 'orbs', in heaven, like the child spirit in Shelley's Prometheus Unbound, and follows shooting stars by moonlight. They are variously associated with rainbow, mist, tempests, earth and the guardianship of the British throne(L1.77-90). They are explicitly related to traditional beliefs, both trivial and profound.

The adaptation of the Rosicrucian machinery in The Rape Of The Lock is indeed an inventive and happy creation. There is no finer gem than this in all the lighter treasures of English fancy. In the ultimate analysis Pope's machinery remains a sure proof of his artistic excellence.

Chapter 18

Further Study Questions

Study Questions:

1. In what ways is *The Rape of the Lock* a mock-heroic poem?
2. What is the background story (occasion) for the poem? To whom does the poet dedicate the poem?
3. In *ll.* 7-8, is the male protagonist well-bred? Can you describe him from his behaviour?
4. Pay attention to the poetic diction Pope uses in *ll.* 7-11. To what does this kind of diction belong? Heroic, gentle, graceful, sarcastic, ironic, cynical, witty, jeering, or satirical? What effect does this create?
5. Comment on the guardian Sylph's speech to Belinda. Is it quite a style?
6. When the Fair expires in all their pride, what happens to them? (Hint: *ll.* 59-60 (fire) fiery termagants—Salamander; *ll.*61-62 (water) soft yielding minds—water nymph; *ll.*63-64 (earth) graver prude—Gnome; *ll.*65-66 (air) light coquettes—Sylph in the air.)
7. Why does the Sylph advise Belinda to remain fair and chaste?
8. Where are the little Sylphs to protect her? To protect her from what kind of men?
9. When the world imagines women go astray, who guides them on their way?

10. What does Ariel predict? Does he know exactly what, how, and where this will happen?
11. How does Belinda end her dream?
12. To what does the poet compare Belinda's dressing up?
13. Pay attention to the poetic diction of the last stanza. What kind of diction is this? (unveiled, silver vase, mystic, robed in white, offerings, curious toil, glittering spoil,¡K)
14. The brief reference of India and Arabia expands the scope and the atmosphere. But what opposite effect does it bring?
15. According to *l.*139, what does the poet portray the lady as here?

Chapter 19

Critical Essays

Anne Finches Opposition to the Rape of the Lock

Anne Finch's Opposition to The Rape of the Lock The Restoration Period (1660-1700) was a period of social, political and philosophical turmoil, which laid the foundation for future centuries. This period was marked by an advance in colonization and trade and by the birth of the Whig and Tory parties. In poetry, works of Alexander Pope and Anne Finch and a number of other poets distinguishes the Restoration. But, there are several objections from these poets; one particular opposition occurs between Pope's The Rape of the Lock and Anne Finch. Pope was born into a Catholic family during a period of intense anti-Catholic sentiment in England. His family was forced to move because Catholics were forbid from living within a certain area of London at this time. While Pope was growing up, Catholicism affected his education although there were very few Catholic schools. His life would soon influence his writing of The Rape of the Lock.

The following comes from the Twickenham Edition of Pope's poem: The families concerned in the Rape of the Lock – The Fermors, Petres, and Carylls—were prominent members of that group of great intermarried Roman Catholic families owning land in the home countries. Most of whom came within the circle of Pope's friends and acquaintances and to whom Pope considered his own family to belong. Some time before 21 March 1712, when Pope sold his poem to Lintott, Robert,

Lord Petre had cut off a lock of Arabella Fermor's hair, and John Caryll had suggested to Pope that he should write a poem to heal the estrangement that followed between the two families. (Twinckenham 83) Alexander Pope is responsible for one of the most comic poems of the eighteenth century, The Rape of the Lock.

This poem was written specifically to resolve a serious falling out between two leading Catholic families. (The cause of the quarrel was the cutting of a lock of hair by Lord Petre from the head of Arabella Fermor.) But, this poem also discussed another theme: the relationship between men and women. The events that Pope describes in this poem occur between Belinda, who is motivated by pride and vanity and Baron, who is driven by ambition. Belinda's energy is driven to attract a man and pretend to be affectionate and then cast him off for another. Baron oversteps his boundaries of acceptable behaviour by acting with force toward the desirable woman. The Rape of the Lock is both a scornful description of a ridiculous social situation and a serious analysis of consequences of flattering self-esteem and desire.

The Rape of the Lock is a staple of neoclassical writing; it includes wit and wit is characterized by parallelism and balance. It contains epic conventions such as war (between the sexes), epic game (played on the "velvet plain" of the card table), a journey (to the underworld), and battle. Pope writes by describing the man as the hero. But Finch writes her poetry in regards to women. When Anne Finch wrote, she followed a particularly intellectual course, not only for women but also for anyone at the time. She wrote about philosophy; her philosophical work had another important source: her own physical pain. She was concerned to provide theodicy for her writers. She attempted to reunite the existence of a compassionate or benign god with the existence of suffering and other evil in the world. Her audience should be prepared to read religious controversy, which is far more intense than other philosophical contemporaries. Ann Finch may have objected to Pope's The Rape of the Lock because Pope's poem is impressed by the force of humour and the style serves to exaggerate how ridiculous "war" is between a man and a woman.

In The Rape of the Lock, the laughter and ridicule do not undermine the importance of good sense and virtue in the relationships between men and women. Finch disagrees and believes the woman is a heroin in this poem. Finch argues that woman rule the race, but men believe that they are the rulers. In most of Finch's works, she "submerges political conflict in an explicitly female lyric voice" (DeMaria 201). "Finch creates both female poetry and poetry of abjection out of this situation- or, rather more accurately, those tangled subjectivies created the abject female poet out of her" (201). She is comfortable criticizing one of the most powerful poets in her period (Pope) while "killing him with kindness". Pope's belief in Catholicism and Finch's belief in philosophy may have also been a cause of Finch's objection to The Rape of the Lock. The two writers had different viewpoints toward religion. Also, Finch may have seen more importance in writing about her own pain, while Pope finds it important to write about others pain. He writes about the pain of Belinda and Baron. In conclusion, there are several examples, as one can observe, of Finch's objection to The Rape of the Lock. The life and beliefs of these two authors were entirely different and this seems to be the major reason Finch may have objected to Pope's poem.

Pope: Bipolar Implication

Near the source of Pope's work is an anxiety understandable in terms of his health and religion. As a Roman Catholic in a Protestant nation, Pope suffered maddening penalties. He could not attend a university or hold a civil office. He paid double the normal tax on land, and the law forbade him to reside within ten miles of London. All Roman Catholics were exposed to charges of conspiring against the government.

But Pope's worst affliction was tuberculosis of the spine, which gave him rickets and a progressive, lopsided curvature of the back. It made him grotesquely short and gradually weakened his thin limbs. It produced much languor, a susceptibility to bad colds, and other painful or unpleasant symptoms which worsened as he aged. Pope had to wear a stiff corset, warm clothes, and (over the skinny legs) three pairs of stockings. Normal sexual relations were out of the question.

Frail, vulnerable, and (in effect) impotent, it was natural for the poet to desire the security of well-placed friends. One of the mainsprings of his imagination was the need to protect himself. Still he was conscious of his genius and wanted fame. He yearned to exercise heroic power over others through the gift of poetry.

To gain the recognition he longed for, Pope had to mask many emotions. As an adolescent, he began a career of seeking out men of talent, rank, or power, winning their friendship and making them serve him. To do so, he learned to charm them with tact and wit, paying careful compliments and accommodating himself to the moods of the mighty.

Not only in his poems but also in his letters and conversation, Pope systematically maintained careful representations of himself that would uphold an appearance of strength, independence, and natural benevolence, all in keeping with the doctrines he recommended in verse. What records we have of his conversation suggest that he hoped his sentiments would be repeated. The rhetoric of Pope's most familiar letters sometimes sounds like that of a senator emitting platitudes for his own obituary. A second reader—Posterity—normally looked over the poet's epistolary shoulder.

I assume that these constraints, added to those of health and religion, nourished a deep resentfulness which compounded the original anxiety. The poetic instinct bent itself to please those whom Pope needed, while the very impulse to create started from subterranean discomforts. Words are a common resource of those who cannot act, but Pope's words had many duties. They vented painful emotions which the poet dared not express simply. They conveyed an air of assurance to cloak a fundamental unease. They made up for a lack of sexual authority. They rewarded friends and punished enemies.

Pope devised methods of attracting and reassuring those who might be hostile to his brilliance, and yet of challenging subtle readers by offering them dangerous thoughts. Wit and irony are known ways of accomplishing these ends, and good critics have examined Pope's use of them. He found other ways as well, which are less familiar.

If we agree that sex, religion, and politics are themes which invite indirection, we may also agree that religion, for Pope, was too risky a subject to experiment with. He did venture on opinions that might trouble his coreligionists, especially a tolerance of non-Catholic positions. He blamed great ecclesiastics for time-serving, avarice, and other vices. But he did not indulge in satire on allegedly false doctrines, as Dryden and Swift had done. In *The Messiah* and *An Essay on Man*, Pope tried, explicitly and implicitly, to avoid controversy.

Sexual themes were treacherous too. The poet's obvious incapacity drove him to adopt conventional poses for fear of becoming too easy a mark for ridicule. Whether he used a rake or a moralist as his mouthpiece, he could hardly afford to sound innovative. Yet if sexual themes particularly excite wordplay, they must have exerted a special charm upon a poet. Pope felt the charm, and characteristically offered both conformist and subversive treatments of those themes.

The association of sexuality with creative power is natural. Keeping this connection in mind, one must notice Pope's tendency to maintain it and yet to separate the imagery of conception from that of sexual intercourse. He liked to refer to his works as his progeny and to the muse as a wife, but not to lovemaking between the creative pair.

In these misty crossings we touch the depths of Pope's identity. He offered several distinct representations of the poetic character. The most familiar is the public idealization of an uncorrupt spokesman for patriotic and social virtue. This is the character he liked to give his own career. Yet implicitly, the ideal public figure depreciates another, viz. the inspired artist celebrated by Horace and recommended by Pope in *An Epistle to Augustus:*

> *'Tis he, who gives my breast a thousand pains,*
> *Can make me feel each passion that he feigns,*
> *Inrage, compose, with more than magic art,*
> *With pity, and with terror, tear my heart.*
>
> *(lines 342–45)*

In these lines "poet" clearly means seductive playwright rather than didactic satirist.

But there is still another figure, for which Pope voices contempt and which he embodies in the persons of failed or inept authors. This alas is the one that excites his greatest energy, his most imaginative language. Therefore, although it alludes normally to writers whom Pope disliked, one may speculate that it also reflects Pope's doubts about his status. He might be a uniquely gifted genius; but putting aside traditional hyperboles, what did the laurel crown amount to when it topped his crazy carcass?

So one may also speculate about the scenes of grotesque fantasy that break out in Pope's best work. Underground, cavernous, and obstetric images, tinged with sexuality, suggest that literary parenthood compensated the poet for the loss of voluptuous pleasure. Pope designed deeply coherent masterpieces around heroines deprived of normal sexual relations: *Eloisa to Abelard, An Elegy to . . . an Unfortunate Lady* ("Of the Characters of Women"). Even Dulness, in *The Dunciad,* is an unwed or parthenogenetic mother. Yet Pope produced no episode of admirable and fulfilled passion.

Two of his most polished works deal sympathetically with women penalized for subversive lust. In *Eloisa to Abelard* the lover has been castrated and the mistress consigned to a nunnery. In the *Elegy . . . to an Unfortunate Lady* a noble heiress has stabbed herself after eloping to a foreign country with a lover whom her guardian uncle had rejected. In both these poems the author encourages us to pity the lawbreaker: "Is it, in heav'n a crime to love too well?" he asks.

In *An Epistle to a Lady* the poet compliments his spinster friend Martha Blount (whom he briefly endows with a mythical husband and daughter) by opposing her to a series of corrupt, passionate mistresses or wives. In *The Rape of the Lock* the male figures are ridiculed and defeated, while the females remain unsatisfied.

Against this pattern it seems significant that the scenes of grotesque fantasy depend on images of unpleasant confusion and procreation. I am thinking of the Cave of Spleen in *The Rape of the Lock,* the Cave of Poverty and Poetry in Book One of *The Dunciad,* the bowers of the mud nymphs in Book Two of *The Dunciad,* and similar material.

Spleen of course means melancholy; and in the seventeenth century, it was commonplace to regard melancholy as the "balm of wit" and the "breath of poetry." When the gnome Umbriel descends to the Cave of Spleen, he is visiting a spring of creative imagination. Here Spleen herself is a goddess who can inspire the "poetic fit." Although the details of this allegorical cave are traditional, Pope colours them with phallic and erotic lights, with hints of perverse coition and gestation. So we get a linking of creativity with displaced sexuality and pain:

Men prove with child, as pow'rful fancy works,
And maids turn'd bottles, call aloud for corks.
(Rape of the Lock IV, 53–54)

In Book Three of *The Dunciad* we meet the laureate Cibber lying with his head in the lap of the goddess Dulness while a dark, soporific dew falls and "raptures" overflow (lines 1–5)—a titillating scene. Two-thirds of the way through Book Three, another genius of false imagination appears—John Rich, producer of pantomimes. Here Pope brings in imagery of miraculous transformations of the universe echoing the representation of Christ in *The Messiah* and suggesting genesis and doomsday at once. The chaos reaches its climax with an egg from which the human race is hatched. Again the work of creative imagination carries hints of asexual conception or parthenogenesis.

We have to notice how often Pope connected the act of composition with discomfort, muddle, misshapen birth and growth, delusive transformation. We do not meet order, dignity, and reality, but chaos, monsterhood, and illusion: "the chaos dark and deep, / Where nameless somethings in their causes sleep" (*Dunciad* I, 55–56, 59, 93–94). Attacking the decline of humanistic education, Pope deplores the standard practice of training schoolboys to compose Latin verses: "We hang one jingling padlock on the mind: / A poet the first day, he dips his quill; / And what the last? a very poet still" (*Dunciad* IV, 163–64).

These examples of disrespect for his vocation are from the last years of Pope's career and refer to bad poetry, not good. In his early work we read similar lines:

Still run on poets in a raging vein,
Ev'n to the dregs and squeezings of the brain;
Strain out the last, dull droppings of their sense,
And rhyme with all the rage of impotence.

This linking of composition to a hard stool and a limp penis also belongs to an attack on bad writing. But the images have too much power to rest in the boundaries prescribed by explicit meaning. When he refers directly to his own career as an author, Pope says, "I've had my purgatory here betimes, / And paid for all my satires, all my rhymes" (*Donne* IV, 5–6). It was only half-jokingly that he once said of the poet's calling, "Must one not be prepared to endure the reproaches of men, want and much fasting, nay martyrdom in its cause". The pleasure of creation loses itself in the toil and humiliation.

If one puts aside the link with authorship and considers unsublimated sexuality, the material points one along a more direct road but not to marriage, parenthood, and stability. The poet offers conventional denunciations of vice. But he also provides vivid descriptions of frustrated passion, titillating coquetry, tenderness outside marriage, and misery born in wedlock. The frailty and quick alterations of carnal appetite strike him more than its fruitfulness. He conveys a deep sympathy with the voluptuous impulse and deep uncertainty as to its consequence.

In *The Rape of the Lock,* disorderly lust glances at us from the first couplet; and it pounds on us in the final canto. "Die" for sexual climax, "thing" for vagina, "hair" displaced from the groin to the head, all remind one that the proper study of nubile girls is men.

"What dire offence from am'rous causes springs, / What mighty contests rise from trivial things, / I sing," says Pope as he begins a story connecting love with theft and war. The couplet sounds plain enough until we hear an echo of Horace joining the same themes and calling the vagina (or lust) a most shameful cause of war (*cunnus taeterrima belli / causa–Satires* I, iii, 107). Once we remember that Pope would translate "cunnus" as "thing," the language of decorum becomes a screen for impropriety.

In Canto Five of *The Rape of the Lock,* the battle of the sexes takes a more liberal form; and when Belinda defeats the Baron with a pinch of snuff, he says,

Thou by some other shalt be laid as low.
Nor think, to die dejects my lofty mind;
All that I dread, is leaving you behind!
(lines 98–100)

Here the poet openly, if indelicately, sympathizes with the natural impulse of young blood. So also in the early cantos of *The Rape of the Lock,* Pope celebrates the delight of Belinda in her own sexually provocative beauty:

Now awful beauty puts on all its arms;
The fair each moment rises in her charms,
Repairs her smile, awakens ev'ry grace,
And calls forth all the wonders of her face.
(I, 139–42)

So also the sylphs—spirits whose job it is to guard Belinda's defensive and offensive weapons—are represented with wholehearted (though smiling) approval. Their humble work is to "tend the fair"; so long as the heroine refrains from matrimony, they strive to protect the arsenal of her beauty—

To save the powder from too rude a gale,
Nor let th'imprison'd essences exhale,
To draw fresh colours from the vernal flow'rs,
To steal from rainbows ere they drop in show'rs
A brighter wash; to curl their waving hairs,
Assist their blushes, and inspire their airs;
Nay oft, in dreams, inventions we bestow,
To change a flounce, or add a furbelo.
(II, 93–100)

Belinda makes us live among changing appearances, unfixed emotions, fascinating discords, elegant but furious rivalries, stylized and comic wars. There is nothing placid, domestic, or parental about *The Rape of the Lock*. Its few snatches of security only prepare us for long passages of delightful uneasiness.

Yet in some masterful lines of elevated reasoning, one of Belinda's friends, named Clarissa, warns her of the transience of voluptuous pleasure and belligerent beauty. She reminds us that courtship ought to fix its goal in stable domesticity, marriage and motherhood:

Since painted, or not painted, all shall fade,
And she who scorns a man must die a maid;
What then remains, but well our pow'r to use,
And keep good humour still whate'er we lose.
(V, 27–30)

This is sane as well as eloquent. Only, as it happens, when the Baron wished to snip off a lock of Belinda's hair, it was the same Clarissa who gave him the scissors.

In *The Rape of the Lock* the poet's obsession with time and change heightens a brief joy in youthful ardor. But ultimately it implies that creative imagination alone can triumph over age and death. The familiar theme of *monumentum aere perennius* brings together the sexual aspect of authorship and the lure of misdirected passion. Elsewhere Pope belittled the theme. Here, by invoking it ironically to close a battle of the sexes, he momentarily resolves his own doubts.

So at the end of the poem, yet once more reviving the exhausted pun on "die," once more identifying the eye of beauty with the eye of heaven, Pope brings nature and art together as he immortalizes the maiden whom he cannot enjoy. Here we meet that ideal of the poet as artist which enabled Pope to transcend his private self-disgust and his public role as guardian of the nation's morals.

For, after all the murders of your eye,
When, after millions slain, your self shall die;
When those fair suns shall set, as set they must,
And all those tresses shall be laid in dust;
This lock, the muse shall consecrate to fame,
And mid'st the stars inscribe Belinda 's name.
(V, 145–50)

Years later, Pope took up the burden of sexuality with rather less of an effort to sound decorous. This was in *Sobre Advice from Horace,* published anonymously in 1734. Here, however, the theme of lust itself becomes part of a political argument; and one should meet that argument before going on to the poem. To Pope, the most challenging aspect of implicit meaning presented itself in his criticism of the highest levels of English vice. From about the time he was forty, and continuing about fifteen years, the poet's judgment of his nation deepened in severity, and he invented subtler, yet keener, ways to reveal it.

The port of embarkation for these expeditions into outrage is unusually apparent in *An Essay on Man*. Here, in the third epistle, the poet displays a vision of the primitive condition of human society. This vision embraces a harmony between various realms of morality and value: private duty and public responsibility, virtue and power, the order of social privilege and the order of natural talent. In the *Essay* Pope represents humanity in the state of nature as embodying the ideal harmony. Kingship, virtue, piety, and wisdom stand united:

'Till then, by Nature crown'd, each Patriarch sate,
King, priest, and parent of his growing state;
On him, their second Providence, they hung,
Their law his eye, their oracle his tongue.
He from the wond'ring furrow call'd the food,
Taught to command the fire, controul the flood,
Draw forth the monsters of th'abyss profound,
Or fetch th'aerial eagle to the ground.
Love all the faith, and all th'allegiance then;
For Nature knew no right divine in Men,
No ill could fear in God; and understood
A sov'reign being but a sov'reign good.

It was from the contemplation of this empyrean that Pope came to judge the rich and the great. What he found of coursewas that the English social order rarely disclosed the correspondences he admired. The directors of the nation set more examples of vice than of virtue. The wealthy class largely overlapped with the frivolous class. The circle of talent bowed to the circle of corruption. Spokesmen for the houses of learning were vain and pedantic; at the head of religious institutions stood worldly, ambitious prelates

Essay on Man III, 215–22, 235–40. The last four lines quoted allude bitterly to the court's easy control over Parliament at the time when the poem was published (May, 1733).

To express his anger or disappointment, Pope used a categorical rhetoric that suited his poetic style. He juxtaposed group to group, example to class, ideal to reality. When he condemned, he described the evil as typical. When he praised, he handled the subject as a rare brightness in a world of shadows.

Pope's methods of satirical implication, therefore, gain strength from the contrast the poet habitually makes between style—including rhetorical forms—and meaning. As a satirist he gave extraordinary attention not only to nuances of implication but to the patterns of sound and rhythm in which he embodied them. These elements he fitted inside the parallels and antitheses of phrase or clause and the analogies or contrasts that shaped his paragraphs. His figures of speech could be pointedly brief, or they could expand the length of a paragraph or even (as a reiterated motif) of a poem, deepening the categorical tendencies of the rhetoric and poetic. So also his arguments moved discursively from general to particular, from example to universal and back. One poem balanced or opposed another, as the first *Moral Essay* (*To Cobham*), on male psychology, balanced the second (*To a Lady*), on female.

On all these levels Pope's constant effort is to redefine, regroup, to undermine old congruities and establish or hint at new ones. In his explicit arguments Pope seldom tried to inculcate fresh doctrines, but relied on traditional wisdom, on commonly accepted moral principles, or formulae. Maynard Mack has demonstrated the fullness of the tradition behind the sentences of *An Essay on Man*. "Its materials," he says, "are painstakingly traditional."[2] Earl Wasserman and Miriam Leranbaum have shown how much the third and fourth *Moral Es-* was that the English social order rarely disclosed the correspondences he admired. The directors of the nation set more examples of vice than of virtue. The wealthy class largely overlapped with the frivolous class. The circle of talent bowed to the circle of corruption. Spokesmen for the houses of learning were vain and pedantic; at the head of religious institutions stood worldly, ambitious prelates

The chief effect of style on meaning in Pope's satires of the 1730s and 1740s is to group persons and ideas in discomforting ways. Since the clusters assembled and disconnected are based on moral relationships, the outcome is a questioning of assumptions often put forward and widely credited. Among these Pope's special tendency is to cast into doubt the proper association of rank with merit, virtue, or even good manners. Again and again in his poems the author invokes a natural hierarchy of established families who benevolently control the landed wealth and the government of the country—recalling the harmonious vision of *An Essay on Man*. But he implies that the social and moral boundaries can no longer be congruent. They have broken down; a heterogeneous mob has replaced the ordered community; and it takes in

> *Whate'er of mungril no one class admits,*
> *A wit with dunces, and a dunce with wits.*
> *(Dunciad IV, 89–90)*

A simple example is Pope's imitation of Horace *Satires* I, ii (*Sobre Advice from Horace*), to which I now return. The Latin poem is a jocular mock-sermon on the dangers of adultery committed with respectable women. Horace directs his satire against men who feel dissatisfied with the sexual opportunities afforded them by slaves, freedwomen, or courtesans, and who insist on pursuing matrons. The individuals whom Horace singles out for explicit reproach are all male. Though he opens by illustrating the theme of excess with instances of prodigality and avarice, once he arrives at the matter of adultery, he focuses his poem on it. While Horace dealt with persons of consequence, he did not draw attention to their rank.

Pope gives roughly equal representation to both sexes but makes his most scandalous examples female. He draws attention to the rank of his characters and connects lust with gluttony and avarice. In a mock-apparatus Pope ridicules the scholarship of Richard Bentley (whose emendations he was nevertheless willing to adopt) and endows him with a prurient sensibility.

The reason for the difference between the two poets is that under the appearance of ridiculing adulterers, Pope is busy endowing the great of the land with the worst vices. He deals with a king's mistress (line 81), a prime minister's infidelities (line 88), the venereal disease of a duchess (line 95), the lust of an archbishop (line 44). Even Bentley, enlisted as annotator *malgré soi*, was himself master of a great college and a cultivator of the Whig ministry in power.

We observe that several of Horace's types of masculine vice turn feminine in Pope's lines. Tigellius the singer becomes Mrs. Oldfield the actress (line 4); Fufidius changes into Fufidia (line 18); Rufillus, Rufa (line 29); Maltinus, Jenny (line 33). In other words, the poet refuses to let the women appear passive, or to imply that only the males of the ruling class are corrupt. Horace had assumed that men were the instigators of vice, and women the persons seduced (though not always resisting). Pope implicitly breaks down the barrier between the sexes, suggesting that on the highest levels women become unnaturally aggressive. To those readers who compared the imitation with the Latin original, Pope would have implied that English ladies of fashion differed from ancient Roman matrons in starting rather than responding to acts of lust. In a sense, this poem leads into Pope's second *Moral Essay, To a Lady*.

Far more broadly, Pope suggests that corruption makes strange bedfellows; and that vice brings together groups that ought to be kept apart. Where Horace blames a few men for disgracing their ancestors, Pope hints that the natural hierarchy which underpins civilized society has yielded to moral chaos. This is also what the effects of style and structure suggest. In his opening lines, the poet uses rhythm and sound patterns to clarify the irony of his tone:

The Tribe of Templars, Play'rs, Apothecaries,
Pimps, Poets, Wits, Lord Fanny's, Lady Mary's. . . .

The catalogue of lawyers, poets, etc., makes the kind of set one might expect to gather in a theater district that lies near the inns of court. But high-placed lords and ladies should have no close ties with actors, pimps, and the healers of venereal disease. Pope marks off "Lord Fanny's, Lady Mary's" with a caesura but places them at the climax of his catalogue. In rhythm and sound patterns they are unlike the earlier series but tied to it. Yet they are, in sound, curiously like each other. Thus Pope implies the ambiguous sexuality of Hervey—the couplet has feminine endings—and the scandalous association of both him and Lady Mary with dubious characters.

Two aspects of the language of the poem add to such effects. Where Horace uses plain words like *inguina, cunnus,* and *muto* (all mistranslated in the Loeb edition), Pope enlists either a suggestive euphemism like *part* (line 87) or a pun like *frigate* (line 62). The consequent dazzle of ambiguities (*rise,* line 88; *stiff,* line 152; above all, *thing,* passim) enriches the suggestion of barriers breaking down. Maynard Mack has pointed out an exquisite instance. When Pope writes,

> *Suppose that honest part that rules us all,*
> *Should rise, and say—"Sir Robert! or Sir Paul!"*
> *(lines 87–88)*

The reference to a prime minister and a statesman evokes question time in the House of Commons; "part" suggests a genital "member," and therefore Member of Parliament; and so a fornicating phallus invades the high process of legislation. Another pair of realms that should be kept apart, merge.

The categories that fascinated Pope, in the satires, were those of public and private, high rank and low. Against these he pitted other categories like good and bad, tasteful and vulgar. Often his rhetoric moves from the personal and private world to that of public responsibility, or from the latter to the former. Invariably, he assumes that a harmony between these worlds is natural.

Such modulations depend on Pope's starting from familiar doctrines (what I should call formulae) and identifiable examples. As a moralist, he may state his doctrine in a paradox, but the teaching itself is likely to be conventional, not difficult and not too subtle. Pope still has a tendency of his own which differentiates him from the usual preacher of Christian doctrine and from most satirists. In searching for models of virtue, he looks instinctively to actors who are offstage—of middle rank or out of flavour. If he must have virtuous kings, statesmen, or bishops, he likes to secure ancients, foreigners, or Englishmen long dead.

By these means Pope can imply harsh judgments on the most powerful figures of his own age without endangering himself. The judgment grows more severe, and the class of corrupt persons more extensive, until we arrive at the *Epilogue to the Satires, 1740,* and the last book of *The Dunciad.* Finally, as in *The Dunciad* (Book IV), Pope was willing to blacken the character of whole orders of humanity. Earlier, he tried to appear selective; for his selectiveness was carefully weighted. Thus in picking names to celebrate, the poet did not always avoid men of rank. Among the subjects of his eulogies are Bathurst, Cobham, Oxford (father and son), and Bolingbroke. But he picked his noble heroes from the files of Jacobites, Tories, and opposition Whigs. Otherwise, he flavoured commoners of middle rank, like Kyrle,[6] Martha Blount,[7] and Dr. Arbuthnot.

Pope usually mentioned bishops only in order to blame them.[8] But when he wished to display his impartiality and bestow compliments on them, he named four, starting with one indeed close to the court but ending climactically with Berkeley, who had been sponsored by the Tory Swift, had been chaplain to the Jacobite Duke of Wharton, and had gained his elevation in spite of his connections:

Ev'n in a Bishop I can spy Desert;
Secker is decent, Rundel has a heart,
Manners with Candour are to Benson giv'n,
To Berkeley, ev'ry Virtue under Heav'n.
(Epilogue to the Satires II, 70–73)

Only the tribute to Berkeley is unequivocal. If we collect all the epithets, the poet drives us into separating the order of bishops from the moral order of decency, charity, candor, and virtue in general. "Ev'n" and "spy" suggest a minute search for the few exceptions to the rule. Berkeley has a strong place in his line, emphasized by the caesura and enriched by the echo of his name's sound and rhythm in "virtue" (*vartue*). Though he ends the series, he makes a contrast to the preceding trio, two of whom divide a line and the third occupies a weak place in a slow line of bathetic compliment.

So also if Pope did praise a very rich government official in Ralph Allen, he went out of his way to call him "low-born";[9] and as Erskine-Hill says, Allen's career rested on genuine service to the nation and was independent of Walpole or party.[10] Although I dwell on the subtle or indirect conveyance of meaning, Pope could be perfectly open at the same time. His gift for innuendo did not keep him from declaring explicitly what he was busy implying:

> *But does the Court a worthy Man remove?*
> *That instant, I declare, he has my Love:*
> *I shun his Zenith, court his mild Decline. . . .*
> *(Epilogue to the Satires II, 74–76)*

Pope's distaste for kings and conquerors is too obvious to need mention. Recently even his respect for the Emperor Augustus as an admirable alternative to the degenerate Georges has been persuasively doubted by meticulous scholars.[11] Miriam Leranbaum pointed out the large number of "great" men alluded to in the first *Moral Essay* (*To Cobham*): "The emphasis is upon rulers, kings, statesmen—exalted figures of all kinds." She observed further that the matching poem, *To a Lady*, also abounds in high personages, and that for part of the poem Pope uses "queen" as a synonym for "woman." Leranbaum connected these poems with the fourth epistle of *An Essay on Man*, which again has a good many allusions to kings in general and to certain rulers and tyrants in particular: Alexander, Caesar, Titus, Marcus Aurelius, Charles XII of Sweden—of whom two are treated as admirable (Titus and Marcus Aurelius) and the others as baneful. The same epistle of *An Essay on Man* opens and closes with a panegyric of Bolingbroke, and the first epistle opens with an apostrophe to him. In all three places he is opposed to kings. Bolingbroke was of course the intellectual leader of the opposition to Walpole's government and to George II's court.

We may infer that the most exciting subject for Pope's ridicule was George II. An analysis of the methods applied to his majesty's character will bring out Pope's methods in general. The operations begin at the level of common nouns. In poems published during the dozen years beginning in 1731, the word "king" constantly appears to point the generalizations about human nature and morality. But somehow the poet uses the name seldom with respect and often with contempt: "the pride of kings," "a lunatic king," "public spirit its great cure a crown."[14] A couplet like that in the fourth epistle of *An Essay on Man* gives the direction of Pope's pressure on the word:

> *Stuck o'er with titles and hung round with strings,*
> *That thou may'st be by kings, or whores of kings. . . .*
> *(lines, 205–6)*

In the *Epistle to Burlington* the poet foresees that some future king will follow the example of the earl, whose ideas are "worthy kings". The notion of the future implicitly excludes the present; and if the projects are suitable for kings, it strikes us that the monarch in power has not seen fit to carry them out. We might infer therefore that kingship as such is a concept excluding George II.

In the *Epistle to Bathurst* the word "king" appears only in connection with avarice (lines 72, 78, 401). The poet suggests that bribes are welcomed by a king and may determine royal policy. In his imitation of Horace *Satires* II, i, Pope uses the word "king" only once and then ambiguously, to say that he himself writes sobre, moral poems such as a king might read (line 152). The remark exudes irony because near the beginning of his poem Pope says that George II does not read poetry. A few weeks later, in the second epistle of *An Essay on Man* (published in February, 1733), "kings" are an instance of presumption (line 244), and "king" is what a lunatic thinks himself to be.

If we now skip to the last epistle of *An Essay on Man*, we see the process speed up, and discover a concentration of "king's" used with offputting connotations: fools fight for kings, wish to be kings, are ennobled by kings, become the flavourites of kings.[15] The poet draws a contrast between the immortal fame of his hero Bolingbroke and the shortlived reputation of kings. The process does not pause here but goes on to the last book of *The Dunciad*, where Pope lets himself ridicule the "*Right Divine* of kings to govern wrong".

When the poet's text failed him, as being too exposed, he could seek refuge in his mock-commentary. In this sanctuary (like Swift in the notes to the fifth edition of *A Tale of a Tub*) he could conjure up not one but two editors quarreling with one another over the meaning of a line, and by this device could produce with safety insinuations against George II. In *The Dunciad* (IV, 181–82) there is a commentators' quibble over a supposed allusion to verses by Claudian that describe liberty as flourishing under a good king. In the course of the disagreement, "Scriblerus" observes that liberty is often confused with monarchy; but "Bentley" retorts that "Liberty was never *lost*, or *went away* with so good a grace, as under a good king"!

In *An Epistle to a Lady* ("Of the Characters of Women") the use of "queen" suffers a similar deformation. Here, in a gallery of female portraits, the only picture of a queen is a flatterer's deception. Pope declares that women generally want power and pleasure: every lady would be queen for life. Thus he makes the word itself into a term of abuse for vicious, megalomaniac females; and we hear the contemptuous phrase, "a whole sex of queens".

As a common noun, of course, "king" easily alternates with its near synonyms. "Tyrant" and "prince" appear alongside it. But all these are mingled with the proper names of various rulers, from Alexander the Great to George II—or with allusions plainly identifying them. Except for Titus and Marcus Aurelius, the names receive ambiguous or sinister overtones. In the *Epistle to Cobham* —published during the same month as the last epistle of *An Essay on Man* —Pope has a passage assembling an ugly gang of individual rulers, as if to balance the use of the common noun in the *Essay* . Although explicitly chosen to illustrate the inconsistency of human nature, almost every one is dispraised in an epithet: buffoon, perjur'd, godless, bigot, faithless, duped, fool.

This example hardly misleads one. Pope's satires do provide momentary glimpses of a king's behaving himself decently, but such acts tend to appear out of character for the particular monarch; and in representing them, the poet seems to want a contrast to the inactivity of George II. Thus Pope describes Charles II, James II, and Louis XIV as tolerating satirical poetry. But he does so in response to a friend who warns him against enraging the present powers;[17] and he treats the phenomenon as contrary to what one might expect of each king. The greatest concentration of admirable royal gestures, in the *Epistle to Augustus* , invites us to set the heroism or patronage of half a dozen kings against the lack of those qualities in King George.[18] And yet several of these examples are themselves ambiguous: Charles I pensioned Quarles; Charles II "debauch'd" the muses ; William III knighted Blackmore.

In the late poems generally, miscellaneous rulers are named to be censured or ridiculed. Pope gives special attention to wicked or stupid figures: kings, usurpers, and emperors whom the poet might freely identify, yet who, by association with the class of kings, would stain the mantle of George II. By admitting his exceptions, the poet strengthens the innuendo against the type.

As early as the *Epistle to Burlington* (published in December, 1731), Pope contrasts the good taste of his lordship with the doubtful taste of Louis XIV and Nero (lines 71–72). In *An Essay on Man* , Epistle IV, along with the common noun, the poet sneers at Caesar three times, as well as Alexander the Great and Charles XII of Sweden. Alexander and Caesar had already been stigmatized in Epistle I as natural disasters (lines 159–60). Midas, in the *Epistle to Arbuthnot* , is cursed by Apollo with the ears of an ass (lines 69–82).

As one reads through the poems, it becomes clear that Pope intends us to refer back and forth among them in order to perfect identifications which are hinted at in separate places. Lord Fanny, Sporus, and Narcissus are thus united. So also the names for Lady Mary Wortley Montagu and her husband. She alone may be Fufidia, Sappho, or simply Lady Mary, which is to say, lustful, unclean, avaricious, and bluestocking. (Sir Edward and she together are Gripus, Shylock, or Avidien and his wife—all usurers.)[1] So when readers are not linking the ambiguous sexuality of Hervey to the florid style of his prose, they may be blending the stinginess ascribed to Lady Mary with her alleged carnality. Alternatively, they may assure themselves that various names allude to the same person because they notice a cluster of traits circulating unchanged. The style of wit and the courtly prominence of Sporus in the *Epistle to Arbuthnot* persuade us that Hervey is the reference of "H——vy" in the *Epilogue to the Satires* .

Even so with Caesar: Pope openly alluded to George II as "Caesar" in an imitation of Horace.A year later, in the last epistle of *An Essay on Man* , he mentioned "Caesar with a senate at his heels," and juxtaposed him to Marcellus in exile—thus inviting us to set George II against Bolingbroke.At the very same time, when he refers to Caesar retreating from Britain and risking his empire for a punk, we may perhaps think of the king leaving England to join Madame Walmoden in Hanover.

Alternatively, Pope may suppress the word "king" and bring together traits well known as marks of his majesty: bearishness, the habit of kicking when angry, the domination of the royal mind (such as it was) by Queen Caroline, the prime minister's power over his master. "'Tis a bear's talent not to kick, but hug," may be an allusion to George II. The following lines (gathering in six of the seven cardinal sins!) certainly are such an allusion:

Know, there are Rhymes, which (fresh and fresh apply'd)
Will cure the arrant'st Puppy of his Pride.
Be furious, envious, slothful, mad or drunk,
Slave to a Wife or Vassal to a Punk
A Switz, a High-dutch, or a Low-dutch Bear—
All that we ask is but a patient Ear.

One of Pope's most mischievous devices is to insult George and Caroline by reviling their flatterers. The obvious example occurs in the earliest imitation of Horace. Here, Pope's friend Fortescue advises the poet to write something in praise of the king. Pope replies with some lines of parody of what

Blackmore, Budgell, and Cibber have written in praise of William III and George II. Fortescue suggests that he praise the queen and the royal children. The poet replies that the ears of majesty are too "nice" to bear his verses. But the satire on bad poets irresistibly attaches itself to the royal persons; and in a closing ambiguity, Pope deliciously evokes his monarch's indifference to literature of all sorts:

And justly Caesar scorns the Poet's Lays,
It is to History he trusts for praise.

Queen Caroline undergoes a similar blackwash in the second *Moral Essay* (*To a Lady*), when Pope ostensibly despairs of finding an honest portrait of her, because flattering authors and artists adorn her always and mechanically with conventional virtues:

One certain Portrait may (I grant) be seen,
Which Heav'n has varnish'd out, and made a Queen:
The same for ever! and describ'd by all
With Truth and Goodness, as with Crown and Ball:
Poets heap Virtues, Painters Gems at will,
And show their zeal, and hide their want of skill.
(lines 181–86)

The innuendo is of course that the artists must manufacture the virtues because Caroline has none of them.

This device can be pointed, as when, in the *Epilogue to the Satires*, the poet denounces those who "make saints of queens, and gods of kings" (II, 225). But it can easily be generalized to apply to other persons of consequence; and in one of the most dazzling passages of his poetry, Pope brings in bishops, judges, and statesmen. This is the first *Moral Essay, To Cobham*. Here, in a justly famous paragraph, Pope argues that most poets (or artists) turn, for their examples of virtue, to the upper levels of society. He then transforms the fact into satire by recommending the practice. Actually, he says, it is so hard to be virtuous in a great position that whoever succeeds in doing so deserves unusual praise:

'Tis from high Life high Characters are drawn;
A Saint in Crape is twice a Saint in Lawn;
A Judge is just, a Chanc'lor juster still;
A Gownman, learn'd; a Bishop, what you will;
Wise, if a Minister; but, if a King,
More wise, more learn'd, more just, more ev'ry thing.
Court-virtues bear, like Gems, the highest rate,
Born where Heav'n's influence scarce can penetrate:
In life's low vale, the soil the virtues like,
They please as Beauties, here as Wonders strike.
(lines 87–96)

The method of implication derives again from the way the technique of verse divides and unites categories: lower clergy and episcopacy are separated instead of being united as the church; so also are a lower justice and the chancellor, who ought to be collected in the law. "Saint in crape" and "saint in lawn" are parallel in form and rhythm. Yet the parson might be a saint while the bishop could only gain promotion through corruption. "Judge-just," as alliteration, balances "chanc'lor-juster," with its repeated endings and sibilants. But the judge is far likelier than the chancellor is to keep his integrity. The categories of true and specious goodness are thus closely joined precisely as they are set apart. "Crape" opposes "lawn" in sound as "judge" opposes "chanc'lor." In the paragraph as a whole the ideas of high and low are similarly split and rejoined.

Such operations bring the whole relation of example to postulate into doubt. Pope can illustrate an aphorism with an instance that weakens it, as when he says that poets want only to enjoy their garden and book "in quiet," and then praises Swift for saving "the rights a court attack'd."[30] More abstractly, he even challenges the distinction between reality and fiction. Thus Pope offers us historical examples, identified by name or otherwise, along with veiled pseudonyms which can be penetrated by a giveaway trait or association, and, as well, with utterly imaginary examples which discourage speculation. Sometimes he combines these various procedures, by using the real name harmlessly and then following it at once with a pseudonym and satiric characterization of the same person: the Addison-Atticus passage in the *Epistle to Arbuthnot* is a cunning example. At his boldest, in dealing with the king, Pope can use the very name of George, but so ambiguously that one reader might think the reference innocuous (or complimentary) while another could see it as an insult:

I sought no homage from the Race that write;
I kept, like Asian Monarchs, from their sight:
Poems I heeded (now be-rym'd so long)
No more than Thou, great George ! a Birth-day Song.
(Epistle to Arbuthnot, lines 220–23)

(That is, the king is so indifferent to poetry that he cannot notice it even when it is in praise of himself.) The magnificent climax of this technique is of course the opening and closing lines of the *Epistle to Augustus*. Both these passages may be read as either eulogy or vituperation.

If we consider the entire range of such innuendoes and the classes of men and ideas to which they are applied, we may say that ultimately, Pope establishes two realms of implication in his satires—one, conventionally didactic; the other, boldly subversive. One shares the orientation of the explicit meaning and develops it in the usual way by imagery, analogy, irony, etc. The other has a different center, different coordinates, from the explicit meaning, which it employs as a code or a screen

Maynard Mack calls the one thematic and the other topical.

Thus although I have made much of the subversive implications of the first *Moral Essay* (*To Cobham*), that poem has a familiar orientation as well, implicitly supported by Pope's choice of images. This design starts from the explicit question whether or not one can secure a true knowledge of the inner characters of men.

Pope offers two points of view, the scepticism of Montaigne and the effort made by Locke to establish an area of demonstrable knowledge. Pope claims that he can arrive at true knowledge by way of the concept of a ruling passion. But for two-thirds of the poem he illustrates the sceptical position.

The imagery of the epistle to Cobham opposes effects of light to elements drawn from external nature: landscape, plants, animals. Pope implies that light and colour are more deceptive than line and shape. He implicitly links human deceitfulness with the ancient principle that line is more reliable than colour. He associates virtue with things that grow naturally, vice with things that blaze.

On this level the poem is not dangerous but quite satisfactory, with the images implicitly bearing out the argument. It is when we shift our attention from the pattern of images to the choice of human examples that the subversive implications rise to trouble us.

The same analysis applies to the last epistle of *An Essay on Man*. Here the poet discusses the best ways for men to achieve happiness, and says that "fled from monarchs, St. John, [it] dwells with thee". Conventionally, this verse alludes to expressions like "happy as a king," and implies that kings are not in fact happy. But subversively, it implies that the corruption of George II is less likely to produce happiness than the integrity of his opponent, Bolingbroke.

So also, expounding the principle that God works in orderly ways and does not often suspend the rules governing the universe, Pope observes that adherence to order may sometimes subject virtuous persons to illness and pain:

Think we, like some weak prince, th'Eternal Cause
Prone for his fav'rites to reverse his laws?
(lines 121–22)

Conventionally, here, Pope is implying that divine justice is the model for earthly justice. But subversively, he implies that under George II, royal mistresses and flavoured courtiers may commit crimes with impunity.

One of the strongest examples of what I may call the bipolarity of Pope's implications is a passage in the *Epilogue to the Satires*. It illustrates his fascination with the connection between private and public realms. Pope starts from the assumption that domestic virtue has a direct relation to public performance, that a faithless husband cannot be an honest statesman. He then proceeds to dissolve the line between the realms, and blame a corrupt politician as if his infidelities sprang from the same cause as his misgovernment. The well-known lines about Vice owned by Greatness make the process splendidly visible:

Vice is undone, if she forgets her Birth,
And stoops from Angels to the Dregs of Earth:
But 'tis the Fall degrades her to a Whore;
Let Greatness own her, and she's mean no more:
Her birth, her Beauty, Crowds and Courts confess,
Chaste Matrons praise her, and grave Bishops bless:
In golden Chains the willing World she draws,
And hers the Gospel is, and hers the Laws. . . .
(Epilogue I, 141–48)

The explicit meaning is deepened by the association of vice with the Scarlet Whore; and as James Osborn has shown, the particular scarlet whore intended was the Empress Theodora. Yet, as Osborn has also shown, there was a hidden, far more scandalous allusion, in these lines, to the marriage of Walpole with his mistress Maria Skerrett; and the description of Vice represents her triumph

The poem does not call upon us to choose between these implications. Conventionally, Pope associates the career of vice with the fall of angels and the rise of the Whore. Subversively, he ties it to the marriage of Molly Skerrett. Neither implication excludes the other, but the two move in different directions. The failure to accept such bipolarity has led some scholars to disregard the topical meaning for the thematic or the latter for the former, whereas the poet usually is playing with both at once, and letting the second peep out from behind the first.

I think we can apply a similar analysis to Pope's concept of heroism. Scholars have noticed his habit of setting up the moral and social values traditionally belonging to the country house as vastly superior to those traditionally assigned to a royal court. This opposition blends with an old political tradition of a country party, based in the gentry, which resisted the measures of the court. When the Tory-Whig alignments emerged in the late 1670s, they cut across the court-and-country alignments, which endured along with them. In poems that seem to place rural contentment before urban activity, Pope is often invoking as well the old political antithesis between country and court. Like Swift, he could distinguish unproductive stockbrokers or financiers from productive merchants or tradesmen. It is the former that he liked to merge with Walpole and the court. If Pope habitually embodied his own values in a cultivated, politically active country gentleman like Arthur Browne,[35] he also assumed that such a figure would for patriotic reasons resist the government in power. Here then is a concept of heroism in keeping with that of Dryden after the Revolution and of Swift after the death of Queen Anne.

In the late satires, however, Pope's bipolarity also shows itself in his treatment of this sort of hero. Ostensibly, he may place the uses of retirement before those of public office during a reign of corruption. The country gentleman may therefore appear to be a truly heroic figure, reminding us of Dryden's cousin John Driden. Yet as T. R. Edwards suggests, the poet as such can be recognized as Pope's hidden hero; and it is for this reason that, so early as *An Essay on Criticism*, we see the poet described as a warrior.[36] I find it significant that in this youthful, hopeful poem, Pope was willing to draw an analogy between writers and monarchs or conquerors:

> *Like Kings we lose the Conquests gain'd before,*
> *By vain Ambition still to make them more. . . .*
> *(lines 64–65)*
> *A prudent Chief not always must display*
> *His Pow'rs in equal Ranks, and fair Array,*
> *But with th'Occasion and the Place comply,*
> *Conceal his Force, nay seem sometimes to Fly.*
> *(lines 175–78)*

In the pessimistic *Epistle to Augustus* the parallel becomes an antithesis:

Yet let me show, a Poet's of some weight,
And (tho' no Soldier) useful to the State. . . .
I scarce can think him such a worthless thing,
Unless he praise some monster of a King. . . .
(lines 203–4, 209–10)

For now it is precisely as an independent gentleman that the poet is heroic. It is by resisting the blandishments of pensions and offices, by refusing to serve a corrupted crown, that the poet shows his virtue:

I cannot like, Dread Sir! your Royal Cave;
Because I see by all the Tracks about,
Full many a Beast goes in, but none comes out.
(Horace Epistles I, i, 115–17)

Thus on the one hand, Pope recommends and identifies himself with "chiefs, out of war, and statesmen, out of place." He celebrates Cobham as a gardener, Bathurst "unspoil'd by wealth,"[40] and the Man of Ross making grandeur blush.[41] He implicitly praises himself for being the friend of men like Caryll and Bethel.

On the other hand, Pope exalts his own heroic character as bold moralist in verse, driving vice before him—"un-plac'd, unpension'd, no man's heir, or slave."[42] It is Pope in his own right who feels proud "to see / Men not afraid of God, afraid of me."[43] As the voice of heroic virtue, or even as "God's deputy" (in the words of T. R. Edwards),[44] he implicitly congratulates men like Burlington for being chosen among the poet's friends:

Enough for half the Greatest of these days
To 'scape my Censure, not expect my Praise:
Are they not rich? what more can they pretend?
Dare they to hope a Poet for their Friend?
(Epilogue to the Satires II, 112–15)

Not only does he become the standard of merit; he records it. So Pope holds the authority that makes Hough and Digby immortal,[45] that damns Sporus and annihilates King George. In this ancient sense it is he who assigns the most splendid rewards for true greatness; honor derives from him as the fountain, and not from the king:

Sages and Chiefs long since had birth
E're Caesar was, or Newton nam'd,
These rais'd new Empires o'er the Earth,
And Those new Heav'ns and Systems fram'd;
Vain was the chief's and sage's pride
They had no Poet and they dyd!

Criticising Pope on Neo-classical Principles: William Wordsworth

There are two main texts in which Wordsworth elaborates his opinion of Pope, the first is his 'Essay upon Epitaphs' (1810), the second is the 'Essay, Supplementary to the Preface' (1815). The core of the first essay, it seems, is a moral and a psychological ideal. "In the mind of the truly great and good," Wordsworth claims, "everything that is of importance is at peace with itself." This peace is, very importantly, connected to a certain orderliness of the mind that could be called integrity, or a harmony of the faculties of the mind. And it is the signs of exactly such mental "peace" that he is looking for in reading writers of epitaphs, and probably all writers.

He speaks, for instance, of his "deep conviction that the excellence of writing, whether in prose or in verse, consists in a conjunction of Reason and Passion, a conjunction which is out of necessity benign." Now, the most important problem with Pope is that his writings seem to offer no signs of this benign conjunction.

Pope's mind had been employed chiefly in observation upon the vices and follies of men. Now, vice and folly are in contradiction with the moral principle which can never be extinguished in the mind: and, wanting this controul, are irregular, capricious, and inconsistent with themselves.

This element of harmony Wordsworth attempts to find as a second step within the language of the epitaphs he discusses. The words used should perfectly coincide with the feelings of the author. In Pope's case, however, "the Reader will perceive at once that nothing in the heart of the Writer has determined either the choice, the order, or the expression of the ideas that the connections are mechanical and arbitrary." If this determining power is at work, however, the poem seems to flow, as it were, of itself. "One half of the process is mechanical, words doing their own work, and one half of the line manufacturing the rest." The most intense articulation of his preference of a poetry of this kind is when Wordsworth claims to be looking for "those expressions which are not what the garb is to the body but what the body is to the soul."

The subject of the poem (the deceased person) should be represented in a similarly unified manner. That is, a complete, living personality should reappear, somewhat uncannily, in the poem.

The Author [Pope] forgets that it is a living creature that must interest us and not an intellectual Existence, which a mere character is. Insensible to this distinction the brain of the Writer is set at work to report as flatteringly as he may of the mind of his subject; the good qualities are separately abstracted (can it be otherwise than coldly and unfeelingly?) and put together again as coldly and unfeelingly."

In other words, Pope is only using the rational part of his mind in composition, and can thus recreate only the same part of his subject. The third problem with this type of poetry is that it does not fulfill its purpose. "The first requisite, then, in an Epitaph is that it should speak, in a tone which shall sink into the heart, the general language of humanity."

In fact, the test is there to enable the reader to see through the text of the epitaph (and probably other pieces of writing as well) and see the whole of a personality, either of the author or of the subject of the poem beneath it; to be able to judge whether they have "inner simplicity", or are, without the control of the "moral principle", "irregular, capricious, and inconsistent with themselves." That the poem should be a communication, as direct as possible, without "the artificialities that have overrun our writings since the days of Dryden and Pope," is most apparent in the best example Wordsworth can give of an ideal epitaph, which is also a good example to show that Wordsworth's ideal, if carried to the extremes, makes writing itself nearly superfluous.

A very small Stone laid upon the ground, bearing nothing more than the name of the Deceased with the date of birth and death, imparting that this was an infant which had been born one day and died the following. More awful thoughts of rights conferred, of hopes awakened, of remembrances stealing away or vanishing were imparted to my mind by that transcription there before my eyes than by any other that it has ever been my lot to meet with upon a Tomb-stone.

In other words, the opposition that was set up between poetry that springs from and activates the whole of the soul and brings it into harmony with itself, and poetry that is only the offspring of the intellect is here treated more narrowly in the context of religion.

The essay, however, is in the most part an attempt to justify the greatness of Wordsworth's poetry in spite of its low sales. The following passage, probably the longest he ever wrote on Pope, is to be read bearing that in mind.

The arts by which Pope contrived to procure for himself a more general and a higher reputation than perhaps any English Poet ever attained during his life-time, are known to the judicious. And as well-known is to them, that the undue exertion of those arts is the cause why Pope has for some time held a rank in Literature, to which, if he had not been seduced by an over-love of popularity, and has confided more in his native genius, he never could have descended. He bewitched the nation by his melody, and dazzled it by his polished style, and was himself blinded by his own success. Having wondered from Humanity in his Eclogues with boyish inexperience, the praise, which these compositions obtained, tempted him into a belief that Nature was not to be trusted, at least in pastoral Poetry.

It is easy to see that Wordsworth's approach has lost some of the subtlety of the previous essay. The style of the attack is much sharper as well. Nature and art are here starkly contrasted. With some exaggeration, it might be said that in this passage Wordsworth seems to identify "art" with dishonest tricks to gain an audience. The "bewitching" effect of Pope's polished style is again emphasized. There is, once again, an attempt to see into the soul of the criticized author, the "dazzling" quality of Pope's verse, which blinded even Pope himself, has eventually no effect on Wordsworth, who sees through the "polished" surfaces of language, to find the misguided person behind them.

The concept of Nature is very much in the foreground here. It is interesting, however, that it does not occur here in the general sense, as something opposed to "art", and which determines the poet to speak "in the general language of humanity." It is used in a narrower sense, as a representation of images from "external nature."

Now it is remarkable that, excepting the Nocturnal Reverie of Lady Winchilsea, and a passage or two in the Windsor Forest of Pope, the poetry of the period intervening between the publication of Paradise Lost and The Seasons does not contain a single new image of external nature. To what a low state of knowledge of the most obvious and important phenomena had sunk, is evident in the style in which Dryden has executed a description of Night in one of his Tragedies, and Pope his translation of the celebrated moonlight scene in the Iliad. A blind man, in the habit of attending accurately to descriptions casually dropped from the lips of those around him, might easily depict these appearances with more truth.

The stress on external nature is also very important. Indeed, the dialectics of external and internal are present all along the essay. At the very beginning, Wordsworth gives the following description of the "business of poetry." "The appropriate business of poetry is to treat of things not as they are, but as they appear; not as they exist in themselves, but as they seem to exist to the senses, and to the passions." From this definition on, the question, how much poetry is an outward movement of the soul or its plying in upon itself is never decided. On the one hand, Wordsworth claims that "of genius, in the fine arts, the only infallible sign is the widening of the sphere of human sensibility," where the key word is obviously "widening." On the other hand, he gives it as the reason of the low popularity of his works, that "in everything which is to send the soul into herself the poet must reconcile himself for a season to few and scattered hearers."

There are basically two strategies with which to discuss such statements. One is to regard them in a psychological light as a "patricide" on Wordsworth's part, as an attempt to suppress all the influence Pope's poetry had on him. Evidence for this is not very difficult to come by. The commentary to his Prose Works offers two important pieces of evidence.

The other approach, however, is to regard Wordsworth as a critic who can be taken seriously, and who has a very strong sense of his position with regard to poetical and critical traditions, which is certainly not unbiased, but still reflective enough to have a thought-provoking power.

The most startling feature of Wordsworth's criticism of Pope is that he finds in Pope many of the problems that his critics seem to find in Wordsworth. That is to say, Wordsworth's present-day critics are applying much the same criteria that he applied in his criticism. The first such characteristic is that Wordsworth is thinking about poetry in moral terms. His problem with Pope is not simply that his style is overly polished, but that it is a lie. The author is not in full earnest. He is only applying a flourishing rhetoric, which is dangerously deceptive. It is important to emphasize this point because it does not fit in with the overwhelming characterization of Wordsworth's poetics as introversive, as "rejecting the very principle of living in society" (as Marilyn Butler expressed it). No, he criticizes Pope exactly for the social effect of his poetry, for the harm he sees it to have caused. Certainly, he sees moral behaviour as beginning within one's own psyche, but he never denies that it is to continue in the social sphere.

In founding his criticism on the "conjunction of Reason and Passion," Wordsworth is following a distinctly classicist tradition. Bertrand A. Goldgar in his introduction the Literary

Criticism of Alexander Pope summarizes the issue in the following way.

. However much the critics may have cautioned against the excess and extravagance wrought by an uncontrolled fancy, they never denied that imagination or invention is essential to the creation of art as well as judgment. What was admired was a proper balance or harmony of the creative and the controlling faculties.

The following lines show Pope's own phrasing of the same idea

For wit and judgment often are at strife, meant each other's aid, like man and wife. 'Tis more to guide than spur the Muse's steed Restrain his fury, than provoke his speed.

What Wordsworth does, from this perspective, is to re-examine and reformulate this classicist teaching in the light of his increased awareness of the probabilities of discord between these faculties. He finds Pope lacking in what Pope himself called the element of "fury" in composition.

A further important element in Wordsworth's critical theory is the requirement that the poet speak "the general language of humanity." This issue remains little explored in these essays, but with historical hindsight, the contrast seems clear enough. As Marilyn Butler makes it clear,

the explicit appeal to a refined élite ceased not long after Pope's death to be the fashionable orthodoxy. the preferred tone now was simple, serious and grand, and the art of the first half of the century, Pope's included, came to be seen as overornamented, clever as opposed to feeling, and meretriciously flattering."

That is to say, Wordsworth maintains that beneath the studied language of Pope's poetry there is a more general, more basic "language of humanity." In effect, his linguistic ideal is indeed a "levelling one."

The last important issue that has to be mentioned is the problem of poetic originality. Wordsworth attacks Dr.

Johnson's praise for an epitaph by Pope as "containing nothing taken from common places." For Wordsworth this is exactly the great shortcoming of such poetry. "It is", he claims, "a primary requisite in an Epitaph that it should contain thoughts and feelings which are in their substance common-place, and even trite. It is grounded upon the universal intellectual property of man." It is very interesting to find that Wordsworth, far from glorifying originality as opposed to poetical tradition, is proposing a counter-canon to poetical tradition, a canon "grounded upon the universal intellectual property of man." If Wordsworth is usually criticized for having abandoned Enlightenment universalism, it might be surprising to realise that in his criticism he applies this very criterion, and in fact against the arguably most representative author of the Enlightenment, Alexander Pope.

To sum it up, Wordsworth, in his insistence on the moral effect of poetry, in the emphasis he lays on the careful balance of the creative faculties in writing, and in his concept of the universality of poetical language is following neo-classical lines of thought. In other words, none of the major criteria that Wordsworth applies in his statements about Pope represent a real turning away from critical tradition, and, thus, they should not be used as a basis for theorizing Romanticism in terms of strong oppositions.

Finding a Place for Pope: S. T. Coleridge

Coleridge never gave an extended discussion of Pope. The Augustan poet's name crops up in his lectures usually as a measure of contrast. He develops his notion of the true nature of poetry in opposition to Pope's work in a lecture of 1813. In later lectures (of 1818) he contrasts Pope to pre-Restoration poets with preference for the earlier authors. He seems to find Pope wanting in a harmony between sense and form on the one hand, and he criticizes the "arbitrariness" of the neo-classical poet's choice of words, on the other. I shall restrict the discussion to his statements on this topic in Biographia Literaria (1817), however, because this is the only one that Byron certainly read.

Coleridge first speaks about Pope in a record of his childhood thoughts and feelings about the neo-classical poet.

> Among those with whom I conversed there were, of course, very many who had formed their taste, and their notions of poetry, from the writings of Mr. Pope and his followers: or to speak more generally, on that school of French poetry, condensed and invigorated by English understanding, which had predominated from the last century. I was not blind to the merits of this school, yet as from inexperience of the world, and consequent want of sympathy with the general subjects of these poems, they gave me little pleasure, I doubtless undervalued the kind, and with the presumption of youth withheld from its masters the legitimate name of poets. I saw that the excellence of this kind consisted in just and acute observations on men and manners in an artificial state of society, as its matter and substance: and in the logic of wit conveyed in smooth and strong epigrammatic couplets, as its form.
>
> intellect, as in the Rape of the Lock, or in the Essay on Man; nay when it was a consecutive narration, as in that product of matchless talent and ingenuity, Pope's Translation of the Iliad; still a point was looked for at the end of each second line, and the whole was as it were a sorites, or, if I may exchange a logical for a grammatical metaphor, a conjunction disjunctive, of epigrams. Meantime the matter and diction seemed to me characterized not so much by poetical thoughts, but by thoughts translated into the language of poetry.

The rhetorical trick in the passage is, of course, that it is impossible to tell how much of this is the opinion of the infantile Coleridge, and how much he retained until the moment of writing. He indicates that his early resistance to Pope was due to his childhood inexperience, but he also emphasises that he had a very subtle insight ("I saw") into this kind of poetry.

The first important novelty in this passage (which is going to reappear in Byron's defence of Pope) is that this kind of writing is, regardless of the actual language, essentially French.

One of the tensions in the passage, which hardly appears on the surface, is the difference in attitude between what Coleridge's associations were regarding anything French at the time of these childhood conversations (probably the seventeen-eighties) and the time of writing.

The second characteristic of Pope's poetry that Coleridge identifies is that it is a poetry that needs experience "of the world", that is, a knowledge of facts. This is, in itself a neutral remark, and one that any reader can easily corroborate: we certainly need many footnotes to appreciate Pope. However, connected to the next remark, that this poetry only focuses on people "in an artificial state of society", this might carry a note of disapproval. This idea can be compared to Wordsworth's criticism that Pope does not go deep enough, he does not manage to touch our common humanity: he is not universal enough.

The third problem that Coleridge touches upon is very important in the entirety of his literary criticism: his consciousness of form. Against Wordsworth's 'Preface' to the Lyrical Ballads he argues very strongly for the importance of metre, which he claims can create "the interpenetration of passion and of will, of spontaneous impulse and of voluntary.

The problem with Pope is that he does not create the unified, organic whole that Coleridge is looking for in a piece of art. He sees this kind of poetry as mechanically producing disjointed couplets.

I have attempted to illustrate the present state of our language, in its relation to literature, by a press-room of longer and smaller stereotype pieces, which in the present Anglo-Gallican fashion of unconnected epigrammatic periods, it requires but ordinary portion of ingenuity to vary indefinitely, and yet produce something, which if not sense, will be so like it to do as well.

Consequently, Coleridge is the worst example for any attempt at setting up an opposition between the first and second generation of Romantics based on their consciousness of form and rhetoric (in the manner of McGann). Indeed, Coleridge everywhere emphasizes the importance of the conscious element in the creative process. He describes Shakespeare, for instance, in the following terms:

> no mere child of nature, no automaton of genius, no passive vehicle of inspiration possessed by the spirit, not possessing it; first studied patiently, meditated deeply, understood minutely, till knowledge, become habitual and intuitive, wedded itself to his habitual feelings.

That Coleridge's overwhelming praise for Pope's Iliad ("that astonishing product of matchless talent and ingenuity"), which is carefully modified later on ("still, a point was looked for at the end of each second line etc."), is disingenuous can be seen from a long footnote later in the Biographia.

> In the course of one of my Lectures, I had occasion to point to the almost faultless position and choice of words, in Mr. Pope's original compositions, particularly in his Satires and moral Essays, for the purpose of comparing them with his translation of Homer, which I do not stand alone in regarding as the main source of our pseudo-poetic diction next to the man who forms and elevates the taste of the public, he that corrupts it is commonly the greatest genius. [it is due to Pope's effect that the audience] had been accustomed, in reading poetry, to receive pleasure from the separate images and phrases successively, without asking themselves whether the whole meaning was sense or nonsense.

A very important problem is raised when Coleridge claims that most of Pope's poetry is structured according to the "logic of wit." Wit, which is indeed often responsible for bringing ideas that seem as far removed from each other as it is possible into unprecedented contact, for which we could borrow Coleridge's term, "conjunction disjunctive." More importantly still, Coleridge probably sees something morally dubious in Pope's satirical talent. "The office and duty of the poet is to select the most dignified as well as 'the happiest, gayest attitude of things.' The reverse is the business of burlesque and travesty, a predominant taste for which has been always deemed a mark of a low and degraded mind." This remark is, in fact, very similar to Wordsworth's identifying the source of Pope's moral instability in his fixation on "vice and folly."

M. H. Abrams, for instance, spoke about the syncretism of Coleridge's mind. That, by his familiar process of desynonimization, Coleridge distinguishes between talents on the one hand, and geniuses on the other. To the first group, characterized by understanding, empirical choice, and fancy, belong Beaumont, Fletcher, Ben Johnson and Pope, while the second, of the rank of reason and imagination, comprises Dante, Shakespeare, Milton, and Wordsworth. The two groups are not in opposition, however, the second includes all that matters in the first.

By way of summary, it might be fair to say that Coleridge, just like Wordsworth, though certainly not sharing Byron's nearly unqualified praise for Pope, articulates his opinion in a way that cannot be said to be standing in a stark opposition to either eighteenth-century classicism or its partial revival by the "younger Romantics." His insistence on form, on the conscious control over the creative process, or on the universal claim of poetry, all link him to that very tradition.

CHAMPIONING POPE: LORD BYRON

As it was noted at the beginning of the essay, this is not an investigation into Pope's reception-history, nor even into the history of the so-called Pope Controversy, still some references to this debate have to be made, because this is the context of Byron's most famous statements concerning Pope. It has to be noted at the outset that the most fundamental difference between Byron's assessment of Pope and that of the two elder poets is that he is contributing to a polemics, and it is anything but certain how much the sentiments he voices here can be assimilated to either his other prose statements or his poetical practice.

The most important name behind these debates is that of Joseph Warton, who published in 1756 a very influential study called An Essay on the Genius and Writings of Pope, which first articulated those criteria in line with which most of the ensuing controversy was to proceed. The following is a cursory inventory of the issues that in the wake of Warton's essay it became almost compulsory to comment upon in treating Pope.

First of all, it was Warton who introduced the method of differentiating between various species of poetry, which became a means of relegating Pope, with due respect to his powers in one class of poetry, to a status which is still below genuine poetry. Warton wishes to distinguish between "species of poetry" according to whether they are the productions of "a man of sense, a man of wit," or of a "true poet." Around the end of the essay, he pushes this opposition a bit further in stating that "the largest portion of them [Pope's works] is the didactic, moral and satiric kind, and consequently not of the most poetic species of poetry.

The second problem that Warton mentions is that "you can reduce" Pope's poetry "to the tameness of prose." Which is to say, versification, the formal perfection of the lines, is in some way external to its meaning, the two have no necessary connection. The third important step in the essay is the introduction of two fundamental requirements: "the sublime and the pathetic are the two chief nerves of all genuine poesy. What is there transcendentally sublime or pathetic in Pope?" The fourth essential remark in the essay is Warton's uneasiness about Pope's formal perfectionism, and about the overwhelming effect his "musical versification" had on even the least talented followers. Fifth, he remarks that "descriptive talent was by no means the shining talent of Pope." The sixth issue is the problem of French influence, more specifically, Pope's adherence to "correctness", that "nauseous cant of the French critics." The final important bit of criticism he raises is that Pope "treats of fashionable follies and the topics of the day", instead of higher subjects.

It falls out of the scope of this essay to treat the various answers to Warton's essay, but it is important to know that it was this debate that William Lisle Bowles renewed when he brought out his ten-volume edition of The Works of Alexander

Pope, with Additional Observations and a Memoir in 1806. Bowles, who "was trained under Joseph [Warton] at Winchester before becoming Thomas's protégé at Oxford," as Amarasinghe remarks, "regarded himself as a conscious disciple of [Joseph] Warton." It is no great surprise, then, that most of his statements are merely a repetition of what Warton had said. The only fundamental difference between the two critics, as Amarasinghe explains, is that of tone of voice: "while Warton's severest criticism was invariably courteously disciplined and moderate, Bowles's strictures are remarkable for their aggressive I shall not pursue the debate to any length, and will confine the discussion to those statements of Bowles that are immediately relevant to Byron's essay.

Byron's engagement with Bowles's strictures goes back to 1807, when he started to compose English Bards and Scots Reviewers. Already in this poem, where he claims to "venture o'er / The path which Pope and Gifford trod before" (lines 93-4), he mocks Bowles for abandoning his poetry (which, by the way, Byron describes as nursery rhymes) and turning to critical prose, and, in specific, to an attack on Pope. What Bowles does, according to Byron, is to "Rake from every ancient dunghill every pearl", only to prove that "the first of poets was, alas! but man" (lines 371, 370).

Byron's private letters, too, abound with references to Pope. Already in 1814, in a letter to Lady Melbourne, (11 February) he compares himself to the classicist poet. In a letter to Leigh Hunt (30 September-October 1815) he takes up the defence of Pope's Homer against Wordsworth. The famous statement, in which he describes himself together with "Scott, Southey, Wordsworth, More, Campbell" as being "upon a wrong revolutionary poetical system", and claims to be "mortified at the ineffable distance" between their production and that of Pope is from a letter to Murray (15 September 1817). It is only in 1820, however, that Byron goes into full attack. "I have taken up the Pope question (in prose) with a high hand", he writes to Hobhouse (29 March) "and you must help me." "It is my intention," he claims "to give battle to the blackguards and try if the 'little Nightingale' can't be heard again."

In fact, already in a very juvenile poem 'Soliloquy of a Bard in the Country' (1806), he presents himself as a bard who shares the tragic fate of Pope, Gray and Dryden; "And thus I fall, though meaner far than they..."

Even when he takes the first important step of the pamphlet, that of identifying the reason of the scandal about Pope's indecent remarks, and a possibly "libertine sort of love" in the general hypocrisy of the day in his famous outcry against cant, he still makes the statement without any direct attack on Bowles himself. The next step, when he objects to the immodest title of one of Bowles's pamphlets, "The Invariable Principles of Poetry", is very important in understanding Byron's consciousness of the ever-changing, instable character of everything human, but it receives no emphasis in this essay.

The first topic of real significance is introduced only after so much preparation. This is the problem of nature. Both Bowles and Byron set up an opposition between the natural and the artificial in a way that can easily be mistaken for the same pair of concepts in Wordsworth, Coleridge, or Hazlitt. It has to be made clear, however, that Byron chooses to attack a very naïve exposition of the problem. For Bowles, this is a very simple matter of thematic concern: the poet, in his opinion, should take his subjects as much as it is possible from nature.

> I presume it will readily be granted, that 'all images drawn from what is beautiful or sublime in the works of NATURE, are more beautiful and sublime than any images drawn from ART;' and that they are therefore, per se, more poetical.
>
> In like manner, those Passions of the human heart, which belong to Nature in general, are, per se, more adapted to the higher species of Poetry, than those which are derived from incidental and transient MANNERS. A description of a Forest is more poetical, than a description of a cultivated Garden: and the Passions which are portrayed in the Epistle of an Eloisa, render such a Poem more poetical (whatever might be the difference of merit in point of execution), intrinsically more

poetical, than a Poem founded on the characters, incidents and modes of artificial life; for instance the Rape of the Lock.

If this be admitted, the rule by which we would estimate Pope's general poetical character would be obvious.

This statement, from Bowles's edition of The Works of Alexander Pope is very important because it precedes all the critical views treated above. Still, the insistence on the importance of nature in Wordsworth, Coleridge, and Hazlitt appears in incomparably more complex discussions of the psychology of composition, the relationship between imagination and politics or ethics, and it appears as primarily a stylistic concern.

Bowles, however, tries to separate this thematic element from all other problems in literary criticism. This one issue precedes everything else, "whatever might be the difference of merit in point of execution." This is exactly the position that, for instance, Marilyn Butler attributes to the first generation of Romantic poets. Their actual statements, however, all made it clear that tradition and form played just as important part in their critical ideas as did nature.

Let me not, however, be considered as thinking that the subject alone constitutes poetical excellency. - The execution is to be taken into consideration at the same time

The subject, and the execution, therefore, are equally to be considered; the one respecting the Poetry, - the other, the art and powers of the Poet. The poetical subject, and the art and talents of the poet should always be kept in mind; and I imagine it is for want of observing this rule, that so much has been said, and so little understood, of the real ground of Pope's character as a Poet.

If you say, that he stands poetically pre-eminent, in the highest sense, you must deny the principles of Criticism, which I imagine will be acknowledged by all.

In speaking of the poetical subject, and the powers of execution; with regard to the first, Pope cannot be classed among the highest order of Poets; with regard to the second, none ever was his superior.

Bowles thus wants to put an end to all debate in critical theory as well as concerning Pope's poetical achievement. He does this by contrasting the poetry and the execution of a poet and, after first claiming that their importance is equal, clarifying that it is only the first that counts as a criterion in establishing if someone belongs to the "highest order of Poets" or not, and the second criterion only serves to place the poet within the limits of the order he or she has been placed in. To highlight the precarious logic of the argument, we could summarize it in the following oxymoron: it is not the poetry alone that makes the poet. And it is this approach that turns Pope into a secondary poet (even if the best within that class), a brilliant stylist who has not much to say, nonetheless: a poet who is all form, and no substance.

Moreover, he does this, keeping to the nearly scholarly and subdued voice he has chosen for the pamphlet, very carefully, building up his position in small steps.

He first attempts to prove that artificial and natural objects play an equal role in poetry. The example used in the controversy before Byron was a ship on the ocean, and the debate was about whether the ship is poetical in itself or only as far as the waves and all the natural surroundings transfer some of their poetry on it (which was Bowles's standpoint). Byron tries to refute Bowles by taking the exactly opposite view. "The 'poetry' of the 'Ship' does not depend on the 'waves &c.' - on the contrary - the 'Ship of the line' confers its own poetry upon the waters - and heightens theirs."

It is after this that Byron comes up with his own examples. He argues basically that the elements of nature, the water, the wind or the sun are in themselves perfectly neutral to human beings. It is only through an interplay with something of immediate concern to us that nature can be made significant. The human concern is "conferred" upon nature, not immediately derived from it.

Other significant element of Byron's argument rests in the nature of his examples. "If the sun shone neither upon Pyramids - nor Fleets - nor Fortresses - would its beams be equally poetical? - I think not - the poetry is at least reciprocal."

Byron founds his examples on the great achievements of civilization and technology (and here Hazlitt's criticism concerning the fascination of human imagination with greatness is perfectly relevant) and contrasts them with everyday phenomena.

They might have seen the poetical 'calm water' at Wapping - or in the 'London Dock,' or in the Paddington canal or in a horsepond - or in a slop basin - or in any other vase - - They might have heard the poetical winds howling through the chinks of a pig-stye - or the Garret-window - they might have seen the Sun on a footman's livery - or on a brass warming pan - but could the 'calm water' - or the 'wind' - or the 'Sun' make all - or any of these 'poetical?' - I think not.

Byron obviously does not want to say the exact reverse of Bowles's idea: he does not want to say that everything artificial is poetical, he simply argues that what poetry there is at all has to be created by human activity. How little it is evident to Byron's mind that nature has anything to say to human beings, that there is any sympathy between the two, is probably most visible in his description of the shipwreck in the Second Canto of Don Juan.

What follows in Byron's argument is a long list of specific examples, mostly of his personal experience, that serve to prove the same thesis: art contributes to the poetry of nature. The element of personal experience will be important later on. Byron claims that he has the authority to settle these matters because he has been there, he has seen the world, he has all the experience. For instance, "I look upon myself as entitled to talk of naval matters at least to poets - with the exception of Walter Scott - Moore - and Southey perhaps - who have been voyagers I have swum more miles - than all the rest of them together now living ever sailed" Byron's is an essay largely about who is "entitled to talk."

Byron, very clearly, has a more important purpose to his attack than to refute Bowles. He sees Bowles's insistence on nature as symptomatic of a much larger issue, and the next move he makes already points in this direction.

The very Cloaca of Tarquin at Rome - are as poetical as Richmond Hill - many will think more so - take away Rome - and leave the Tyber and the seven Hills - in the Nature of Evander's time - let Mr. Bowles - or Mr. Wordsworth or Mr. Southey - or any of the other "Naturals" make a poem upon them - and then see which is more poetical - their production - or the commonest Guide-book which tells you the road from St. Peter's to the Coliseum - and informs you what you will see by the way.

It is this passage that connects Bowles's principles to those of the Lake Poets. The connection, however, as we have seen, is superficial, it has more to do with the fact that Bowles, Southey and Coleridge happened to be friends, than with any deep theoretical affiliation. It might be argued that Byron simply chooses the target, which is easiest to attack. A more interesting approach, however, is to suggest that Byron is attacking the Lake School exactly because he thinks that they are responsible for the production of phenomena like Bowles, and some even worse than him.

The next move of the argumentation is to present Bowles's depreciation of anything artificial as a distinctly primitivistic gesture, as ultimately the rejection of culture. Bowles maintained that already Homer was a poet of nature, and gave the following example:

The shield of Achilles derives its poetical interest from the subjects described on it, far more than from its workmanship, and these are the subjects of the creation of the heaven and earth, scenes of Pastoral and Military life, the rural dance, &c. Besides, was the age of HOMER an æra of refinement or artificial life?

Byron answers by stretching Bowles's idea as far as possible, to show its inherent dangers (once again, without any abstract arguments, only by overwhelming his opponent with examples).

And from what does the Spear of Achilles derive its interest? and the helmet and the Mail worn by Patroclus - and the celestial armour - and the very brazen greaves of the well-booted Greeks? - Is it solely from the legs and the back and the breast - & the human body which they enclose? - In that case - it would have been more poetical to have made them fight naked - and Gulley and Gregson as being nearer to a state of nature - are more poetical boxing in a pair of drawers - than Hector and Achilles in radiant armour and with heroic weapons. Why not represent the Greeks & Trojans like two savage tribes - tugging and tearing - and kicking - and biting, and gnashing - foaming grinning and gouging in all the poetry of martial Nature - unincumbered with gross prosaic artificial arms - an equal superfluity to the natural warrior and his natural poet.

Byron is interested in the social, even political element in Bowles's rejection of anything connected with art. He clearly sees his opponent's poetical ideas as inseparable from a social commitment, basically, a return to "a state of nature." Byron describes the vision, which is the ultimate consequence, to his mind, of the uncritical commitment to nature: a stripping off of all the clothes of civilization, a revolutionary attempt to start history anew.

The classic example of such a use of the metaphors of clothing is Edmund Burke's Reflections on the Revolution in France. The two instances of this imagery may seem perfectly unconnected, but it is arguable that the thrust of the two pieces of argumentation is not dissimilar altogether. To Burke's mind the fact that the queen of France had to undergo such humiliation as had very recently happened to her is symptomatic of a crisis in culture.

Now all is to be changed. All the pleasing illusions, which made power gentle, and obedience liberal are to be dissolved by this new conquering empire of light and reason. All the decent drapery of life is to be rudely torn off. All the super-added ideas, furnished from the wardrobe of a moral imagination, which the heart owns, and the understanding ratifies, as necessary to cover the defects of our naked shivering nature, and to raise it to dignity in our own estimation, are to be exploded as a ridiculous, absurd, and antiquated fashion.

On this scheme of things, a king is but a man; a queen is but a woman; a woman is but an animal; and an animal not of the highest order.

What Burke is concerned about is the possibility that all exterior, visible signs of social status may be effaced. From this, Byron moves on to expressing his allegiance for Pope's special branch of poetry. "In my mind the highest of all poetry is Ethical poetry - and the highest of all earthly objects must be moral truth." It must be clear, however, that Byron is not proposing didactic poetry (a term that he also uses) in the usual sense. He defends a kind of poetry, which relies upon the social facts of its subject matter, he proposes a kind of realism, which is also apparent in the arguments he puts forth in justifying a number of his works. To this ideal, he opposes what he sees as the present-day focus on imagination.

"It is the fashion of the day to lay great stress upon what they call 'Imagination' and 'Invention' the two commonest of qualities - an Irish peasant with a little whisky in his head will imagine and invent more than would furnish forth a modern poem." This witticism is perhaps the first overt indication of the politics of Byron's commitment to poetical tradition. The contrast between "the commonest of qualities", that enables even "an Irish peasant" to produce poetry is in sharp contrast to the huge learning and experience of the world Byron has given so many examples of throughout the article.

The attempt of the poetical populace of the present day to obtain an Ostracism against Pope is as easily accounted for as the Athenians Shell against Aristides they are tired of hearing him always called "the Just" - - They are also fighting for Life - for if he maintains his station - they will reach their own - by falling. —They have raised a Mosque by the side of a Grecian temple of the purest Architecture - and more barbarous than the Barbarians from whose practice I have borrowed the figure - they are contented with their own grotesque edifice - unless they destroy the prior and purely beautiful fabric which preceded and which shames them & theirs forever and ever. — I shall be told that amongst these -

I have been (or it may be still am) - conspicuous; - true - and I am ashamed of it; - I have been amongst the builders of this Babel attended by a confusion of tongues - but never amongst the envious destroyers of the classic temple of our Predecessor. - I have loved and honoured the fame and name of that illustrious and unrivalled man - far more than my own paltry renown - and the trashy Jingle of the crowd of "Schools" and upstarts - who pretend to rival - or even to surpass him.

It is in this passage that Byron finally names those against whom the pamphlet is written. It is not, in fact, Bowles, nor is it any of the great Lake Poets; Byron calls them "upstarts." This essay provides an exceptional glance into the genuine concern Byron feels over the emergence of those who destroy the "purity" of Pope's heritage, a heritage that he sees as representative of the whole of civilization. The, as yet unspecified, upstarts unleash a confusion of tongues. They produce a diversity that threatens to disrupt all social organization, that has a revolutionary potential.

The upstarts are identified only in the addenda to the article. "Now is it not a shame to hear our Lakers in 'Kendal Green' and our Bucolical Cockneys crying out " Pope had seen all of Nature that England alone can supply." He goes on, somewhat later, to elaborate on this same attack on the Cockneys.

There have sprung up two sects of Naturals - the Lakers - who whine about Nature because they live in Cumberland - and their under-Sect - (which someone has maliciously called the 'Cockney School') - who are enthusiastic for the country because they live in London. It is to be observed that the rustical founders are rather anxious to disclaim any connection with their metropolitan followers I can understand the pretensions of the aquatic gentlemen of Windermere to what Mr. Braham terms 'enthusymusy' for lakes and mountains and daffodils - and buttercups - but I should be glad to be apprized of the foundation of the London propensities of their imitative brethren to the same 'high argument'? - Southey Wordsworth - & Coleridge - have rambled over half Europe - and seen

Nature in all her varieties - (although I think that they have occasionally not used her very well) - but what on Earth - of Earth - and Sea and Nature - have the others seen? Not a half nor a tenth part so much as Pope. - While they sneer at his Windsor forest - have they seen any thing of Windsor except its Brick?

Here, finally, are the ultimate reasons of his disparagement of Bowles and the Lake poets: they make such poetry as that of the Cockneys, who have no experience in the world and no learning, legitimate. The Lakers disown this connection, but in this essay Byron's aim is to make their responsibility visible to everyone. The reference to the social position of the Cockneys is also unmistakable; they are regarded as only qualified for working in factories, making bricks, and not for writing poetry. The most important element in Byron's denouncement of the Cockneys is only made explicit around the end of the letter.

The grand distinction of the Under forms of the New School of poets - is their Vulgarity. - By this I do not mean that they are Coarse - but 'shabby-genteel' - as it is termed. A man may be coarse & yet not vulgar - and the reverse. - Burns is often coarse - but never vulgar. —Chatterton is never vulgar; nor Wordsworth nor the higher of the Lake School, though they treat of low life in all it's branches.

- It is in their finery that the New-under School - are most vulgar; and they may be known by this at once - as what we called at Harrow - 'a Sunday Blood' might be easily distinguished from a Gentleman - although his cloathes might be better-cut and his boots the best blackened of the two - probably because he made the one or cleaned the other with his own hands.

What Byron is concerned with, more importantly than anything, is transgression. What if this new under School should become the upper school? What if the whole distinction should disappear? What if the illusion these poets create by their finery manages to deceive people? Byron sees it as his task to unmask these attempts. He wants to remove the splendid costumes and show the man of the working class beneath them, who make their own clothes and clean their own shoes. This attempt at "undressing" people contrasts sharply with the Lake poets' attempts to undress all human beings, show them without the costumes of civilization, and show the common human element underneath. Byron, on the contrary, wants to fix them in their proper clothes, he wants to diminish all revolutionary potential in the Cockneys' attempts at appropriating the traditional "fineries" of poetry. Byron will, of course, deny that he has anything personally against the unnamed authors, or, in fact, against their social class, but he finds it hard to define what their "shabbygenteelness" exactly consists in.

In the present case I speak of writing, - not of persons. — Of the latter I know nothing - of the former I judge as it is found. Far be it from me to presume that there ever was or can be such a thing as an Aristocracy of Poets - I do not mean that they should write in the Style of the Song by a person of Quality but there is a Nobility of thought and of Style - open to all Stations - and derived partly from the talent - & partly from education If I were asked to define what this Gentlemanliness is - I should say that it is only to be defined by examples, — of those who have it - & those who have it not. It does not depend upon low themes - or even low language - for - Fielding revels in both - but is he ever vulgar? - No - you see the man of education the gentleman and the Scholar sporting with his subject - it's Master - not it's Slave. - Your vulgar Writer is always most vulgar - the higher his subject But to the proof - it is a thing to be felt - more than explained.

The aristocracy of poets may not exist, but there certainly is (to Byron's mind) a style proper to a person of quality, which is a style that will be always vulgar if used by a person of the under-class. Still, nobility is not fully a matter of stylistic "surface", since that is too much "open to all Stations:" It is mysterious "thing to be felt." However, the most palpable element is the issue of education.

A very important recent study into the relationship of poetry and politics around the Peterloo year in the work of Byron and Shelley on the one hand (who had the classical education, and the "appropriate" social background for poets), and the Cockney school on the other (who did not), can be found in Richard Cronin's The Politics of Romantic Poetry. Cronin's ideas are very interesting because (unlike Butler) he does not try to present politics and poetics as reducible to each other, but as standing in a deeply problematic elationship.

with regard to changes in the political climate, Cronin points out that since Byron had left England, the ways of doing politics changed fundamentally. "[Henry] Hunt and Cobbett were busy in these years trying to put an end to political life as Byron understood it, a life conducted by men who differed in their views but shared the same manners. For them politics was not a conflict between opinions but a conflict between classes." Byron, as his letters make it obvious, was outraged by this change and hurls abuse on the "dirty levellers." Cronin emphasizes that there was only one thing that could provoke such an intemperate fury from Byron at the time, and this was the poetry of John Keats. For Byron "the attack on Pope in which Keats had had joined was an attempt to 'level' the reputation of a great poet."

Hunt's and Cobbet's politics and Keats's poetry were both attempts to break down the social distinctions on which polite society and polite literature alike depended. Hence the vigour with which Byron rushed to Pope's defence in his two letters to Murray, and hence too, their manner, in which, as Hazlitt shrewdly noticed, critical argument is almost wholly subordinated to expansive display by Byron of his own lordliness.

Byron admits his complicity in the building "of this Babel attended by a confusion of tongues," and Babel is, of course, the classic example of human transgression. Consequently, as Cronin says, "Byron's present concern is to re-establish the cultural barriers that he feels himself to have assisted in demolishing," and the standard by which he attempts to redraw these barriers is "classical education." "Why, our classical education alone - should teach us to trample on such unredeemed dirt [Henry Hunt and Cobbett]."

Cronin then goes on to discuss how Byron draws the consequences of all this in his revival of the classical drama (here his argument is somewhat weakened by failing to address the problem that Byron kept on writing a very different form of drama at the same time, the mystery), and to analyse the extent to which Byron was right in sensing the disruptive potential of Cockney poetics, which, in a sense, Keats carried to its utmost perfection. It shall suffice here to exemplify in a couple of his statements about Keats the utmost importance Byron attributed to the issue of education, and, specifically, the younger poet's lack of it.

John Keats, who was killed off by one critique, Just as he really promised something great, If not intelligible, - without Greek

Contrived to talk about the Gods of late,

Much as they might have been supposed to speak. (Canto XI)

Here too, Byron's acclaim for the greatness of Keats's production cannot silence, that, although this is not at all visible from the poem itself, it was written by someone, who has not, after all, the proper qualifications to become a poet.

The weakness of Cronin's argument is that he tries to connect Byron's indignation against Leigh Hunt and Keats too strongly to the political events of 1819. In fact, Byron was full of despise already for their "vulgarity" a year earlier, when in a letter to Th. Moore (1 June 1818) he stated that "Hunt's letter is probably the exact piece of vulgar coxcombry you might expect from his situation. He is a good man, with some poetical elements in his chaos; but spoilt by the Christ-Church and a Sunday newspaper When I saw Rimini in MS., I deemed it good poetry at bottom, disfigured only by a strange style." The strangeness that Byron identifies is probably the same that Cronin describes as the quintessence of Cockney poetics. "In

The Story of Rimini Hunt invents cockney poetry as an inverted pastoral. Instead of courtly poets appropriating the language and sentiments of rustics, Hampstead poets appropriate the manners of the court, and infect its language with the cant terms of their own ordinary discourse." This, for Byron, amounts to a complete misunderstanding about one's identity. "He (Leigh H.) is an honest charlatan, who has persuaded himself into a belief of his own impostures, and talks Punch in pure simplicity of heart, taking himself for Vates in both senses, or nonsenses, of the word."

Much Byron was concerned by the problem of similar "appropriations" is visible from a letter to Murray (1 August 1819) on a completely different topic. Here he speaks about his liaison with Maria Cogni, and complains about her love of fineries. "She had a thousand fooleries: in her fazziolo, the dress of the lower orders, she looked beautiful; but, alas! she longed for a hat and feathers, and all I could say or do (and I said much) could not prevent this travestie." Such a "travestie" in the "lower orders" is indeed something against which Byron has a lot to say.

It is interesting to see that Byron was far from being alone in concentrating on the problem of education in literary criticism; neither was he alone in connecting it to social stratification. In fact, the notorious early Tory criticism that Keats received is dominated by similar preoccupations. John Gibson Lochart, for instance, in his article on 'The Cockney School of Poetry' in Blackwood's Edinburgh Magazine (August 1818) called attention to the fact that Keats wrote his Endymion without reading "a single line either of Ovid or of Wieland." Lochart also wants to make Keats ridiculous for his attempt to transgress his social position by what Byron calls "travestie." "His Endymion is not a Greek shepherd loved by a Greek goddess; he is merely a young Cockney rhymester Costume, were it worthwhile to notice such a trifle, is violated in every page of this goodly octavo." But, this is only what "might be expected from persons of their [Keats's and Hunts's] education." Most importantly, the conclusion of this article, as the conclusion of Byron's would be, explicitly political. "We had almost forgot to mention that Keats belongs to the Cockney Rimini to be the first poem should believe The Examiner to be the first politician of the day."

On the basis of the issue of education, we find Byron not only in the perhaps unexpected company of "reactionary" Tory critics, but also in the company of Coleridge, one of the first-generation romantics that Byron is usually opposed to. In Biographia literaria Coleridge often invokes education as the antidote to "the spirit of Jacobinism," which may be lurking among the uneducated people. "Whether the spirit of Jacobinism, which the writings of Burke exorcised from the higher or from the literary classes, may not, like the ghost in Hamlet, be heard moving and mining in the underground chambers admits of a question." He refers to his own classical education as the supreme influence that withheld him from "enthusiasm." "In part from constitutional indolence, which in the very hey-day of hope kept my enthusiasm in check, but still more from the habits and influence of classical education and academic pursuits." These attitudes of Byron, in other words, hardly oppose him to conservative or "reactionary" Romanticism.

CONCLUSION

In this paper I have tried to revisit some of the conceptual oppositions with the help of which recent criticism has reinstated Byron as one of the most important authors of the romantic period. My claim was that together with the great gain in Byron's canonical position, there has been an important loss in the subtlety of the approaches to his oeuvre. The most influential accounts of Romanticism usually construe a position they call Byronic, which is invariably presented as a counter-position. Byron is characterised as the opposite of "reactionary" first-generation Romanticism in politics, as the opposite of Wordsworthian sincerity in his poetics; as the opposite of anti-Enlightenment, anti-neoclassical early Romanticism in short.

I have tried to show that these oppositions do not hold either if we examine them from the perspective of Coleridge or Wordsworth or if we concentrate on Byron's contribution to the Pope Controversy. Following Hazlitt's inspiration, I was searching for some common ground beneath the many differences between Byron and the most important firstgeneration romantics. Evidence suggests that the importance of classical education as the background and legitimatisation of poetry is an important connection between these diverse authors.

Bibliography

A Collection of Pieces in verse and prose, which have been publish'd on occasion of the Dunciad. By Mr. Savage. 1732.

Abbott, Edwin. A Concordnace to the Works of Alexander Pope. With an introduction. 1875.

Another occasional Letter from Mr. Cibber to Mr. Pope, Wherein the new hero's preferment to his throne in the Dunciad seems not to be accepted. 1744.

Beljame, A. Le Public et les Hommes de Lettres en Angleterre au dix-huitième siècle (1660–1744). Paris, 1881.

Coleridge, S. T. Biographia Literaria. 1817.

Conington, John. The Poetry of Pope. Oxford Essays. 1858. Rptd. in vol. 1 of his Miscellaneous Works, 1872.

Courthope, W. J. A History of English Poetry, vol. V. 1905.

Crousaz, J. P. de. Examen de l'Essai de M. Pope. 173.

Deetz, Albrecht. Alexander Pope. Ein Beitrag zur Literaturgeschichte des achtzehnten Jahrhunderts, nebst Proben Pope'scher Dichtungen. Leipzig, 1876.

Dennis, John. Remarks on Mr. Pope's Rape of the Lock. 1728.

Dobson, A. Dialogue to the Memory of Mr. Alexander Pope. Collected Poems, 1897 (p. 301).

Elton, O. The Augustan Ages. Edinburgh, 1899.

English Poetry from Dryden to Cowper. The Quarterly Review. July, 1862.

Hazlitt, William. Dryden and Pope. Lectures on the English Poets. 1818. Collected Works. Edd. Waller, A. R. and Glover, Arnold, 1902–6. (Vol. V, pp. 68–85.)

Lloyd, Charles [Lamb's friend]. Poetical Essays on the Character of Pope. 1821.

Lowell, J. R. Pope. My Study Windows. 1871.

Maack, R. Über Popes Einfluss auf die Idylle und das Lehrgedicht in Deutschland. Hamburg, 1895.

Mead, W. E. The Versification of Pope in its relation to the 17th century. Leipzig, 1889. (Diss.)

Saintsbury, G. A History of English Prosody, vol II. 1908.

Spence, Joseph. An Essay on Pope's Odyssey: in which some particular Beauties and Blemishes of that work are considered. London and Oxford, 1726.

Stephen, Sir Leslie. Pope as a Moralist. The Cornhill Magazine. 1873. Rptd. in Hours in a Library, vol. 1, 1874.

Taine, H. A. Histoire de la Littérature anglaise. 8th edn. Paris, 1892.

Traill, H. D. Pope. Chambers's Encyclopaedia, vol. VIII. 1908.

Vater, P. Ein Beitrag zur Kenntniss des Dichters und des Philosophen. Halle, 1897. (Diss.)

Verses addressed to the imitator of the First Satire of the Second Book of Horace. By a Lady. [1733. By lady Mary Wortley Montagu, assisted, probably, by lord Hervey.]

Wakefield, Gilbert. Observations on Pope. 1796.

Warton, Joseph. An Essay on the genius and writings of Pope. Vol. 1, 1756; vol. II, 1782.

Weiser, C. S. Pope's Einfluss auf Byron's Jugenddichtungen. In Anglia, vol. 1. Halle, 1878.

Wordsworth, William. Preface and Appendix to Lyrical Ballads. 1798.